THE Baseball ◇ Research JOURNAL

The Eighteenth Annual
Historical and Statistical Review
of the Society for American Baseball Research

ARE THERE ANY TWO institutions that deserve each other more than SABR and the Hall of Fame? Probably not. Maybe that's why the 1989 SABR convention went to the Hall on the fiftieth anniversary of its opening. And maybe that's why conversation on the bus from Albany, New York, convention headquarters to Cooperstown waxed downright metaphysical.

Several SABRites were debating the relative merits of hitting against overhand pitching at sixty feet, six inches, to facing underhand throwers at forty-five feet. Where was Bill James when we needed him? "I had a dream," BRJ author Jim Skipper said. "I was at the Hall looking at Pete Rose's plaque. All his relevant stats were on it, but not his name or face."

We like to think we have a Hall-of-Fame issue, one complete with relevant names, faces, and facts. Among many Hall-oriented pieces are ones on the fellow best qualified to select Negro-league immortals (page 6), a standard for Cooperstown membership (11), Hall-of-Fame managerial nicknames (36) and teams (47), the immortal Bill Terry as a minor-league pitcher of all things (53), and a major-league hurler one of our authors would like to see enshrined (55). The issue also contains several pieces on the nineteenth century, the results of a major SABR research project on the 1930 Negro National League, the last word on clutch hitting, an amusing trivia "sting," and whimsical work on everything from the Rabbi of Swat to Joe Charboneau.

In all, this is the most extensively authored BRJ ever, with 35 names on the contents page and several more accompanying boxes and fillers. Heartfelt thanks to Publications Director Paul Adomites, Associate Editors Len Levin and Elizabeth McGrail, Deb Wilds and her crew at Ag Press, and the incomparable E.P. (Pete) Palmer, winner of the 1989 Bob Davids Award and statistical guru for this edition. And a special nod to the membership for contributing the labors of love that fill these pages.

Jim Kaplan

Editor: Jim Kaplan
Associate Editors: Len Levin, Elizabeth McGrail

Cover Art by Bob Carroll

Photo sources: Pages 6, 7, and 8, Tweed Webb; Page 28 and 78, John Thorn; Pages 33, 53, 57, 59, 80, and 88, National Baseball Library; Page 68, George E. Brace.

The Forgotten Winning Streak of 1891

ROBERT L. TIEMANN

Ranking with the 1951 Giants and the 1978 Yankees, the Boston Beaneaters won 18 straight to win a National League pennant in a stirring and controversial comeback.

ALTHOUGH THEIR 18-game winning streak in 1891 is ignored by most record books, the Boston Beaneaters won the National League pennant with one of the most dramatic and controversial stretch drives in baseball history. On September 15, with just sixteen playing dates left in the season, Boston trailed Chicago in the standings by 6½ games. Then Boston won 18 games in a row to leap to the pennant by 3½ games. The victory, however, was accompanied by suspicion and accusations. Chicago complained that Boston had played four doubleheaders, which required special permission from the rest of the league. There was also evidence to suggest that the other Eastern clubs had purposely lost many of their games with Boston. That evidence looks convincing nearly a century later, but the 1891 pennant still belongs to Boston.

The Beaneaters got off to a slow start, playing below .500 ball as late as June 10. Then a nine-game winning streak vaulted them into the race. Their chief competition came from the veteran New York Giants squad and the upstart Chicago Colts, led by forty-year-old Adrian C. (Cap) Anson. The Giants exchanged the lead with the Colts six times in July, but the Beaneaters kept inching closer to the top. On the morning of August 15, only four percentage points and one game separated the three leaders. Then Chicago ran off 11 consecutive victories to pull away.

By early September, Chicago seemed sure to win the National League pennant. On the fourth, Anson was feeling so frisky that he showed up at the game wearing a white wig and a false beard that flowed down over his ample chest. To the delight of the Chicago crowd, he wore the costume for the entire game and his Colts beat the Beaneaters 5-3. At that point, Chicago had a 70-41

record and a seven-game lead over second-place Boston, which was at 62-47.

The Beaneaters salvaged the final game in Chicago but were still far behind as they headed home for the last four weeks. With first baseman Tommy Tucker swinging a hot bat, the Beaneaters won three of four from Cleveland and three straight from Cincinnati during the next week.

On September 14, the Chicago Colts came to town for the final three games between the two contenders. After the Colts won the opener, 7-1, the Chicago Tribune crowed, "The good captain's men are champions and no mistake." After another victory in the second game, the Tribune claimed that even "the Boston cranks [fans] give it up." Anson was jolly enough to give a billiards demonstration in South Boston that evening.

The morning newspapers on Wednesday, September 16, showed Chicago leading the league with a 76-44 record, while Boston was second at 69-50. In the Boston Globe, Tim Murnane, a player-turned-sportswriter, exorted Beaneater manager Frank Selee to "wake up your hired men and make them hustle for old Anson's scalp." But the prospects for the final game of the series were not encouraging. Boston was scheduled to pitch Charles 'Kid' Nichols whose lifetime record against Chicago was 0-9. His opponent, Hutchison, had already beaten Boston eight times in 1891. Yet it was in those inauspicious circumstances that the Beaneaters launched their long winning streak. A day-by-day account of the streak fol-

---

Robert L. Tiemann has done complete day-by-day research of all major-league pennant races and is the author of "Dodger Classics" and "Cardinal Classics." Chairman of SABR's Nineteenth Century Research Committee, he is co-editor (with Mark Rucker) of "Nineteenth Century Stars."

lows: (Note: At the time the home team had the choice of batting first or last.)

September 16

Chicago	76-45	.628	-	Lost to Boston, 7-2
Boston	70-50	.583	5½	Beat Chicago, 7-2

	r	h	e	Batteries
Boston	000 211 111 =	7	10	1 Nichols and Bennett
Chicago	100 100 000 =	2	8	7 Hutchison and Shriver

According to the headline in the Globe, "Nichols was on his pitch" and was backed by fine fielding. Doubles by Harry Stovey and Bobby Lowe, a triple by Tommy Tucker, and a homer by Charlie Bennett led to runs.

September 17

Chicago	76-46	.623	-	Lost at New York, 3-1
Boston	70-50	.583	5	Tied Pittsburgh, 7-7(10)

	r	h	e	Batteries
Boston	200 100 004 0 =	7	11	2 Staley and Ganzel
Pittsburgh	103 000 210 0 =	7	11	5 Galvin and Miller

Boston was lucky to gain a tie in this game, scoring four runs in the ninth aided by three errors and a base on balls. Charley Ganzel got the key hit in the rally. Darkness halted the game an inning later. This was no way to start a winning streak, but at least Chicago lost and was held to six hits by Amos Rusie.

September 18

Chicago	76-47	.618	-	Lost at New York, 9-3
Boston	71-50	.587	4	Beat Pittsburgh, 9-3

	r	h	e	Batteries
Boston	101 006 001 =	9	13	4 Clarkson and Ganzel
Pittsburgh	100 000 002 =	3	4	4 Baldwin and Miller

Mark Baldwin pitched like a man "drawing salary on suspicion," much to the chagrin of his foghorn-voiced batterymate, George Miller. Fly balls hit to rightfielder Bud Lally were "as good as hits," and Baldwin's own throwing error allowed Boston to score the go-ahead run. John Clarkson "didn't pitch a speedy ball during the game," but his slow drops, curves, and changeups baffled the Burgers. John Ewing and the Giants beat Chicago.

September 19

Chicago	76-48	.613	-	Lost at New York, 8-0
Boston	73-50	.593	2½	Beat Pittsburgh twice,
				11-3, 11-2 (5)

	r	h	e	Batteries
Game 1 -				
Boston	000 126 002 =	11	12	1 Nichols and Bennett
Pittsburgh	200 001 000 =	3	6	3 King and Mack
Game 2 -				
Boston	012 08 =	11	9	4 Clarkson and Ganzel
Pittsburgh	200 00 =	2	2	7 Baldwin and Mack

(called on account of darkness)

Pittsburgh scored early in each game, but Boston won both with ease. Herman Long hit a two-run home run in the first game, and little Joe Quinn hit a three-run homer over the right-field fence in the opener and a grand-slam over the left-field fence in the nightcap. (The fences down both lines at South End Park were notoriously close.) In New York, the Chicagos succumbed to Rusie again, losing on just three hits.

Sunday, September 20, was an off day, since the National League forbade Sunday ball.

September 21

Chicago	77-48	.619		Won at Cincinnati, 5-4
Boston	74-50	.597	2½	Beat Brooklyn, 6-1

	r	h	e	Batteries
Boston	000 000 051 =	6	8	2 Staley and Kelly
Brooklyn	000 001 000 =	1	4	4 Inks and T. Daly

Harry Staley "put on the steam" and handcuffed the Bridegrooms. Lefthander Bert Inks also pitched well until the eighth, when captain John M. Ward booted a double-play ball. Inks then failed to cover first base on a grounder to the right side, Ward let a throw go through him, and Staley capped the five-run rally with a home run. In Cincinnati, the Colts rallied to edge the Reds.

September 22

Chicago	78-48	.619	-	Won at Cincinnati, 4-1
Boston	75-50	.600	2½	Beat Brooklyn, 3-0 (8)

	r	h	e	Batteries
Boston	000 100 20 =	3	5	1 Nichols and Bennett
Brooklyn	000 000 00 =	0	4	2 Lovett and Kinslow

(called on account of darkness)

Ward's wild throw to the plate allowed the first run to score, and Bennett's two-run single clinched the victory. Brooklyn could do nothing with Nichols' delivery. Chicago beat Cincinnati, behind Tom Vickery's four-hitter.

September 23

Chicago	79-48	.622	-	Won at Cincinnati, 9-0
Boston	77-50	.606	2	Beat Brooklyn twice,
				5-1, 9-2

	r	h	e	Batteries
Game 1 -				
Boston	200 210 000 =	5	11	2 Clarkson and Ganzel
Brooklyn	000 010 000 =	1	12	7 Foutz and C. Daily
Game 2 -				
Boston	100 001 520 =	9	11	0 Staley and Kelly
Brooklyn	020 000 000 =	2	6	4 Inks and T. Daly

Boston won a pair as "Brooklyn stumbled about like a drunken man on stilts." Six Bridegrooms were caught napping on the bases in the first game, and shortstop Fred Ely made four errors. In the nightcap, Long of Boston scored from first base on a misplayed bunt and from second on an infield tap. Chicago won its third straight.

September 24

Chicago	80-48	.625	-	Beat Pittsburgh, 7-4 (7)
Boston	78-50	.609	2	Beat Philadelphia, 5-2

	r	h	e	Batteries
Boston	200 020 001 =	5	4	3 Nichols and Bennett
Philadelphia	000 100 010 =	2	6	5 Keefe and Fields

The Phillies presented a weak nine, with catcher Jack Clements and first baseman Willard Brown both hurt. Charles Esper, the only Phillie pitcher with a winning record against Boston for the season, was not even brought along on the trip. Still, Tim Keefe baffled the Beaneaters with his change of pace and would have shut them out with decent support. As it was, bad errors by Sam Thompson, Billy Hamilton, and Ed Mayer gave Boston its runs. Chicago rallied to beat Pittsburgh.

September 25

Chicago	81-48	.628	-	Beat Pittsburgh by forfeit
Boston	79-50	.612	2	Beat Philadelphia, 6-3

		r	h	e	Batteries
Boston	012 002 010 =	6	10	3	Clarkson and Ganzel
Philadelphia	100 020 000 =	3	8	5	Gleason and Fields

Fielding once again made the difference. An "old-gold muff" by Phillie first baseman Jerry Denny and two wretched throws by third baseman Mayer gave Boston five of its runs. Chicago won by forfeit when Pittsburgh refused to remove an ejected player. The Boston Reds, in the other league, mathematically clinched the American Association pennant with a victory in Baltimore.

September 26

Chicago	81-48	.628	-	Tied Pittsburgh, 6-6 (8)
Boston	80-50	.615	1½	Beat Philadelphia, 8-6

		r	h	e	Batteries
Boston	201 400 001 =	8	7	3	Staley and Kelly
Philadelphia	410 000 100 =	6	11	8	Kling (4) Thornton (5) and Fields

The Bostons were once again "pulled out of a hole by their opponents' errors." Mayer was shifted to shortstop, where he contributed two errors. Catcher Jocko Fields, not to be outdone, made four, including two on throws to the plate. John Thornton pitched one-hit relief after rookie Bill Kling had been routed, but it was too late.

September 28

Chicago	81-49	.623	-	Lost at Cleveland, 4-2
Boston	81-50	.618	½	Beat New York, 11-3

		r	h	e	Batteries
Boston	111 520 100 =	11	14	2	Nichols and Bennett
New York	010 010 001 =	3	10	8	Coughlin and Buckley-Burrell

The Giants arrived in Boston accompanied by manager Jim Mutrie and club president John B. Day. Day quickly held a conference with Boston president Arthur H. Soden. The Giants had failed to bring their two best pitchers, Amos Rusie and John Ewing, and their slugging first baseman Roger Connor. Ewing was nursing a sprained ankle. Connor had been given a day off to attend to personal business in his home town of Waterbury, Connecticut. And Rusie, who had beaten Chicago twice in three days a week before and had pitched both games of a doubleheader on September 26, was allowed to go home a week early, Day and Mutrie agreeing that "he was entitled to a rest." In the opening game of the series, according to Sporting Life, "the New Yorks beat all records for indifferent and rocky playing." Even the Boston partisans were disgusted and roundly hissed the visitors' work. Meanwhile, Cy Young snapped Chicago's winning streak.

September 29

Chicago	82-49	.626	-	Won at Cleveland, 14-13
Boston	83-50	.624	-	Beat New York twice, 13-8, 11-3 (7)

	r	h	e	Batteries

Game 1 -

		r	h	e	Batteries
Boston	303 011 230 =	13	16	4	Clarkson and Ganzel
New York	020 050 100 =	8	11	8	Welch and Clark

Game 2 -

		r	h	e	Batteries
Boston	330 310 1 =	11	10	2	Staley and Kelly
New York	000 030 0 =	3	6	5	Sullivan and Burrell

Boston had no trouble winning both games, since the Giants' work was so dubious as to threaten baseball's "present high standing among outdoor games." Connor was again absent; this time the excuse was a train wreck. For Boston, Long and Lowe both scored three runs in each game. Stovey went four for five in the opener and hit a three-run triple in the nightcap.

September 30

Boston	85-50	.630	-	Beat New York twice, 16-5, 5-3 (8)
Chicago	82-50	.621	1½	Lost at Cleveland, 12-5 (8)

	r	h	e	Batteries

Game 1 -

		r	h	e	Batteries
Boston	200 271 040 =	16	16	3	Nichols and Bennett
New York	200 000 012 =	5	13	9	Coughlin (4) Welch (5) and Clark

Game 2 -

		r	h	e	Batteries
Boston	001 202 00 =	5	7	3	Staley (5⅓) Clarkson (2⅔) and Ganzel
New York	000 001 02 =	3	10	3	Sullivan and Burrell

(called on account of darkness)

Boston took over the league lead with a double victory. Connor was finally in the New York lineup, but the Giants still "played without much heart." In the second game they had four men thrown out at the plate and two cut down at third. The Beaneaters played spirited ball, led by four hits each by Quinn and Steve Brodie. Chicago lost to Young and Cleveland again, but filed a protest against the doubleheaders in Boston. Club president James A. Hart made no outright accusations of crookedness, but he did say, "Things look suspicious."

October 1

Boston	86-50	.632	-	Won at Philadelphia, 6-1 (7) CLINCH TITLE
Chicago	82-51	.617	2½	Lost to Cincinnati, 6-1

		r	h	e	Batteries
Boston	000 402 0 =	6	6	3	Clarkson and Bennett
Philadelphia	000 100 0 =	1	6	4	Esper and Clements

(called on account of darkness)

Although the Beaneaters were finally facing a team fielding its strongest nine, they were still able to come out ahead. Shortstop Long was brilliant, turning five double plays in seven innings and contributing a timely single in the four-run fourth. Tucker poled a triple in the same frame but had to come out for a pinch runner. When it was announced that the usually boisterous Tucker was sick to his stomach, a wag in the bleachers yelled, "So were we when Tommy was coaching," bringing a roar of laughter from the stands and benches alike. Chicago was whipped by Cincinnati, and Boston had clinched the pennant with two games still to play.

League president Nick Young addressed the Chicago protest by reviewing the rule about double games. Since only six teams needed to approve additional games, Chicago need not have been asked or informed before the event. Then Young admitted that the league president need not be informed either. Still, he assumed that Boston president Soden had "amply protected himself."

October 2

Boston	87-50	.635	-	Won at Philadelphia, 5-3
Chicago	82-52	.612	3½	Lost to Cincinnati, 17-16 (7)

	r	h	e	Batteries
Philadelphia	110 100 000 =	3	10 3	Gleason and Clements-Gray
Boston	010 110 02x =	5	7 1	Nichols and Bennett

The Beaneaters made it 18 in a row. In the top of the fifth, two Phillies were thrown out at the plate while in the bottom Long circled the bases on errors. A double by Nichols drove in the go-ahead run in the eighth.

October 3 (end of season)

Boston	87-51	.630	-	Lost at Philadelphia, 5-3 (6)
Chicago	82-53	.607	3½	Lost to Cincinnati, 15-9

The streak ended when King Kelly allowed three passed balls and made four errors to hand the game to the Phillies. But there were still the protests and accusations to be dealt with. President Hart of Chicago said that the Eastern teams had deliberately lost to Boston to deprive Chicago of the pennant. The Colts had one of the lowest payrolls in the league, and the high-salaried Easterners did not want the humiliation of losing the pennant to Captain Anson's youngsters. Furthermore, Anson had stood steadfastly against the late, lamented players' Brotherhood, and the old Brotherhood boys resented this. Both the Boston and New York correspondents of The Sporting News agreed that the Giants, at least, had deliberately "laid down" against the Beaneaters. As for the protest about double games, Soden told Sporting Life on October 1 that he held telegrams of consent from six clubs. But the Boston Globe's interviewer was convinced that Soden did not actually have such telegrams.

Investigations were ordered. The first was made by the New York club, concerning its own doubtful player absences in the Boston series. Not surprisingly, the club exonerated itself. When the league's board of directors looked into the matter in November, the New York report was accepted. Apparently Soden also was able to produce sufficient authorization for the protested double games as well, so all charges were dismissed and the pennant officially awarded to Boston.

But the odium remained. The Boston fans held the Reds in generally higher esteem than they held the Beaneaters, especially since Soden and his partners absolutely refused to have their team meet the AA champs in a World Series. Nine years later Anson wrote in his autobiography that "a conspiracy was entered into whereby New York lost enough games to Boston to give the Beaneaters the pennant." And even today, the tainted 18-game winning streak, tied for fifth longest in National League history, is generally left out of the record books.

Individual Statistics Compiled During the Boston Beaneaters' 18-Game Winning Streak in 1891

	G	R	RBI	AB	H	2B	3B	HR	BB	HB	SO	BA	SB	PO	A	E	FA	DP
Herman Long, ss	19	23	14	80	24	0	2	2	11	2	2	.300	13	52	63	14	.891	15
Bobby Lowe, cf	19	22	14	82	23	5	1	3	5	2	8	.280	9	34	4	0	1.000	1
Harry Stovey, lf	19	23	13	74	22	8	3	0	15	1	6	.297	14	34	2	9	.800	0
Steve Brodie, rf	18	17	19	74	24	7	0	1	8	1	7	.324	6	18	8	2	.929	2
Billy Nash, 3b	19	15	10	77	26	3	1	0	7	2	1	.338	5	29	31	1	.984	5
Tommy Tucker, 1b	19	14	11	71	18	1	2	0	6	5	5	.254	3	160	6	2	.988	17
Joe Quinn, 2b	19	14	16	73	21	0	2	3	7	1	3	.288	6	42	55	8	.924	12
Charley Ganzel, c-rf	8	4	4	30	8	0	0	0	2	1	3	.267	0	34	9	1	.977	2
Charlie Bennett, c	8	6	3	22	3	0	0	1	7	1	7	.136	1	49	8	2	.966	0
Mike Kelly, c	5	4	1	16	3	0	0	0	3	0	5	.188	1	27	5	3	.914	1
Kid Nichols, p	7	4	6	27	6	1	0	0	0	0	6	.222	0	2	43	1	.978	1
John Clarkson, p	7	5	2	25	5	0	0	0	0	0	6	.200	0	2	27	1	.967	1
Harry Staley, p	6	3	3	21	4	0	0	1	2	0	3	.190	0	2	36	0	1.000	0
Boston Totals	19	154	116	672	187	25	11	11	73	16	62	.278	58	485	297	44	.947	22
Opponents' Totals	19	58	.46	617	148	20	5	6	47	4	79	.240	27	481	317	101	.888	10

	W-L-T	ERA	G	GS	CG	IP	H	R-ER	BB	SO
Nichols	7-0	2.18	7	7	7	62.0	57	18-15	16	36
Clarkson	6-0	1.78	7	6	6	50.2	47	20-10	21	14
Staley	5-0-1	2.55	6	6	5	49.1	44	20-14	11	29
Total	18-0-1	2.17	19	19	18	162	148	58-39	48	79

These statistics include the tie game September 17.

Tweed Webb:
'He's Seen 'Em All'

JAY FELDMAN

---

*Anyone interested in researching the Negro leagues should contact this man. Former player, manager, and historian, he **has** seen nearly all the great black stars.*

A COUPLE OF YEARS AGO, when there was a vacancy on the National Baseball Hall of Fame Veterans Committee, SABR's Negro Leagues Committee submitted the names of several candidates who could be expected to promote the cause of former Negro-league stars worthy of Cooperstown enshrinement but thus far overlooked. Nominees included ex-players such as Hall-of-Famers Hank Aaron, Willie Mays, Ray Dandridge, and Buck Leonard; noted sportswriter Sam Lacy, and historian Normal (Tweed) Webb.

At age eighty-four, Tweed Webb is possibly the oldest living chronicler of black baseball. He's certainly one of the most dedicated and vocal. His motto — "I've seen 'em all" — bears testimony to his more than seventy-five years of service as a fan, batboy, player, manager, sportswriter, officer scorer, historian, and, still today, tireless crusader for black baseball.

Webb, who acquired his nickname from a tweed suit worn in grade school, was introduced to baseball in 1910, when his father, a semi-pro ballplayer, took him to a game between the hometown St. Louis Giants and the Indianapolis ABCs. His career began in earnest seven years later, at age twelve, when he worked as batboy for Rube Foster's visiting Chicago American Giants. The Giants were one of the all-time great clubs, with a lineup that included such stars as Bingo De Moss, Dave Malarcher, Jimmy Lyons, and Carlos Torrienti.

In 1919, Webb lived in Cleveland, where his uncle Pete Miles, a major stockholder in the Cleveland Tate Stars, introduced him to greats like Ben Taylor, Turkey Stearnes, John Donaldson, and future Hall-of-Famer John Henry Lloyd. On his return to St. Louis, Webb began organizing ballgames between local street teams. "I was always an organizer, always trying to get things going," he says. "I'd form up a team from my street and get a game with a team from another street."

Tweed Webb in 1924

Those pick-up games also provided the first outlet for two of Webb's later passions: sportswriting and baseball history. "I'd write up a little story, 'Tweed Webb Stars at

---

Jay Feldman is a freelance writer and an organizer of the "Baseball for Peace" trips to Nicaragua.

Shortstop,' "he relates with an elfish grin. "I got a kick out of seeing my name. I wished I could be a writer." The historian in him kept the scorecards from those games (he still has several); it was about this time that he also began clipping and compiling newspaper articles.

In 1920 and '21, Webb played shortstop for the St. Louis Black Sox, a semipro team managed by his father. Next year the squad entered the newly-formed Tandy League — St. Louis' first black semipro circuit that would become a training ground for the Negro leagues. They competed under several names before becoming the St. Louis Pullmans, and dominating the league for a decade.

The apex of Webb's playing career came in 1926, with the Fort Wayne Pirates, an associate member of the Negro National League. "I was a good ballplayer, a smart ballplayer," he asserts. "I was 5'3", 140 pounds, little bitty guy, but I stood ten feet tall. Littlest man out there, with the biggest mouth. Hard to strike out. Good bunter. Good arm. I was a hustler.

"But to tell the truth, I didn't like that life. Bad travelling conditions, bad accommodations. The professional players were a rough bunch. I didn't drink or smoke, and I didn't like the women that hung around the players. And the pay was low — twenty-five dollars a week."

So he returned to St. Louis, became a sign painter, and resumed his association with the Tandy League — a connection that would continue until 1966 and earn him the sobriquet "Mr. Tandy." In his more than forty years as player, manager, official scorer, and publicity director, he had a hand in developing numerous future major leaguers, including Luke Easter, Al Smith, Sammy Pendleton, Sam Jethroe, Nate Colbert, and Ted Savage. (In the late forties, Webb also founded the short-lived Rube Foster League, the best known graduate of which was Elston Howard.)

In 1934, Webb branched out into sportswriting with a weekly column for the St. Louis Argus, one of the city's two daily black newspapers (he also wrote for the St. Louis American for a couple of years in the mid-thirties). Except for 1943-5 when he was in the Navy, Tweed Webb's "Hot Stove League" was a fixture for the next thirty-seven years. During the 1940s, he also covered the annual East-West all-star games and Negro League World Series.

As a reporter for the Argus and the official scorer for the St. Louis Stars' home games in 1932-49, Webb compiled records and photographs that would prove valuable decades later, when the history of the Negro leagues became a subject of serious study.

As anyone who has ever approached the field knows, black baseball history presents a problematic discipline, the main difficulty being the lack of reliable statistical data. "I get requests almost on a weekly basis from SABR members wanting statistics or other information on differ-

ent players or teams or leagues," relates Negro Leagues Committee chairman Dick Clark. "I'm not sure people really understand that we just don't have the information, that we can't just go out and find it in a book. We have to look for it. And Tweed has been one of our main sources. He was one of the first to start researching black baseball."

Webb in the Navy

"People are always asking me about specific records, for example, whether Josh Gibson or Turkey Stearnes hit more home runs," says Webb. "I hate to say it, but the records of black baseball are inadequate. In many cases, the true statistics just don't exist. It's hearsay; anybody that's got any sense knows there's nothing to prove it. But now, what happens sometimes is that some writer will go talk to John Doe and the guy will tell him, 'I hit .400 that year,' or, 'I hit 500 home runs,' and he'll go and write the story that way, but there's no proof."

Still, Webb has been a source for many writers and researchers, providing records, anecdotes, personal recollections, and photographs for numerous projects, including Charles Whitehead's biography of Rube Foster ("A Man and His Diamonds") and Phil Dixon's forthcoming comprehensive pictorial history of black baseball. "He's probably more knowledgeable about St. Louis [black] baseball than anybody," states Dixon, "and overall, he's one of the most knowledgeable people around the country. As far as a writer of [black] baseball, he's certainly one of the oldest around."

In his tireless, decades-long crusade for the affirmation of black baseball Webb has made his greatest mark. Says Bob Burnes, retired sports editor of the St. Louis Globe-Democrat, who has known Webb for more than thirty years, "Tweed Webb has done more in bringing recognition to the black player than anyone else. Cool Papa Bell is in the Hall of Fame because of Tweed's insistence."

In addition to his campaign for the induction of his longtime close friend Bell, Webb has also worked doggedly for the inclusion of other former Negro leaguers, including 1981 inductee Rube Foster. "Everybody talks about how I campaigned for Cool Papa Bell and Rube Foster for the Hall of Fame," says Webb with uncharacteristic shortness, "but I shouldn't have **had** to campaign for Rube Foster — he should have been the first. Not only was he a great pitcher and manager, but he was the founder of the Negro National League, the father of modern Negro baseball. There wasn't anybody did more for black baseball than Rube Foster. And they waited until 1981 to put him in. That was nothing but a joke."

His crusade far from over, Webb remains determined to see the great players and teams receive their due. "There are about a dozen men from the Negro leagues in the Hall of Fame, but some of the greatest have yet to be inducted. When most people talk about the Negro leagues, they know Satchel Paige, Josh Gibson, and Cool Papa Bell, and that's about all. Well, I've seen greater ballplayers than them."

Webb's immediate candidate for the Hall is Smokey Joe Williams, a flamethrower who starred in 1910-32. "I've been campaigning for him for the last five, six years. He was the greatest fastball pitcher I ever saw. Faster than Paige. He pitched a no-hitter against the New York Giants in 1919 in an exhibition game — struck out 24 and lost the game on an infield error. That was all swept under the rug. It's a mystery to me why he's not in the Hall of Fame."

After Williams, Webb has a lengthy list of other nominees. "There was Bruce Petway, a tremendous catcher with Rube Foster's club — a great hitter and he could throw. There was a series of exhibition games in Cuba where he threw out Ty Cobb sixteen out of seventeen tries. I wrote about that fifty years ago. People just can't believe it. Most places you'll read that he threw him out two out of three times.

"There's Biz Mackey, another catcher, who played ball for the Newark Eagles till the age of fifty. He was something. He should be in the Hall of Fame without a doubt.

"Almost nobody knows about John Donaldson; Chester Brewer; Bullet Rogan; Turkey Stearnes, who hit as many home runs as anybody; Jimmy Lyons, the fastest man in baseball before Cool Papa Bell; Pete Hill; Willie (Devil) Wells, one of the great shortstops; Dick London, another great shortstop. You have pitchers: Hilton Smith and Newt Allen, both of whom wrote to me asking me to put their names before the Hall of Fame. There's Willie Foster, Rube's brother.

"And there are plenty of other great players, but the problem is that not enough people saw the old-timers play. That's about it, right there. [Veterans Committee members] Roy Campanella and Monte Irvin don't know anything about those players, except what they've heard. They have no business being on that committee. **I'm** qualified to be on that committee."

Webb in 1984

Webb continues his crusade from his home, lobbying for the election of Smokey Joe Williams, answering the letters he receives from around the country, and reporting on special events — particularly illnesses and deaths of old-time players. In 1970, he organized the Oldtime Negro Baseball Players Association to aid former players, and he remains available, as he has been for the last fifty years, to deliver a tribute at a ballplayer's funeral. "If the family calls me, I drop everything to be there."

In the past fifteen years, as the history of black baseball has found a widening circle of enthusiasts, Webb's contribution has become more generally known. In 1974, he was the first black to be inducted into the St. Louis Amateur Baseball Hall of Fame. The same year, he appeared on "The Joe Garagiola Show" with Cool Papa Bell and Satchel Paige and selected his all-time Negro-leagues team. On July 9, 1975, St. Louis congressman William Clay read a tribute to Webb into the Congressional Record, and in 1986, he was the recipient of a "SABR Salutes" award.

The personal honors please him, but his devotion is to the cause: "I'm a dedicated man," he says proudly, hauling out his well-thumbed scrapbooks, notebooks and files, and spreading them out for perusal. "This is what I've done with my life."

Joe Charboneau: Far-Out Phenom

JACK KAVANAGH

---

*There are phenoms, and there are phenoms. Super Joe
could drink beer through his nose and open bottles
with his teeth — and, for a year, hit like blazes.*

WHEN A PLAYER blazes into view with an eye-catching performance, we call him a "phenom." Great things are expected from him and, sometimes, they follow. Joe DiMaggio, Ted Williams, and Stan Musial were first hailed as "young phenoms." As playing careers lengthen and a player who debuted as a "young phenom" becomes a steady star, he ceases being "a phenom." The players we remember as phenoms are the ones who promised stardom but faded after streaking into prominence. They are like comets.

Some disappeared because their talents were inadequate; they had a weakness others discovered. Many were tragically cut down by an injury; some even by death. Others became victims of their own weaknesses.

The best known phenoms are familiar to many baseball fans. There was Louis Sockalexis, who shone for only half the 1897 season with the Cleveland Spiders but left a legacy: The team was later renamed Indians in his honor. There was Harry Agganis of the 1955 Red Sox, the celebrated "Golden Greek" who died of pneumonia just as he was becoming a star first baseman. There was Bob (Hurricane) Hazle, who helped the 1957 Braves win the National League pennant, then faded fast as a squall. There was Cub second baseman Ken Hubbs, the 1962 Rookie of the Year who died in a plane crash after his second season. And there was Mark (The Bird) Fidrych, who won 19 games for the 1976 Tigers and almost singlehandedly reinvented the curtain call, only to succumb to arm trouble.

Oddly an even more recent phenom is slipping from memory. He deserves better because his may be the weirdest phenom story of all.

"Super Joe" Charboneau was a single-season phenom who fell from grace as colorfully as he zoomed to temporary stardom with the 1980 Cleveland Indians. When a player's accomplishments are great enough to win Rookie-of-the-Year honors, and he provides writers and broadcasters volumes of bizarre publicity, he becomes a gold-plated phenom.

A signal that Charboneau's off-beat antics were more than baseball management was willing to tolerate came when the Philadelphia Phillies virtually gave him away in 1978, even though he'd batted .350 in the California League.

The Indians closed their eyes to Joe's eccentricities, preferring to see in him the second coming of Rocky Colavito. And what eccentricities! Writers told about such off-field activities as pulling out his own tooth with a pair of pliers, opening beer bottles with his eye socket, and removing an unwanted tattoo with a razor blade. Not to mention winning bets by eating lighted cigarettes, swallowing eggs in their shells, and downing glasses of beer through his nose.

Having led one minor league in batting in 1978, Charboneau moved up to the Southern Association, and topped that league, too, batting .352 for Chattanooga.

His batting alone would have drawn the press. Arriving at spring training in 1980, he hit as if he were still in Chattanooga. He gave interviews, demonstrated some of his clubhouse stunts, and made the starting lineup. When the team reached Cleveland, the city was ready for him. A rock group had turned out a record, "Go, Joe Charboneau," which was played incessantly. The Cleveland Plain Dealer, dubbing him, "Super Joe," made Charboneau a cover feature in their Sunday magazine. Other publications ran features about him. He hit a 500-foot shot

---

Jack Kavanagh is enjoying "retirement" as a busy sports historian and writer, after a career as an advertising and broadcast executive and administrator in services for the handicapped.

off Tom Underwood at Yankee Stadium and seemed to bat best against the league's best pitchers. Joe's hitting feats were written up daily.

Despite a long slump, he finished with a .289 average, 23 home runs, and 87 runs batted in. These are fine marks for a first-year player only twenty-five years old. He was named American League Rookie Of The Year by the Baseball Writers' Association and The Sporting News.

Joe Charboneau's "rookie card" in the 1981 bubble-gum sets became a gilt-edged premium, bought up by collectors and dealers sure they had gotten in on the ground floor of an investment certainty. As Charboneau marched to Cooperstown, his first baseball card would increase in value many times. However, like most "penny stocks" shoestring investors buy, the Charboneau card today isn't an investor's dream. His career bubble burst like an overchewed wad of Topps gum.

Super Joe was again the center of attention in spring training of 1981. This time it was for what he had done, not what he might do. He stopped telling about removing teeth and tattoos and consuming indigestibles. He concentrated on his batting. But now was no longer hitting.

Charboneau floundered. By mid-season he had been sent to Charleston of the International League, having hit only .210 in 48 games, with only four home runs. Disgruntled by his demotion, he hit .217 with Charleston, with no home runs in 14 games before heading home to California to ruminate on his change in fortune.

The Indians brought him to spring training again in 1982. This time the interviews focused on what went wrong and, as the 1982 season began, why they were still going wrong. Joe hit only .214 in 22 games, with a pair of home runs. He returned to Charleston and failed. Even dropped down to the scene of earlier glory, Chattanooga, Joe couldn't hit. Another season was gone.

The next season found Joe Charboneau assigned to Cleveland's Buffalo farm club, in the International League. All he got from this circumstance was an extra's role in the Robert Redford movie, "The Natural." The player who had once seemed a natural himself was suspended for a week for making obscene gestures to the Buffalo fans. They had jeered him for not running out a ground ball.

Joe could have claimed a back injury had pointed the fickle finger of fate at him. Instead, he gave the finger back to the fans and demanded to be released. Having rejected winter trade offers and an inquiry from Japan, the Indians now freed Joe to accept whatever offers came his way. None came.

Joe joined a local semi-pro team to keep in shape and played in a tournament that involved four games in a single day. His team won. When they tried to drink a toast after the final game, no one had brought a bottle opener. Not to worry; Joe opened the beer bottles with his teeth.

Eventually, Joe got an offer. It came from the San Jose Bees, hoping a return to the California League would restore Joe to greatness. The general manager, Harry Steve, scheduled a returning-hero welcome. When the plane landed, however, no passenger named Charboneau got off. Joe had returned to his wife and two children in Santa Clara. He might not have known the way to San Jose. More likely, he wanted to recover from his back injury first.

During the winter, doctors at Duke University Hospital removed two and a half discs from Joe's back. The prognosis was that Joe would be lucky to walk, let alone run and swing a bat. Joe lost twenty-five pounds after the operation and waited for another chance. He is still waiting.

Looking back, the irrepressible Joe Charboneau pointed out how few athletes achieve as much as he did: just making the major leagues and having one starring season. "It took a good break to get there," Joe said, "and a bad break to keep me from getting back."

RIPKEN AND LaVALLIERE — THE SECOND GENERATION

Cal Ripken Sr., who has spent his entire career in the Baltimore organization as a minor-league player and manager and a major-league scout, coach, and manager, began as a twenty-one-year-old player for Phoenix of the Arizona Mexico League in 1957. Guy LaValliere, two years older than Ripken, was the first-string catcher for Phoenix. Ripken was a back-up catcher and a third baseman and outfielder. After that season Ripken and LaValliere drifted apart. In 1960, LaValliere was catching for Charlotte of the South Atlantic League. On August 18, 1960, his son Mike was born in Charlotte. That night, at Charlotte's Griffith Park, Guy celebrated the birth by going 2-for-2, with a double and two runs scored in a 5-1 win over Jacksonville. Six days later, on August 24, Cal Jr. was born in Havre de Grace, Maryland. Cal Sr., playing at Topeka for Earl Weaver's Fox Cities club in the Three-Eye League, celebrated by driving in the lead run in Fox Cities' 7-4, 10-inning victory.

Cal Jr. reached the majors with the Orioles in 1981 and today is one of the premier shortstops in the American league. Mike reported to the majors with Philadephia in 1984, spent several years with St. Louis, and after being traded to Pittsburgh in 1987 established himself as one of the best catchers in the National League.

— Al Kermisch

Who Belongs In The Hall?

RICHARD KENDALL

Has Cooperstown been admitting too many unqualified candidates, as some critics have been charging lately? Here's a system to evaluate the worthy—and unworthy...

MY PURPOSE in this study is to make an objective determination of players who belong in the Hall of Fame by comparing them to Hall of Famers at their position.

All Hall of Famers were classified by position and their career totals in eleven hitting and fielding categories (runs, hits, home runs, runs batted in, batting average, total bases, runs created,[1] stolen bases, assists, range factor,[2] and fielding percentage) were listed. Then for the players at each position a mean and standard deviation for each of the eleven categories was computed.[3] Each player was rated by how many SDs each of his career totals were from the mean of that category for that position.

An equivalent season[4] for those eleven categories for each player was computed. Each player was ranked according to his mean and standard deviation for each seasonal stat; this was compared to the mean and SD for Hall of Famers at that position. This moderated some extremes found when rating players by career totals only. Players who had relatively short but brilliant careers ranked somewhat lower than would be expected because their career totals were not especially high. Joe DiMaggio, Roy Campanella, and Hank Greenberg are good examples. On the other hand, a player who compiled large totals because of a long career will rank higher than his equivalent seasons would suggest. Carl Yastrzemski and Pete Rose are good examples of these. Combining career stats and equivalent seasons gives a total of a player's career and peak value.

The positive and negative career and seasonal SDs for each player were added and divided by 22, (the total number of SDs[5] from the mean). This gives a rating of a player relative to the average Hall of Famer at his position. This was computed for players at that position who are not in the Hall. For example—Mike Schmidt's career run total was 1.09 SDs above the mean for Hall-of-Fame third basemen, his seasonal run total was 1.17 SDs above the mean, but his BA was 1.06 SDs below the Hall-of-Fame third basemen's mean, and so forth. Considering those SDs above the mean as positive numbers and those below the mean as negative, Schmidt's total SDs were +12.65. Divide that by 22 and his overall SD is +0.58, the highest among third basemen past or present.

Pitchers were rated in regard to career and seasonal wins, winning percentage, earned run average, and strikeouts as well as strikeout-to-walk ratio, career shutouts, number of 20-win seasons, winning percentage compared to team's winning percentage minus their own (some pitchers with modest winning percentages did so while toiling for teams with low winning percentages), and lastly, career ERA as a percentage of the league's ERA (this adjusts the rather high ERAs of lively-ball eras and the extremely low ERAs of certain dead-ball eras).

Among Hall of Famers I did not consider players who spent the majority of their careers in the nineteenth century. Seasons were shorter, rules differed, and the statistics for these players skewed the means and SDs rather extremely. I also left out certain players who were elected to the Hall as managers.

[1]
$$\frac{(H + BB)\ (TB)}{AB + BB} = \text{Runs Created}$$

[2] Range Factor equals assists plus putouts divided by games at that position.

[3] Mean is the average for the category. Standard Deviation is the average variance from the mean. The number of standard deviations above or below the mean is a

Richard Kendall is a middle-school social studies teacher in Buffalo, Wyoming.

measure of how far above or below the average player a player places in a category: If a player is one SD above (or below) the mean, he is better (or worse) than about two-thirds of all players in that category. If he is two SD above (or below) the mean, he is about 95 percent better (or worse) than all players in that category.

[4] Equivalent seasons are determined by dividing the player's career total of games by 162. You then divide this number of equivalent seasons into each of the player's career stats to find out what his stats would be if he played a 162-game schedule. Runs Created, Range Factor, and Equivalent Seasons are courtesy of "Bill James Baseball Abstract," the source of much of my statistical ideas and information.

[5] I had only 20 SDs to divide by for catchers and first basemen, because I did not include a range factor for them since range is not especially important at those positions. For outfielders I also had only 20 SDs because I only had four fielding stats as compared to six for 2B, SS, and 3B (the most important fielding positions). Outfielders were rated on seasonal assists, seasonal putouts, season and career FP.

THE RANKINGS

Catcher

Yogi Berra	+0.77
Bill Dickey	0.70
Joe Torre	0.68
Johnny Bench	0.66
Mickey Cochrane	0.55
Ted Simmons	0.53
Carlton Fisk	0.46
Gabby Hartnett	0.40
Ernie Lombardi	−0.17
Roy Campanella	0.27
Roger Bresnahan	0.38
Bill Freehan	0.43
Manny Sanguillen	0.44
Wally Schang	0.49
Rick Ferrell	0.59
Ray Schalk	0.63
Al Lopez	0.77

NOTE: Fielding statistics are projected from years for which stats are known to career stats, except for Torre and Ferrell, for whom no fielding stats were found.

Joe Torre, Ted Simmons, and Carlton Fisk ranked high among catchers. Torre and Simmons were heavy hitters, but neither was considered a strong catcher and each spent a lot of time playing other positions. How much this will reduce their support for the Hall of Fame remains to be seen. Fisk, on the other hand, has been a fine all around catcher, entirely deserving of election to the Hall.

On the negative side, was Al Lopez elected to the Hall

as a manager or simply because he had caught more games than any other catcher? There don't seem to be any flagrant omissions among eligible catchers.

First Base

Lou Gehrig	+1.00
Jimmie Foxx	0.82
George Sisler	0.28
Hank Greenberg	0.14
Bill Terry	0.07
Johnny Mize	0.00
Steve Garvey	−0.11
Orlando Cepeda	0.15
Bill Buckner	0.21
Tony Perez	0.25
Joe Judge	0.31
Gil Hodges	0.31
Jim Bottomley	0.33
Mickey Vernon	0.38
Joe Kuhel	0.50
Willie McCovey	0.52
Joe Kelly	0.52
Jake Daubert	0.52
Stuffy McInnis	0.52
Lee May	0.53
Ted Kluszewski	0.53
Charlie Grimm	0.86
Frank Chance	0.90

It took a long time for Johnny Mize to be elected. Why? It looks like Steve Garvey has had a Hall-of-Fame career. Will Orlando Cepeda's baseball pluses outweigh his criminal minuses? Joe Judge and Gil Hodges did not rank very high but they out-ranked four Hall of Famers. Willie McCovey ranked surprisingly low. Frank Chance is the first of the Tinker to Evers to Chance infield to rank at the bottom of the rankings.

Second Base

Rogers Hornsby	+0.70
Charlie Gehringer	0.55
Nap Lajoie	0.40
Frankie Frisch	0.36
Eddie Collins	0.29
Bobby Doerr	−0.07
Joe Morgan	0.09
Billy Herman	0.39
Jackie Robinson	0.43
Toy Lazzeri	0.46
Rod Carew	0.51
Joe Gordon	0.53
Buddy Myer	0.53
Nellie Fox	0.64
Bobby Grich	0.64
Red Schoendienst	0.64
Marty McManus	0.79
Del Pratt	0.85
Bill Mazeroski	0.94
Larry Doyle	1.24
Tony Taylor	1.39
Johnny Evers	1.41

The difference in the ranking of Bobby Doerr and Joe Gordon is a surprise. Doerr has been underrated. Tony Lazzeri and Nellie Fox seem to be marginal Hall-of-Fame candidates at best and Bill Mazeroski seems to be completely out of consideration.

Shortstop

Honus Wagner	+ 1.25
Ernie Banks	0.42
Joe Cronin	0.26
Arky Vaughan	0.19
Luke Appling	0.17
Vern Stephens	0.08
Luis Aparicio	− 0.11
Travis Jackson	0.14
Dick Bartell	0.19
Rabbit Maranville	0.21
Joe Sewell	0.21
PeeWee Reese	0.26
Lou Boudreau	0.27
Dave Bancroft	0.28
Alvin Dark	0.33
Bobby Wallace	0.35
Maury Wills	0.42
Bert Campaneris	0.58
Dick Groat	0.60
Joe Tinker	0.69
Art Fletcher	0.81
Phil Rizzuto	0.88

The biggest surprise here is Vern Stephens, never given much credit as a potential Hall of Famer. But there he is, at or above the mean for shortstops. Only five had a higher ranking.

Let's give Rowdy Dick Bartell some credit for being a top shortstop. It was extremely hard to accept Phil Rizzuto's low ranking. His career offensive stats were low but he would be expected to rise in the ranks when fielding stats and seasonal offense were included. But that was not the case. Subjectively he was one of the top shortstops of his era but the numbers don't show that. Tinker, Evers, and Chance still make one ask, Why?

Third Base

Mike Schmidt	+ 0.66
George Brett	0.58
Eddie Mathews	0.46
Pie Traynor	0.24
Frank Baker	0.13
Ron Santo	0.07
Dick Allen	0.01
Jimmy Collins	− 0.04
Brooks Robinson	0.05
Ken Boyer	0.07
Freddie Lindstrom	0.21
Stan Hack	0.25
George Kell	0.25
Harlond Clift	0.27
Harmon Killebrew	0.29
Bob Elliot	0.30
Graig Nettles	0.31
Pinky Higgins	0.40
Tommy Leach	0.42
Al Rosen	0.46
Heinie Groh	0.61
Larry Gardner	0.62
Jimmy Dykes	0.81
Eddie Yost	0.90

Wow! Mike Schmidt, Eddie Mathews, and George Brett ahead of the great Pie Traynor. Well, get used to the idea. Ron Santo has certainly been overlooked, as well as Dick Allen, Ken Boyer, Darkie Clift, Bob Elliot, and yes, Graig Nettles. Sure, Graig has a low batting average, but he was top-notch in power and fielding.

Outfielders

Ty Cobb	+ 1.18
Babe Ruth	1.14
Hank Aaron	0.79
Ted Williams	0.71
Willie Mays	0.69
Stan Musial	0.67
Tris Speaker	0.66
Joe DiMaggio	0.55
Al Simmons	0.54
Mel Ott	0.32
Frank Robinson	0.27
Mickey Mantle	0.17
Pete Rose	0.13
Paul Waner	0.05
Carl Yastrzemski	− 0.01
Willie Keeler	− 0.01
Goose Goslin	− 0.01
Harry Heilman	0.02
Al Kaline	0.03
Earl Averill	0.05
Jim Rice	0.05
Joe Medwick	0.06
Kiki Cuyler	0.09
Roberto Clemente	0.11
Joe Jackson	0.15
Chuck Klein	0.15
Heinie Manush	0.20
Fred Clarke	0.20
Hack Wilson	0.21
Sam Rice	0.25
Duke Snider	0.25
Bob Johnson	0.26
Sam Crawford	0.29
Billy Williams	0.30
Zack Wheat	0.32
Vada Pinson	0.34
Max Carey	0.34
Bobby Bonds	0.37
Al Oliver	0.37
Richie Ashburn	0.37
Earl Combs	0.38
Lou Brock	0.41
Ken Williams	0.47
Reggie Jackson	0.47
Amos Otis	0.51
Ralph Kiner	0.54

Babe Herman	0.56	Jesse Tannehill	0.16
Reggie Smith	0.56	Don Drysdale	0.18
Lloyd Waner	0.57	Vic Willis	0.24
Larry Doby	0.58	Robin Roberts	0.26
Edd Roush	0.58	Lefty Gomez	0.30
Doc Cramer	0.59	Hippo Vaughn	0.30
Minnie Minoso	0.59	Luis Tiant	0.31
Sherry Magee	0.59	Carl Mays	0.31
Enos Slaughter	0.61	Jim Bunning	0.32
Willie Davis	0.62	Doc White	0.33
Bobby Veach	0.63	Catfish Hunter	0.33
Tony Oliva	0.65	Phil Niekro	0.35
Del Ennis	0.66	Stan Coveleski	0.36
Elmer Flick	0.67	Urban Shocker	0.40
Willie Stargell	0.69	Hal Newhouser	0.41
Gee Walker	0.72	Bill Donovan	0.44
Harry Hooper	0.73	Babe Adams	0.45
Bing Miller	0.76	Mort Cooper	0.46
Dixie Walker	0.76	Bob Lemon	0.49
Charlie Keller	0.86	Vida Blue	0.49
Jimmy Sheckard	0.87	Dave McNally	0.54
Rusty Staub	0.88	Wilbur Cooper	0.56
Carl Furillo	0.97	Allie Reynolds	0.59
Cy Williams	1.01	Mickey Lolich	0.62
Roy Thomas	1.02	Early Wynn	0.64
		Tommy John	0.65
		Tommy Bridges	0.66
		Bob Shawkey	0.66
		Billy Pierce	0.67
		Mel Stottlemyre	0.68
		Jack Coombs	0.73
		Milt Pappas	0.75
		Red Faber	0.75
		Art Nehf	0.76
		Slim Sallee	0.77
		Red Ruffing	0.82
		Jim Kaat	0.82
		Jack Powell	0.82
		Bucky Walters	0.85
		Herb Pennock	0.86
		Burleigh Grimes	0.86
		Virgil Trucks	0.86
		Rube Marquard	0.88
		Wes Ferrell	0.90
		Schoolboy Rowe	0.91
		Eppa Rixey	0.94
		Freddie Fitzsimmons	0.95
		Lou Burdette	0.98
		Waite Hoyt	0.98
		Jerry Koosman	0.99
		Jim Perry	1.00
		Paul Derringer	1.00
		Ted Lyons	1.02
		Eddie Rommel	1.02
		Hooks Dauss	1.03
		Jesse Haines	1.13
		Dolph Luque	1.30

Well, the traditional favorites still come out on top: Cobb, Ruth, Speaker, Aaron, Mays, Williams, Musial, and DiMaggio. What took them so long to elect Earl Averill? Jim Rice should be a shoo-in. Why not Indian Bob Johnson? How about my old favorite, Vada Pinson?

Pitchers

Walter Johnson	+1.51
Christy Mathewson	1.46
Cy Young	1.19
Grover Alexander	1.04
Tom Seaver	0.70
Eddie Plank	0.70
Ed Walsh	0.68
Three Finger Brown	0.60
Lefty Grove	0.58
Addie Joss	0.55
Sandy Koufax	0.54
Juan Marichal	0.53
Rube Waddell	0.42
Whitey Ford	0.40
Warren Spahn	0.38
Bob Gibson	0.37
Jim Palmer	0.32
Steve Carlton	0.28
Chief Bender	0.15
Carl Hubbell	0.10
Fergie Jenkins	0.10
Bob Feller	0.08
Ed Reulbach	0.07
Dizzy Dean	0.02
Sam Leever	0.01

Gaylord Perry	−0.01
Don Sutton	0.03
Dazzy Vance	0.03
Deacon Phillippe	0.06
Nolan Ryan	0.07
Jack Chesbro	0.11
Bert Blyleven	0.16

Walter Johnson's +1.51 SDs was the highest of any player at any position. Anyone could have predicted Johnson, Mathewson, Young, and Alexander topping the list. But who would have guessed Eddie Plank? Notice how many pitchers of the last twenty years ranked very high: Seaver, Gibson, Koufax, Marichal, Ford, Carlton, Palmer, Jenkins, Perry, et al. Someone must have forgotten about Ed Reulbach and Sam Leever and Deacon Phillippe and Jesse Tannehill.

Then you look at the bottom of the list and wonder what Pop Haines and Ted Lyons and Waite Hoyt and Eppa Rixey and Herb Pennock and Red Ruffing and Marquard and Grimes and Faber are doing down there. They're Hall of Famers, aren't they?

Top Eligible Candidates

1. Joe Torre   +0.68
2. Ferguson Jenkins   .10
3. Ron Santo   .07
4. Dick Allen   .01
5. Gaylord Perry   −0.01
6. Ken Boyer   0.07
7. Orlando Cepeda   0.15
8. Luis Tiant   0.31
9. Jim Bunning   .31
10. Vada Pinson   .34
11. Bobby Bonds   .37
12. Maury Wills   .42

Veteran's Committee

1. Vern Stephens   +0.03
2. Ed Reulbach   0.07
3. Sam Leever   0.01
4. Deacon Phillippe   −0.06
5. Jesse Tannehill   0.16
6. Dick Bartell   0.19
7. Vic Willis   0.24
8. Stan Hack   .025

MEANS AND STANDARD DEVIATIONS

		CAREER		SEASON	
		Mean	SD	Mean	SD
Catcher	R —	777.6	201.38	73.4	19.5
	H —	1647.3	307.2	153.1	17.78
	HR —	146.5	110.98	13.6	10.37
	TB —	2466.9	624.53	229.7	47.23
	RBI —	908.7	290.58	83.8	22.6
	SB —	65.4	66.23	6.4	7.2
	BA —	.2872	.02066		
	RC —	925.2	225.22	86.9	19.86
	A —	1042.2	341.61	106	39.01
	FP —	.9833	.00535		
First Base	R —	1223.3	735.06	104.2	18.39
	H —	2158.9	472.83	184.4	22.74
	HR —	287.8	177.08	23.4	12.55
	RBI —	1336.9	396.16	113	23.11
	TB —	3625.4	958.29	306.6	46.87
	SB —	126.1	133.92	12.2	15.02
	BA —	.3145	.02176		
	RC —	1490	450.26	126.1	24.72
	A —	1052.5	256.84	96.3	14.72
	FP —	.9899	.00202		

		Mean	SD	Mean	SD
Second Base	R —	1369.89	325.39	103.78	10.01
	H —	2530.44	629.35	190.67	18.21
	HR —	126.67	89.22	10	7.23
	RBI —	1162.33	357.28	88.11	19.68
	TB —	3601.89	906.18	272.56	39.19
	SB —	277.78	205.41	20.33	11.99
	BA —	.31544	.02509		
	RC —	1504.89	439.48	113.22	18.47
	A —	5634.33	1489.07	475	30.37
	RF —	5.5322	.2497		
	FP —	.97033	.00835		
Shortstop	R —	1172.29	242.94	87.5	10.49
	H —	2313.36	452.15	172.43	13.15
	HR —	107.93	119.94	8	7.81
	RBI —	1046.93	322.95	78.36	18.86
	TB —	3263.43	737.54	243.07	29.28
	SB —	218.79	186.92	15.43	11.15
	RC —	1247.5	340.41	93.21	17.16
	BA —	.28764	.02246		
	A —	5727.64	1278.22	500.5	26.5
	RF —	5.3729	.3437		
	FP —	.95293	.01154		
Third Base	R —	1115.63	212.43	90.88	11.22
	H —	2163	331.55	177.13	21.05
	HR —	218.63	197.17	16	12.25
	RBI —	1163.75	273.85	93.63	10.99
	TB —	3344.5	736.41	269	16.96
	SB —	103.88	74.7	9.63	7.61
	RC —	1215.75	300.41	97.75	12.06
	BA —	.2915	.02216		
	A —	3417	1426.44	308.25	20.63
	RF —	3.11	.3079		
	FP —	.95163	.01351		
Outfield	R —	1492.23,	339.57	106.1 ,	13.66
	H —	2667.65,	571.72	189.28,	17.14
	HR —	269.13,	204.58	18.83,	12.96
	RBI —	1361.93,	423.82	96.68,	23.33
	TB —	4210.88,	1002.76	297.93,	31.68
	SB —	226.1 ,	225.66	15.45,	14.28
	RC —	1701.2 ,	493.37	120.225,	21.15
	BA —	.31515,	.02		
	A —			14.4 ,	4.71
	PO —			318.63,	45.59
	FP —	.972 ,	.00968		
Pitcher	W —	255.39	60.44	20	2.12
	PCT —	.60103	.04325		
	ERA —	2.93	.5181		
	SO —	1869.4	637.5	149.08	45.9
	K/W Ratio —	1.96	.6528		
	ShO —	45.68	19.04		
	20 W —	5.55	3.3		
	WPAT —	.06548	.04109		
	BR/9 Inn —	10.82	0.9772		
	ERA % L —	.8213	.0782		

10,000 Plate Appearances
TED DiTULLIO

THE FOLLOWING is a list through 1989 of every major-league player who came to bat at least 10,000 times in his career. The category I/O refers to interference or obstruction and has been verified for every player but Jake Beckley. Zack Wheat finished his career four appearances short of 10,000.

	AB	BB	HBP	SH	SF	I/O	TOTAL
1. Rose	14053	1566	107	56	79	29	15890
2. Yastrzemski	11988	1845	40	13	105	1	13992
3. Aaron	12364	1402	32	21	121	0	13940
4. Cobb	11436	1249	92	296			13073
5. Musial	10972	1599	53	35	53	0	12712
6. Mays	10881	1463	44	13	91	0	12492
7. E. Collins	9946	1503	77	511			12037
8. Speaker	10196	1381	101	309			11987
9. B. Robinson	10654	860	53	101	114	0	11782
10. F. Robinson	10006	1420	198	17	102	2	11745
11. Wagner	10427	963	57	221			11668
12. Kaline	10116	1277	55	45	104	0	11597
13. R. Jackson	9864	1375	96	13	68	1	11417
14. Ott	9456	1708	64	109			11337
15. J. Morgan	9277	1865	40	51	96	0	11329
16. Maranville	10078	839	39	300			11256
17. Brock	10332	761	49	47	46	5	11240
18. Aparicio	10230	736	27	161	76	0	11230
19. Staub	9270	1255	79	56	119	0	11229
20. T. Perez	9778	925	43	9	106	0	10861
21. Max Carey	9363	1040	77	290			10770
22. P. Waner	9459	1091	38	174			10762
23. Darrell Evans (A)	9973	1605	35	35	89	0	10737
24. Ruth	8397	2056	42	113			10608
25. S. Crawford	9579	760	10	242			10591
26. Carew	9315	1018	25	128	64	0	10550
27. Beckley	9476	616	164(E)	290		1?	10547
28. B. Williams	9350	1045	43	8	73	0	10519
29. Lajoie	9590	516	113(E)	220	•		10439
30. Pinson	9645	574	54	52	78	0	10403
31. Banks	9421	763	70	45	96	0	10395
32. Fox	9232	719	142	208	48	1	10350
33. Dahlen	9019	1064	44	202			10329
34. Hooper	8785	1136	76	248			10245
35. S. Rice	9269	709	54	213			10243
36. Appling	8857	1302	10	74			10243
37. Gehringer	8860	1185	51	141			10237
38. Nettles	8986	1088	50	12	90	1	10227
39. Clemente	9454	621	35	36	66	0	10212
40. G.S. Davis	9027	870	65(E)	200			10162
41. Mathews	8537	1444	26	36	58	0	10101
42. Frisch	9112	728	31	229			10100
43. Anson	9067	952	32	46			10097
44. Schmidt	8352	1506	79	16	108	0	10061

NOTE: HBP data for Wagner, Crawford, Dahlen and Anson are incomplete. All pre-1950 players' SH/SF are combined and Interference/Obstruction data is missing. A-Active. E-Estimated.

Ted DiTullio is SABR's only fur designer.

Will The Real Rabbi Of Swat Please Stand Up?

LOUIS JACOBSON

The cult-inducing slugger failed with the Giants, but not for reasons previously reported. Nor did he go by the name in the Baseball Encyclopedia. Herewith the facts.

HIS STORY WAS THE STUFF of legends. His name was Mose Solomon. He hit 49 home runs in Hutchinson, Kansas, of the Southwest League in 1923 — and only Babe Ruth had ever hit more. John J. McGraw's New York Giants bought him for (depending on what newspaper article you quote) $4,500 up to $100,000, planning to make him a rival gate attraction to Ruth and hoping that New York's burgeoning Jewish population would come out to see one of their own. He immediately became a darling of the Gotham press, who promptly gave him (or at least publicized) such nicknames as "The Jewish Babe Ruth" and "The Rabbi of Swat."

He played in three games at the end of that 1923 season, batting .375 (3 for 8) and outhitting rookie benchmates (future Hall of Famers) Bill Terry (.143) and Hack Wilson (.200).

What could go wrong with this movie-like script? Well, it didn't turn out as planned: He was sold to Toledo in the American Association before the next season, never to play in the majors again.

These are primarily facts that make a legend; unfortunately, published speculations about Solomon's premature downfall have proved to be incorrect, initiating a legend of their own.

Howard Lavelle, in "Moses Solomon, the Rabbi of Swat" (published posthumously in the 1976 "Baseball Research Journal"), wrote, "The king abdicated. The clouting colossus of the southwest collapsed. His fielding was atrocious. He couldn't catch a fly without flypaper. He was a hazard on defense, not only to himself but also to his teammates. The king was soon exiled to the minors, shorn of his tinsel and glamour. The Rabbi of Swat had become a rabbit of swatters; the long-ball touch was gone."

And Bill James, also of SABR, in his "Historical Abstract," wrote, "Seems like he had a lot of trouble with the glove and a certain amount of trouble with the curve ball."

"The reason they sent him down was so simple you wouldn't believe it," Mose's son Joseph Solomon told me in December 1987.

"He came up at the end of the season [in] 1923. The Giants made the World Series. McGraw asked my dad to stay and attend the Series, even though he wasn't eligible to play. He hadn't played enough games to be eligible."

There was a problem. Solomon was a top football player, good enough to play on teams such as Jim Thorpe's Carlisle Indians and the Portsmouth (Ohio) Spartans, which evolved into today's Detroit Lions.

"Football season was starting," Joseph Solomon said. "My dad made more money playing football than baseball. He asked McGraw, 'Am going to get paid?' McGraw said, 'No.' And [Mose] said, 'Then I'm going to play football.' He played for Portsmouth.

"McGraw said, 'If you go play football, you will not be on the Giants. You're either going to be a baseball player or a football player.' My dad read about it in the papers: He was sold to Toledo."

There is more to the legend of the Rabbi of Swat, though. Let's go back to the beginning.

He was born on Hester Street, on the Lower East Side of Manhattan, on December 8, 1900. The midwife who delivered him made a mistake on the birth certificate.

"[T]he midwife didn't record the certificate until February or something," says Joseph Solomon. "It was a cold winter, and she went out with a whole pile [to be recorded at the same time]. She put 'Morris' on [the certificate]."

The problem was, his name wasn't Morris; it was Mose.

"It created a lot of problems through the years," says Joseph. "Such as in dealing with his insurance policies. He knew the birthdate; it happened in a period near Hanuk-

---

Louis Jacobson, a sophomore at Princeton, is researching a book on the sociological aspects of Jews in baseball.

kah, and his whole family knew."

Neither was his given name Moses, Joseph says. "As far as he was concerned, it was 'Mose.' All his friends called him Mose. But sometimes the newspapers called him Moe, further complicating the issue."

His parents were poor (his father was a peddler), and they moved to Columbus, Ohio, when Mose was young. His mother had emigrated from Austria, and his father from Russia. Though the parents were religious, the piety didn't rub off on Mose.

BASEBALL AND FOOTBALL were not the only sports to run in the family. One of his brothers, who fought under the name Harry Sully, was an Ohio boxing champion. Joseph relates that Sully said, "You know, I could lick everybody in Ohio — and my kid brother [Mose] could whip my ass from the time he was fifteen."

Sully's son became an all-around athlete, the only one at his Ohio high school ever to earn twelve athletic letters.

Mose was so talented at football that Ohio State took serious notice of him. "He was offered the first football scholarship from Ohio State University that I know of," says Joseph. He says he believes that never before had the university offered somebody free tuition simply because of football prowess.

Unfortunately, Mose couldn't accept: The family needed his income.

Joseph maintains Mose's aging scrapbook, and one page that has since been lost had an article that described a one-punch fight under the stands. "He knocked the guy cold," says Joseph. "It said the word finally got around the league: Better lay off the big Jew. He told me that was typical: It [occurred in] every town. He had to prove that he was [equal to the challenge]."

Times hadn't changed much by the time Joseph was playing ball. He too had some notable experiences with his Jewish identity. When he was pitching for South Miami in the Dade County League, he was razzed by the opposing bench — the Naval Reserve squad — about being Jewish. "I just politely went off the mound, went over to our bat rack, picked up a bat. I went over [to the bench] and I said, 'All right now. If anybody has anything more to say, come on out and say it.' That was the end of it." The Naval Reserve was subsequently kicked out of the league.

Mose never hid his Jewish identity in the face of anti-Semitism. But he did hide it once for another reason.

"He played [football] one year with the Carlisle Indians, with Jim Thorpe," says Joseph. The team was supposed to be an all-Indian team. "They were barnstorming, and they were down near the end of the ballgame and it was 0-0. They were playing in Dayton, Ohio, which is far enough from Columbus [that Mose wouldn't be recognized]. My dad was playing under an assumed name — Red Bill or Red Hawk, or something."

Mose was an outstanding drop-kicker — a now extinct art that flourished in the early days of pro football. In fact he used to give exhibitions of his skill at drop-kicking, in which the ball is dropped, allowed to bounce, and then is kicked on its upward flight.

"They needed a field goal," Joseph said. "My dad drop-kicked the field goal, and they won the ballgame.

"There happened to be a sportswriter from Columbus in the stands," says Joseph. "He came down to the locker room afterwards, and he told my dad, 'I'll never tell on you, but you can't do this!' And that was the end of his playing with [the Indians].

"Now, there may have been other guys on the team who weren't Indians, too. But I don't think there were too many Jews on the team!"

Still, neither football nor baseball was an accepted occupation among most Jewish parents of Mose's time. When people asked his parents what Harry was doing for a living, they wouldn't hesitate to say "boxing." But when people asked what Mose was doing, his parents said, "He's out West working."

"It was society," says Joseph. "It hadn't yet become acceptable. Boxing already had Jewish champions, like Benny Leonard and Lew Tendler. But baseball was not the type of work a Jewish boy did."

MOSE, IT SEEMED, was chronically injured, which makes his success — the 49 home runs, the seven seasons in the minors batting over .300 — even more incredible. "He was in the hospital twenty-three times," says Joseph. "He had kind of brittle bones in his ankles, and he broke his ankles a lot. But when he broke his collarbone in 1924 playing football, he told me, it kind of changed his swing. He had a hard time pulling the ball after that."

He retired when he was only twenty-seven years old, playing in the Eastern League with Albany, New York. "[That was] when I was born," says Joseph, "and that was one of the reasons he quit when he did."

Mose died in 1966 of heart failure — perhaps, as Lavelle writes, "richer and happier." Some would say he lived the American dream. One thing is sure, though. The Rabbi of Swat lived the life of a legend.

The Joe Cronin Trade And the Senators' Decline

JERRY HANNAN

WASHINGTON IS THE ONLY city to have lost *two* major-league teams. In its last twenty-five years as an American League franchise, the nation's Capital never even reached the first division. But its greatest single misfortune may have taken place on October 26, 1934, when owner Clark Griffith sent Joe Cronin to the Red Sox for $225,000 and Lyn Lary. In terms of Washington infamy, that date ranks second only to Pearl Harbor Day.

Was this the worst trade ever? How did it compare with the trade of Lou Brock (and some never-to-be-heard-of's-again) for Ernie Broglio? Or Nellie Fox for Joe Tipton? Hard to say. In any case, the circumstances that dictated the Cronin trade included more than just playing talent. Clark Griffith surely was astute enough to know that Lyn Lary wasn't comparable in any way with Cronin, but in that Depression era Griffith probably needed the $225,000 to stay in business. Yet it's hard to imagine any deal that resulted in a faster unraveling of a franchise.

To understand the enormity of that trade, it's necessary to appreciate what had transpired in the preceding years. Washington entered the American League in 1901 and struggled for respectability for more than two decades. In 1924 the Senators won the pennant and defeated the New York Giants in the World Series. They also won the pennant in 1925 and had the Pirates down 3 games to 1 before losing the Series. There followed seven years in which the Senators did well, but never as well as the Yankees or Philadelphia Athletics. During that period the Senators were not really serious contenders despite having some quality players.

Cronin became a regular in 1929—not just a regular but a good fielder and an excellent hitter. During his first four years there was a steady correlation between his batting and the team's standing in the league:

Year	Cronin's Average	Senators' standing
1929	.281	5th
1930	.346	2nd
1931	.306	3rd
1932	.318	3rd

In 1933, Cronin was named the playing manager. He was all of twenty-six years old. Help immediately arrived,

as Griffith acquired lefthanded pitchers Earl Whitehill and Walter Stewart and reliever Jack Russell. In lesser transactions Griffith picked up Fred Schulte, Luke Sewell, and Goose Goslin—the latter having been a Senator standout in their glory days. With Cronin hitting .309, driving in 118 runs, turning double plays with Buddy Myer, and baiting the umps—in dramatic contrast to his deliberate predecessor, Walter Johnson—the Senators won the pennant. They were no match for the Giants in the World Series, losing 4 games to 1, but Washington fans could not have been disappointed with the 1933 season.

In 1934 the bubble broke. Cronin's average dropped 25 points, Joe Kuhel's fell 33, General Al Crowder degenerated from a league-leading 24 wins to 4, and Whitehall won 14 games instead of 22. The team dropped to seventh place in one of the more dramatic turnarounds in baseball history. Many veterans had lost the touch after their one blockbuster of a season. There was some hope for the 1935 season, however, because Cecil Travis had shown that he could hit (.319) and Johnny Stone had a good year at .315. Maybe with a little luck and a few off-season deals by the Old Fox, the Senators could be back in the hunt. Instead, Clark Griffith, short of cash, disposed of his most valuable asset by peddling Cronin to the Red Sox for the aforementioned $225,000 and Lyn Lary. To put this in perspective, imagine the Baltimore Orioles trading Cal Ripken for a truckload of cash and Mike Fischlin! Lary didn't finish the 1935 season, and the Senators finished in sixth. Succeeding years saw them finish fourth, sixth, fifth, sixth, seventh, seventh, and seventh before rising to second in the 1943 war year.

None of those teams would have won the pennant, but with Cronin at shortstop they might well have contended. An infield of Kuhel, Myer, Cronin, and Travis would have been among the league's best until Kuhel was traded after the 1938 season. Their contact-hitting style was perfect for Griffith Stadium's vast outfield. But once Cronin was gone, the Senators were on their way out, too.

Jerry Hannan is a chemist at the Naval Research Laboratory in Washington, D.C.

Evaluating Pitchers' Won-Lost Records

STEPHEN FINLAN

© 1989, by Stephen Finlan

A pitcher's record is a common — and imperfect — gauge of his performance. Weighing factors other than pure wins and losses gives us a better way to judge success.

THE WON-LOST RECORD is the most-often-cited pitcher's stat, despite its obvious flaw: going 20-12 for the 1927 Yankees is not as good as going 20-12 for the 1988 Rangers. The Wins-Above-Team (WAT) statistic measures how many more wins a pitcher had than his team would have had with its other pitchers in the same number of decisions. If a pitcher goes .600 for a .500 team, he has a good WAT, but this stat is misleading because it fails to separate the element of hitting support from the element of how good that pitching staff happens to be. If the team has great hitting but poor pitching, a pitcher will probably have to go only 13-10 to get a good WAT rating. WAT compares a pitcher to the other pitchers on the same staff, rather than comparing him to the rest of the league.

This system introduces a way of evaluating a pitcher's wins and losses with respect to the run-scoring ability of his team (and also its fielding ability). In 1985, Rick Reuschel's 14-8 for the poor-hitting Pirates was a little better than Joaquin Andujar's 21-12 for the good-hitting Cards or Charlie Liebrandt's 17-9 for the average-hitting Royals.

The system assigns points to given W-L records, varying in accordance with the hitting and fielding support the team gave its pitchers. It is not based on how much above average a pitcher's record is, because "above average" does not win pennants. The system is based on the idea that the team's goal is to win the pennant. Therefore, positive points are only awarded to records that are at, or close to, a pennant-winning caliber.

Assuming an average-hitting team, and ignoring for now the factors of complete games, saves, and the era in which the season occurred, look at the logic of gauging pennant-winning performance. First, award points for W-L records over .600. A pitcher who goes 17-11 (.607) for an average-hitting team has a season of pennant-winning caliber and is awarded one point. If the rest of the pitching staff accumulates a similar percentage, the team will win 98 games and contend for the pennant. If a pitcher maintains that percentage, he deserves more points. Thus, 26-17 (.605) is worth one and one-half points. The system is configured on the basis of the question: How close to a pennant does his won-lost record take the team?

A 23-10 record is better than an 18-7 record in this system, even though the percentage is lower (.697 compared to .720). If a pitcher is 18-7 on September 1, and then goes 5-3 for the remainder of the season, he added eight more decisions at a .625 rate, and pushed his team closer to a pennant. Or consider that when a pitcher goes 23-10, the rest of the staff needs only to accumulate .581 over the remaining 129 games to get 98 wins. If a pitcher goes 18-7, the rest of the staff must achieve .584 over 137 games. Therefore, 23-10 is a 3.5 point season; 18-7 is a 3-pointer.

The Basic Point System and its Adjustments

Appendix A shows a chart of points awarded for seasons with 15 to 29 wins, and 0 to 21 losses, including negative points for some seasons, and zeroes for seasons in the middle. Appendix B also discusses how these numbers are adjusted for hitting and fielding support, and the era in which the season occurred.

Saves are a different case. As a general rule, a pitcher is awarded an additional win for every four saves, or for every five saves if he has over 19. If the pitcher has a negative season, then a win is awarded for every three saves (even if

---

Stephen Finlan is a typesetter and a student of Biblical history. "BRJ" readers interested in printouts of their favorite pitchers should write him, enclosing a self-addressed stamped envelope.

more than 20), in order to help him get out of negative territory. Also, if a pitcher's record is a "high zero" and he had three to seven saves, a win is awarded for every three saves in order to give him a positive rating for the season.

Important adjustments are made according to era. There is a very significant increase in these figures for years after 1947, and a major reduction for seasons pitched before 1893, when the mound was moved to 60'6". More details are given in Appendix B.

It must be admitted, however, that the system is more effective for rating starters than relievers, and more useful for the era before relief pitching became so important. Some people may feel these factors affecting W-L are one reason why ERA is a more useful stat, but ERA has as many flaws as W-L: it can be pushed up by one bad game; it ignores unearned runs, as though pitching effectiveness becomes irrelevant once an error is made; and it ignores the dynamics of individual games. W-L measures something ERA does not: a pitcher's competitiveness in **each** game — his ability to pitch well enough to win, whether that means 1-0 or 5-4. W-L also incorporates a pitcher's hitting and fielding ability, which can help his team to win.

Additional Points

The main component in this point system is the total of the points gained or lost in all of a pitcher's seasons. However, points are added at the end for other achievements, including a tenth of a point for every 10 wins, and another tenth of a point for every hundred wins, so that a 13-10 is not simply a "zero," but results in about .13 being added to the pitcher's total.

Other points added at the end include: total saves divided by 200; complete games divided by 600 if the pitcher pitched in 1894 or later; complete games divided by 300 if he pitched in 1965 or later; and 1.5 points for every "ERA year." To get an ERA year a pitcher must finish in the top three in his league in one of the following: ERA, runs-prevented (called "pitcher's runs" in Palmer's Linear Weights System), either of these when adjusted for home-park factor, or in overall pitcher-rating in Palmer's system ("The Hidden Game of Baseball").

A sum of .03 points is given for every year with a poor-hitting team, regardless of W-L record; and -.02 for every year with a good-hitting team, regardless of record. A total of .15 points is awarded for post-season wins, -.1 for post-season losses, and there is a system for awarding additional tenths of points for post-season ERA. Several tenths of points are awarded for the pitcher's lifetime park-adjusted normalized ERA (see "Hidden Game," page 181). These make little difference except in settling the rating question when two pitchers are otherwise evenly matched.

Appendix A: Points Assigned to Some Win-Loss Records, Avg-Hitting Teams

Win ◊ Loss ◊	15	16	17	18	19	20	21	22	23	24	25	26	27	28	29
0	5.5	6.0	6.1	6.5	7.0	7.5	8.0	8.2	8.5	9.0	9.5	10.0	10.2	10.5	11.0
1	5.0	5.5	5.6	6.0	6.5	7.0	7.5	7.6	8.0	8.5	9.0	9.5	9.7	10.0	10.5
2	4.5	5.0	5.1	5.5	6.0	6.5	7.0	7.1	7.5	8.0	8.5	9.0	9.2	9.5	10.0
3	4.0	4.5	4.6	5.0	5.5	6.0	6.5	6.6	7.0	7.5	8.0	8.5	8.7	9.0	9.5
4	3.5	4.0	4.1	4.5	5.0	5.5	6.0	6.1	6.5	7.0	7.5	8.0	8.2	8.5	9.0
5	3.0	3.5	3.6	4.0	4.5	5.0	5.5	5.6	6.0	6.5	7.0	7.5	7.6	8.0	8.5
6	2.5	3.0	3.1	3.5	4.0	4.5	5.0	5.1	5.5	6.0	6.5	7.0	7.1	7.5	8.0
7	2.0	2.5	2.6	3.0	3.5	4.0	4.5	4.6	5.0	5.5	6.0	6.5	6.6	7.0	7.5
8	1.5	2.0	2.0	2.5	3.0	3.5	4.0	4.1	4.5	5.0	5.5	6.0	6.1	6.5	7.0
9	1.0	1.5	1.5	2.0	2.5	3.0	3.5	3.6	4.0	4.5	5.0	5.5	5.6	6.0	6.5
10	.05	1.0	1.0	1.5	2.0	2.5	3.0	3.1	3.5	4.0	4.5	5.0	5.1	5.5	6.0
11	0.0	0.5	1.0	1.0	1.5	2.0	2.5	2.6	3.0	3.5	4.0	4.5	4.6	5.0	5.5
12	0.0	0.0	0.5	0.8	1.0	1.5	2.0	2.0	2.5	3.0	3.5	4.0	4.1	4.5	5.0
13	0.0	0.0	0.0	0.5	0.5	1.0	1.5	1.5	2.0	2.5	3.0	3.5	3.6	4.0	4.5
14	0.0	0.0	0.0	0.0	0.0	0.5	1.0	1.0	1.5	2.0	2.5	3.0	3.1	3.5	4.0
15	0.0	0.0	0.0	0.0	0.0	0.0	0.5	0.8	1.0	1.5	2.0	2.5	2.6	3.0	3.5
16	-1.0	0.0	0.0	0.0	0.0	0.0	0.0	0.3	0.5	1.0	1.5	2.0	2.0	2.5	3.0
17	-1.0	-1.0	0.0	0.0	0.0	0.0	0.0	0.0	0.1	0.5	1.0	1.5	1.5	2.0	2.5
18	-1.5	-1.0	-1.0	-0.5	0.0	0.0	0.0	0.0	0.0	0.1	0.5	0.8	1.0	1.5	2.0
19	-1.5	-1.5	-1.0	-1.0	-0.5	0.0	0.0	0.0	0.0	0.0	0.0	0.1	0.5	1.0	1.5
20	-2.0	-1.5	-1.5	-1.0	-1.0	-0.5	0.0	0.0	0.0	0.0	0.0	0.0	0.1	0.5	1.0
21	-2.5	-2.0	-2.0	-1.5	-1.0	-1.0	-0.5	0.0	0.0	0.0	0.0	0.0	0.0	0.1	0.5

18-18 commences negative points for 'break-even' years

To get points, wins must be 5 more than losses, from 5 to 18 wins

For 19 to 24, there must be a margin of 6 between W and L

For 25 to 28, there must be a margin of 7 between W and L

Appendix B: Adjustments to Point-Chart

Positive-point seasons pitched before 1893 (when the mound was moved to 60' 6") in the NL are valued at 60 percent of the figure given in Appendix A, or at 55 percent in the American Association (though negative years are the same as shown on the chart.) National Association records are valued at 30 percent.

Seasons after 1947 are multiplied by 1.06. NL seasons after 1962 are multiplied **again** by 10.03; expansion years are multiplied **again** by .975. Also, every season is given a small increment for every year beyond 1900 (a negative increment for nineteenth-century years). A record that is worth 4.5 points in 1900 would only be worth 2.69 in 1887, or 5 for an NL team in 1980.

Hitting and Fielding Support Adjustments

A pitcher's won-lost record is influenced by the offensive and defensive support he gets. In any given year, a chart can be created showing that some teams stand out in supporting a pitcher with the bat and glove, and others lag behind.

For every season since 1876, compare each team's total runs and errors with the rest of the teams in its league (taking into consideration the home-park factor, though to a lesser degree than in Palmer's system). Most teams have been assigned to one of three categories: good, average, or poor; two rarer categories are very good and very poor. In 1988 in the AL, the A's, Twins, Red Sox, and Yankees gave good support to a pitcher; the Indians, White Sox, and Rangers gave poor support; the Orioles **very** poor.

In Appendix C this category is called "Support." Under this heading, 4-2 means the pitcher had four years with good or very good hitting and fielding teams, two with poor teams and the rest with average. The next column is total points, then the number of good years, and the points accumulated in those years. Lastly is the ranking the pitcher would have had if good years were the only thing counted (Carlton would have been first among post-1958 pitchers).

Points assigned to a W-L record are reduced by 25 percent or more when achieved with a good-hitting team. Points are increased 45 to 140 percent when with a poor-hitting team, and more still for years with **very** poor teams (any non-losing record for a very poor team results in points). Negative points for losing years with poor teams are considerably less than for the same record with an average team.

One peculiarity about this list is the scarcity of pitchers with good teams. This "under-rewarding" of the pitcher with a good-hitting team compensates for the fact that he will have **more** positive seasons than a comparable pitcher with a poor-hitting team. What the latter lacks in **number** of "scoring" years is made up for by the higher **value** given to his winning years.

Appendix B: Most Points in a Season

	Name	Yr	Tm	W-L	HtgSupp.	Pts.
1.	Carlton	1972	PHN	27-10	Poor	11.7
2.	Radbourn	1884	PRN	60-12	Avg.	10.3
3.	Johnson	1913	WSA	36-7	Avg.	10.2
4.	Grove	1931	PHA	31-4	Avg.	10.2
5.	Chesbro	1904	NYA	41-13	Avg.	9.6
6.	G. Perry	1978	SDN	21-6	Poor	9.0
7.	Meekin	1894	NYN	36-10	Avg.	8.7
8.	Young	1895	CLN	35-10	Avg.	8.5
9.	Dean	1934	SLN	30-7	Avg.	8.5
10.	Riddle	1941	CNN	19-4	Poor	8.3
11.	Walters	1944	CNN	23-8	Poor	8.2
12.	Walsh	1908	CHA	40-15	Avg.	8.2
13.	Koufax	1964	LAN	19-5	Poor	8.1
14.	Wood	1912	BSA	34-5	Good	7.9
15.	Koufax	1963	LAN	25-5	Avg.	7.7
16.	McGinnity	1904	NYN	35-8	Good	7.6
17.	Vance	1924	BKN	28-6	Avg.	7.5
18.	Clemens	1986	BSA	24-4	Avg.	7.5
18.	Roberts	1952	PHN	28-7	Avg.	7.4
20.	Face	1959	PTN	18-1	Avg.	7.4
21.	Gomez	1934	NYA	26-5	Avg.	7.3
22.	McLain	1968	DTA	31-6	Good	7.2

This point system indicates that the following pitchers may be underrated: Nichols (#6 all-time), Seaver (#8), Ford (#11), Newhouser (#22), Tannehill (#25), Guidry (#28), Leever (#33), and Allie Reynolds (#51).

1,000 Games Caught (Through 1989)

TED DiTULLIO

1. Bob Boone (A)	2195	22. Hemsley	1482	43. Chief Zimmer	1239	64. Cy Perkins	1111
2. Fisk (A)	1928	23. Del Crandall	1479	44. Ivy Wingo	1231	65. Tebbetts	1108
3. Sundberg	1927	24. Roseboro	1476	45. Steve Yeager	1230	66. Masi	1101
4. Al Lopez	1918	25. Cochrane	1451	46. Severeid	1225	67. Battey	1087
5. Gary Carter (A)	1822	26. Wally Shang	1431	47. Walker Cooper	1223	68. Stanage	1074
6. Rick Ferrell	1806	27. Ruel	1413	48. Terry Kennedy (A)	1216	69. Jack Clements	1073
7. Hartnett	1790	28. Lance Parrish (A)	1405	49. Seminick	1213	70. Ed Bailey	1064
8. Ted Simmons	1772	29. Johnny Edwards	1392	50. Tom Haller	1199	71. Scioscia (A)	1040
9. Bench	1744	30. McCarver	1387	51. George Gibson	1196	72. Jody Davis (A)	1035
10. Ray Schalk	1726	31. Gus Mancuso	1360	52. Kittredge	1196	73. Milt May	1034
11. Bill Dickey	1712	32. Jimmie Wilson	1359	53. Dooin	1194	74. John Jos. Warner	1032
12. Yogi Berra	1699	33. Grote	1348	54. Campanella	1183	75. Sammy White	1027
13. Jim Hegan	1629	34. O'Farrell	1338	55. Mickey Owen	1175	76. Hundley	1026
14. Deacon McGuire	1611	35. Wilbert Robinson	1316	56. T. Peña (A)	1174	77. Mike Tresh	1019
15. Freehan	1581	36. Frankie Hayes	1309	57. Johnny Kling	1168	78. Buck Martinez	1009
16. Sherm Lollar	1571	37. Spud Davis	1291	58. Whitt (A)	1167	79. Bill Killefer	1006
17. Luke Sewell	1561	38. Ashby	1280	59. Smoky Burgess	1139	80. Clay Dalrymple	1003
18. Ernie Lombardi	1542	39. Munson	1278	60. Ellie Howard	1138	81. Duke Farrell	1003
19. Steve O'Neill	1528	40. Del Rice	1249	61. Cerone (A)	1135		
20. Dempsey (A)	1515	41. Frank E. Snyder	1249	62. Billy Sullivan Sr.	1121	A = Active	
21. Darrell Porter	1506	42. Wynegar	1247	63. Sanguillen	1114		

Appendix C: The Greatest Pitchers Of All Time

Rank	Name (L = Lefty)	W — L	Sv	Support	Total Pts.	# Gd Yrs.	Gd Yrs Only	Rank Gd Yr.
1	Mathewson	373-188	27	6-2	72.4	12	50.2	1
2	Cy Young	511-313	16	5-3	71.0	13	45.8	2
3	L - Grove	300-141	55	7-1	67.6	12	43.4	3
4	Walter Johnson	416-279	34	1-7	64.3	12	42.9	4
5	Alexander	373-208	31	2-1	62.9	12	40.4	5
6	Kid Nichols	360-203	16	6-0	48.8	10	34.7	7
7	Brown	239-129	48	3-1	47.4	9	31.7	8
8	Seaver	311-205	1	4-7	47.2	10	31.7	9
9	Feller	266-162	21	2-2	47.2	9	31.6	10
10	L - Spahn	363-245	29	6-2	45.5	12	28.8	12
11	L - Ford	236-106	10	11-0	43.8	12	28.3	14
12	Palmer	268-152	4	9-0	42.7	12	24.9	16
13	L - Koufax	165- 87	9	1-1	40.9	6	30.3	11
14	L - Carlton	329-244	2	6-4	40.6	11	35.5	6
15	Gibson	251-174	6	2-3	39.2	9	23.2	17
16	L - Hubbell	253-154	33	0-0	38.1	8	22.1	19
17	L - Plank	327-193	23	7-1	35.8	12	28.8	13
18	Marichal	243-142	2	5-0	35.4	8	28.2	15
19	Keefe	344-225	2	5-2	33.7	8	19.9	27
20	McGinnity	247-144	23	4-1	32.2	8	21.2	22
21	L - Gomez	189-102	9	7-0	32.1	8	19.8	28
22	L - Newhouser	207-150	26	1-2	32.0	6	21.0	24
23	Rusie	243-160	5	1-0	30.8	5	19.1	30
24	Radbourn	308-191	2	3-1	29.2	6	19.6	29
25	L - Tannehill	197-116	7	3-3	28.7	7	22.6	18
26	Lemon	207-128	22	3-0	28.2	9	17.7	37
27	Clarkson	326-177	5	7-0	28.2	9	18.5	34
28	L - Guidry	170- 91	4	8-0	27.1	8	22.0	20
29	Mays	208-126	31	3-0	26.8	8	18.2	35
30	Walsh	195-130	36	1-2	26.7	6	13.3	47
31	Roberts	286-245	25	0-4	26.5	7	15.0	45
32	Dean	150- 83	30	2-0	25.7	4	15.9	42
33	Leever	193-101	12	5-0	25.3	9	21.8	21
34	Griffith	240-141	6	4-0	24.9	8	17.9	36
35	Ruffing	273-225	16	10-5	24.7	10	18.8	31
36	Reulbach	181-105	11	3-0	24.6	8	20.2	25
37	G. Perry	314-265	11	4-5	24.6	5	18.6	33
38	L - Vance	197-140	10	0-2	24.5	6	15.6	44
39	L - Pennock	240-162	32	8-2	24.4	8	16.1	41
40	Ferrell	193-128	13	0-3	24.0	7	15.7	43
41	Hunter	224-166	1	7-3	24.0	6	16.3	40
42	Joss	160- 97	5	2-1	23.9	5	13.0	49
43	L - John	286-224	4	8-4	23.7	10	21.2	23
44	Bender	210-127	24	5-2	23.4	10	20.1	26
45	Grimes	270-212	18	3-3	23.3	9	18.6	32
46	Coveleski	217-141	19	6-0	23.2	7	11.2	51
47	Wilhelm	143-122	227	1-6	23.2	7	13.8	46
48	Cicotte	208-149	25	4-2	23.0	6	16.9	39
49	Adams	194-140	15	3-2	22.9	7	13.0	48
50	Lyons	260-130	23	0-8	22.5	7	12.7	50
51	Reynolds	182-107	49	8-2	22.5	8	17.5	38

The Best Pitchers From 1958 To Present

Rank	Name (L = Lefty)	W — L	Sv	Support	Total Pts.	# Gd Yrs.	Gd Yrs Only	Rank Gd Yr
1	Seaver	311-205	1	4-7	47.2	10	31.7	2
2	L - Ford	236-106	10	12-0	43.8	12	28.3	4
3	Palmer	268-152	4	9-0	42.7	12	24.9	6
4	L - Koufax	165- 87	9	1-1	40.9	6	30.3	3
5	L - Carlton	329-244	2	5-4	40.6	11	35.5	1
6	Gibson	251-174	6	2-3	39.2	9	23.2	7
7	Marichal	243-142	2	5-0	35.4	8	28.2	5
8	L - Guidry	170- 91	4	8-0	27.1	8	22.0	8
9	G - Perry	314-265	11	3-5	24.6	5	18.6	10
10	Hunter	224-166	1	7-3	24.0	6	16.3	13
11	L - John	286-224	4	8-4	23.7	10	21.2	9
12	Wilhelm	143-122	227	1-6	23.2	7	13.8	20
13	Tiant	229-172	15	9-4	20.6	8	14.4	18
14	Gossage*	110- 97	302	3-1	20.6	10	16.1	14
15	Sutton	324-256	5	7-3	20.6	9	15.4	15
16	McLain	131- 91	2	5-1	19.9	4	15.2	16
17	L - McNally	184-119	1	7-1	19.5	7	16.5	12
18	Sutter*	66- 71	300	1-5	19.4	6	11.1	37
19	Hershiser*	83- 49	4	0-3	19.2	3	11.2	36
20	Quisenberry*	53- 44	238	2-3	18.8	6	14.2	19
21	Gooden*	91- 35	0	4-0	18.7	5	13.4	23
22	L - Lyle	99- 76	238	7-0	18.6	7	14.9	17
23	Niekro	318-274	30	6-7	18.5	5	10.2	39
24	Bunning	224-184	16	4-3	18.5	5	13.3	25
25	L - McDaniel	141-119	172	1-1	18.3	9	17.4	11
26	Jenkins	284-226	7	6-3	17.8	7	11.8	31
27	L - Cuellar	185-130	11	5-1	17.2	7	13.7	22
28	Blyleven*	254-226	0	3-2	17.0	3	5.6	96
29	Clemens*	78- 34	0	1-0	16.9	4	11.7	33
30	Drysdale	209-166	6	1-3	16.7	3	8.3	57
31	L - Candelaria*	164-102	15	4-0	16.0	7	12.5	28
32	L - Blue	201-153	2	6-3	15.8	5	10.7	38
33	Tekulve	94- 87	191	1-3	15.7	6	12.8	27
34	Morris*	177-118	0	3-0	15.4	7	12.4	30
35	L - McGraw	96- 92	180	4-3	15.4	7	11.2	35
36	Fingers	114-118	341	5-3	15.3	7	9.6	43
37	Maloney	134- 84	4	4-0	15.0	6	12.9	26
38	L - Valenzuela	118- 90	1	2-3	15.0	6	7.5	70
39	L - Gullett	109- 50	11	7-0	14.6	7	13.4	24
40	Regan	96- 81	92	3-1	14.2	4	13.8	21
41	Face	104- 95	193	3-2	14.1	5	11.8	32
42	L - Kaat	283-237	18	11-2	13.7	6	9.2	47
43	L - Higuera*	69- 38	0	1-2	13.6	4	8.8	52
44	L - McGregor	138-108	5	3-3	13.5	4	9.8	41
45	Pascual	174-170	10	4-7	13.0	4	7.1	73
46	Stieb*	131-109	1	1-2	13.0	4	4.5	106
47	Messersmith	130- 99	15	1-3	12.8	3	6.6	83
48	L - Tudor*	105- 68	0	2-3	12.7	3	6.9	78
49	L - Lolich	217-191	11	5-2	12.7	7	12.4	29
50	Welch*	132- 95	8	4-2	12.3	5	7.7	66
51	Chance	128-115	23	1-3	12.0	4	8.5	54
52	Grant	145-119	23	3-1	11.6	4	7.5	68
								Active

Shutouts:
Final Year, Final Game
WILLIAM RUIZ and LYLE SPATZ

It's tough enough to throw a shutout in your final season — fewer than 300 pitchers did — and almost impossible to zip the opposition in your final game.

IN 1901, BILL CRISTALL, a rookie lefthanded pitcher and a native of Odessa, Russia, started six games for the Cleveland Blues of the new American League. He lost five, but his one win was a shutout. Although he was only twenty-two years old, Cristall never appeared in another major-league game. With fellow American Leaguers Jerry Nops of Baltimore, Ted Lewis of Boston, Dale Gear of Washington, Cleveland teammate Pete Dowling, and National Leaguer Roger Denzer of the Giants, he shares the distinction of being the first major leaguer to throw a shutout in his final year. Of the thousands of big league pitchers who have retired since 1901 fewer than 300 have earned a place on this select list.

Injuries caused Sandy Koufax to retire following the 1966 season, a season in which five of his 27 wins for the Dodgers were shutouts. Koufax was only thirty years old and on his way to being perhaps the greatest pitcher ever when his career prematurely ended. Certainly no pitcher ever ended his career in more spectacular fashion. He led the league in wins (27), earned run average (1.73), games started (41), complete games (27), innings pitched (323), strikeouts (317), and shutouts (5). Yet the five shutouts he had only tied the record for the most in a final year. Four other pitchers had done so previously.

In 1903, Henry Schmidt, a thirty-year-old righthander spent his one and only year in the big leagues. Pitching for fifth-place Brooklyn, he won 21 games while losing 13, and became the first pitcher to end his big-league stay with five shutouts.

In 1905 a righthanded pitcher named Herbert Briggs, whom everyone in the National League called Buttons, duplicated Schmidt's accomplishment. Briggs, who like Koufax and Schmidt was thirty in his final year, had pitched for Chicago in 1896, 1897, 1989, and 1904. In 1904 he had won 19 games and pitched his first three shutouts. The five shutouts he threw in his final year of 1905 were the only bright spots in a season in which his record was a mediocre 8-8.

Hall of Famer Joe McGinnity, at age thirty-seven, ended his brilliant ten-year career by winning 11 and losing 7 for the 1908 New York Giants. McGinnity also had five shutouts in a year best remembered for the Fred Merkle incident.

In 1915 George Kaiserling pitched five shutouts while compiling a 13-14 record for the Newark Peps of the Federal League. Kaiserling was a twenty-two-year-old righthander whose only other year in the majors was in 1914 with the Indianapolis Hoosiers of the Federal League. When the Federal league folded following the 1915 season, Kaiserling was gone from the major leagues. He died in 1918 at the age of twenty-four.

Since 1915 only Koufax, in 1966, has pitched five shutouts in the last year of a career. Larry French had four as a member of the 1942 Dodgers before he left to enter the Navy. When the war ended he chose to retire. The five-shutout feat has yet to be turned in the American League. Among AL pitchers with four are Ed Cicotte of the 1920 White Sox, banned following that season for his part in the Black Sox Scandal; Allie Reynolds, who was thirty-nine when he did it for the 1954 Yankees; and most recently, Britt Burns of the 1985 White Sox. Traded to the Yankees, Burns was hampered by a bad hip and was never able to pitch again.

Only five pitchers threw shutouts in their final game. On Oct. 5, 1929, the next-to-last day of the season, Rube Ehrhardt, age thirty-four, won his only start by allowing five hits and issuing one walk in blanking the league champion Chicago Cubs 9-0.

Lew Krausse Sr. made his final appearance in the big leagues a memorable one. Pitching for the Philadelphia Athletics, he shut out the Red Sox 15-0 on Sept. 2, 1932. Five days later he pitched in an exhibition game against

William Ruiz is a research associate at the Hall of Fame. Lyle Spatz is a regional economist for the U.S. Dept. of Commerce. They were assisted by Ray Gonzalez.

Stroudsburg. Although he was only twenty years old, his major-league career was over. Twenty-nine years later his son, Lew Krausse Jr. of the then-Kansas City Athletics, made his major-league debut. Eighteen years old and just graduated from high school, he shut out the Los Angeles Angels 4-0, limiting them to three singles. This gave Lew Krausse Sr. and Jr. back-to-back shutouts twenty-nine years apart.

In the first game of a season-ending doubleheader at Boston, on Sept. 30, 1945, Don Fisher of the Giants shut out the Braves 1-0. Fisher pitched the entire 13 innings, scattering 10 hits and three walks. Nap Reyes' homer in the top of the 13th was the game-winner. Fisher, who was twenty-nine, had been recently picked up from a semipro league in Cleveland. As was the case with Ehrhardt, this was his only start of the season. In Fisher's case it was also his only start in the major leagues. He was replaced by the servicemen returning to the majors the next season.

Don Wilson was a first-rate pitcher for the lackluster Houston Astros from 1966 through 1974. In '74 he had an 11-13 record with four shutouts, including one in his last appearance. On September 28 he defeated Atlanta 5-0, allowing only two hits. A strikeout pitcher, Wilson oddly had none that day. On January 5, 1974, Wilson, not yet thirty, died in a tragic accident in his Houston home.

The most recent pitcher to throw a shutout in his last major league game was Brian Denman of the 1982 Red Sox. At Yankee Stadium, on October 2, he defeated Dave Righetti by shutting out New York 5-0 on six hits. Denman was back at Pawtucket the next year, spent several more seasons in the minor leagues, and never again pitched in the majors.

It's sad to think that with the possible exception of Ehrhardt, none of these men knew that the shutout they had just pitched would be their last major league appearance. But it was.

Homer Leaders By Letter

Fluffy Saccucci

Letter	Player	Home Runs
A	Hank Aaron	755
B	Ernie Banks	512
C	Orlando Cepeda	379
D	Joe DiMaggio	361
E	Darrell Evans (A)	414
F	Jimmie Foxx	534
G	Lou Gehrig	493
H	Frank Howard	382
I	Pete Incaviglia (A)	100
J	Reggie Jackson	563
K	Harmon Killebrew	573
L	Greg Luzinski	307
M	Willie Mays	660
N	Graig Nettles	390
O	Mel Ott	511
P	Tony Perez	379
Q	Jamie Quirk (A)	37
R	Babe Ruth	714
S	Mike Schmidt	548
T	Frank Thomas	286
U	Del Unser	87
V	Mickey Vernon	172
W	Ted Williams	521
X	No Players	
Y	Carl Yastrzemski	452
Z	Gus Zernial	237

A = Active

Eye Injury Handicapped Young Babe

Al Kermisch

When Babe Ruth broke into Organized Baseball it didn't take him long to establish himself as an outstanding pitcher and a hitter with exceptional power. But was the young Babe satisfied with his batting? Apparently not. On April 25, 1919, the following item appeared in C. Starr Mathew's column "Playing the Game," in the Baltimore Evening Sun:

"Once upon a time before Babe Ruth became famous, a newspaperman complimented him on his batting and the Baltimore slugger said: 'I'm handicapped in batting because one of the boys at school smacked me in the eye with a brick. If I could see better I could hit better.'

"Few persons ever guessed that Babe was handicapped to such an extent. It is a very sad thing, of course, but there are many American League pitchers who just hate to think what Ruth would do but for that 'bad' eye."

The above item appeared about a week after the Babe had culminated a sensational slugging spring by hitting six home runs in six official times at bat in two exhibition games between the Red Sox and Orioles in Baltimore.

Chris Von der Ahe: Baseball's Pioneering Huckster

RICHARD EGENRIETHER

© 1989, Richard Egenriether

Move over, Charlie Finley and Bill Veeck — the old Browns' owner was baseball's first great promoter. And move over George Steinbrenner — Von der Ahe was a meddler supreme.

PERHAPS THE GREATEST DAY of Chris Von der Ahe's life occurred in the spring of 1882, when he dedicated his new Sportsman's Park on Grand Avenue and Dodier Street in north St. Louis. Leading his fellow American Association owners to the mound, the portly magnate, glowing with pride, is alleged to have said: "Look around chentlemen [sic], because this the largest dimundt in the welt ist." Charlie Comiskey, the St. Louis Browns captain, tactfully reminded Chris that baseball diamonds were the same size. "Vot I meant to say," said the "Boss President," hastily correcting his grand claim, "vas this the larchest infield in the welt ist."

This vignette is characteristic of Chris Von der Ahe, the German immigrant who knew virtually nothing about baseball, yet was one of the few owners in the early professional era to earn a substantial profit from his investment. Popular with his employees and the public as a magnanimous entrepreneur and flamboyant character, he was detested by many of his rival magnates as an interloper who degraded the "truly American" character of the pastime of baseball by charging lower admission rates, promoting Sunday play, and instituting beer concessions at the ballpark. National League magnates like Albert G. Spalding were dismayed by the marketing strategies of American Association owners like Von der Ahe and eventually forced Chris out of the game. But Chris's impact is felt to this day. Quirky promotions like the installation of a shoot-the-chute, a "stadium club," and sideshow attractions were later imitated in the modern era by the likes of Larry MacPhail, Charles O. Finley, and Bill Veeck. Even the conservative conglomerates of today, desiring a profitable return on their investments, offer premiums and extra-baseball entertainment to their customers. Yet for all of their efforts, today's promotions pale in comparison to those of Chris Von der Ahe, baseball's pioneering huckster.

Sources conflict as to exactly when Chris was born. Lee Allen tells us that Chris arrived at New York at seventeen in 1864. The Sporting News and the St. Louis Globe-Democrat in their obituaries say that Chris was born at Hille, Germany in 1850. By 1870, he was in New York. Later he moved to St. Louis, where he worked as a grocery clerk and eventually became the proprietor of a saloon on Sullivan and Spring Avenues at the western edge of the city. Within a few years he bought real estate in the neighborhood and made money as a landlord. Von der Ahe was also involved in neighborhood politics and used the back room of his tavern as a ward headquarters.

Just east of his saloon was a lot first used by German immigrants as a shooting park and later converted to a makeshift baseball field known as Sportsman's Park. The games there were amateur events but drew large crowds, many of whom would repair to Von der Ahe's saloon for friendly imbibing afterwards.

Alfred H. Spink, who would later know success in the establishment of The Sporting News, backed a professional independent club known as the Browns — a name recalling an earlier St. Louis ball club that held membership in the National League. In the spring of 1881, Spink contacted Cincinnati sportwriter O. P. Caylor and asked him to organize a club for an exhibition at St. Louis. Caylor readily accepted the invitation and had little trouble finding players in a town that had become baseball-starved. (An 1880 NL ban on Sunday games had effectively removed Cincinnati from the league.) The game at Sportsman's Park was a tremendous financial success. "Vot a fine pig crowd [sic]," Chris, holder of the concession nights, said to Spink after the game. "But the game, Al, how vas the game? You know, Al, I know

---

Richard Egenriether is a graduate student in American studies at the University of Minnesota.

nawthing." Whether the game was good or not made no difference to Chris and Al, but the success at the gate indicated to Spink that it would be profitable to arrange for other exhibitions with other independent clubs. So successful were these exhibitions that these clubs came together in the fall of 1881 to create a formal relationship. A meeting held at Cincinnati resulted in the formation of the American Association, which granted franchises to Baltimore, Cincinnati, Louisville, Philadelphia, Pittsburgh, and St. Louis.

The constitution of the Association was based along the same lines as the National League. Although the American Association copied the National League in respect to the philosophy of honest play, it was far more liberal in other respects. Member clubs could play outside clubs on open dates. Players were not bound to the reserve clause as were their National League brethren. Indeed, a player could be released from his club without prejudice, given two weeks salary, and allowed to sign immediately with any Association club that desired his services. Other distinctions were two innovations in play: that the club with the highest percentage instead of the most wins was champion, and the hiring of a permanent staff of umpires. But the greatest differences between the League and the Association were that the interlopers allowed Sunday ball, charged twenty-five cent admission, (half that of the League), and sold beer and liquor. The latter was not surprising, given the brewery and distillery money behind several clubs.

Spink approached Von der Ahe in early 1882 and asked him to sell 180 shares of stock in the Browns at ten dollars a share. Von der Ahe had bought the stock himself as an opportunity to expand his bar business. From the beginning, the Browns were a success. During the exhibition season of 1881, Spink had spotted a talented first baseman named Charles A. Comiskey playing for the Dubuque Rabbits. Persuaded to sign with the Browns, "Commy" was given a free reign to manage the club. By 1885, Comiskey built the Browns into baseball's most dominant club. They won four consecutive pennants between 1885 and 1888, a feat that was not matched until John McGraw's New York Giants of 1921-1924 and not surpassed until Casey Stengel's New York Yankees of 1949-1953. Von der Ahe was fortunate to have Comiskey, a good player and intelligent leader who got the most out of his talented players. Among them were Arlie Latham, a clownish but dazzling third baseman; Bob Carruthers and Dave Foutz, two outstanding pitchers who over three years won 195 games; and Tip O'Neill and Curt Welch, two staples in the outfield who provided power and finesse. Von der Ahe fawned over his Browns during the glory days. He paid them well and outfitted them in broad-stripe

blazers that served as warm-up jackets. Chris always got some of his money back from his players by insisting that they live in his boarding houses and do their drinking in his saloon. The players, however, were not always willing to spend their free time under the Boss's constant eye and frequently sneaked across the street to a rival public house.

Chris Von der Ahe

Von der Ahe tried vainly to keep tabs on those players by occasionally visiting the rival. But the recalcitrant players always managed to evade detection because Chris could easily be spotted under the tavern's short-bottomed swinging doors. His spatted shoes and ever-present greyhounds were dead giveaways. Seeing trouble, the players would hightail it out the back door.

Von der Ahe was not a baseball man in the sense Spalding or NL founder William A. Hulbert were, but an entrepreneur. As such, he saw the value of postseason exhibitions for his champions. A three-game series was established in 1884 in which Providence of the National League beat New York of the Association. In 1885, the Browns played a series of touring exhibition games with Chicago. The Browns won three games of seven played, one ended in a tie because of darkness, and a second was forfeited by the Browns when Comiskey took them off the field after an adverse umpiring decision. In search of larger receipts, Von der Ahe suggested to Al Spalding in 1886 that the series be played on the contestants' fields. Spalding, whose White Stockings were the perennial League champions, agreed to the format and set forth other conditions to avoid "the misunderstandings of last year" in a winner-take-all series. Spalding promised his players half of the receipts and new suits if they won. Inspired by such a magnanimous promise, the White Stockings won two of the the first three games at Chicago. But the Browns came storming back, sweeping three at Sportsman's Park. The last game was won in the tenth inning after Chicago blew a 3-0 lead in the seventh. The Browns rallied, scoring one run followed by a single by Comiskey and a bunt single by Curt Welch. Arlie Latham, known as "the freshest man on earth," came to bat with the calm confidence of Thayer's Casey silencing the crowd by saying, "Don't worry folks, I'll tie it up." And he did with a two-run triple. The Browns scored in the tenth to win the series when Welch stole home with the famous "$15,000" slide. Spalding was reported to be so upset with his players that he refused to pay their train fare home. Von der Ahe was so elated with his Browns that he arranged a parade in which the club rode in a large carriage bearing a huge woolen pennant proudly proclaiming: "St. Louis Browns: Champions of the World."

During the 1880s a baseball game featuring the Browns was an event almost akin to the Fourth of July. At home or on the road, the Browns virtually guaranteed a full house. Going to the game was as momentous as the game itself. "The Boss President," as Chris liked to call himself, personally led his club to the ballpark. In those days, many parks did not have clubhouses, so players dressed in their hotel rooms or apartments. In St. Louis, the Browns would assemble at Von der Ahe's saloon and march down to Sportsman's Park. A silk-hatted, swaggering Chris would lead the formation, flanked by his two sleek greyhounds, Snoozer and Schnauzer. Chris would beam as he acknowledged cheers, but he was always bewildered by the laughter that followed him. Had he ever bothered to look back, Chris would have seen third baseman Latham aping the Boss's gait and wearing a bright red false nose reminiscent of Chris's bulbous proboscis.

The festivities continued on the field with an aggressive brand of play. Consistent with the American value of achieving success at any cost, baseball players in the 1880's seemingly observed only one rule: Everything was fair. One contemporary umpire noted that only the closest watch of players could keep them from tricks like sliding spikes-high, which became such a hazard that spikes were barred from the major leagues for several years. The Browns were not the only club that resorted to such tactics, but because they won so many pennants they were singled out for rowdy play and accused of "stopping at nothing" to win.

Following the action on the field, Chris would lead his customers back up Sullivan Avenue for a nightly wassail. Chris would even occasionally spring for drinks, declaring

"money, dot [sic] ist to schpend!"

The 1880s were heady days for Von der Ahe and the Browns; not even the threat of a third league could slow the Von der Ahe juggernaut. The key behind the Browns' success was that Comiskey could deal diplomatically with the mercurial Von der Ahe and prevent the Boss from interfering with running the club on the field.

The Browns' fortunes, however, turned with the formation of the Players League in 1890. Comiskey was one of 30 AA stars to defect. The PL's collapse did not help the AA, and after the 1891 season, Von der Ahe and his Browns were begrudgingly accepted into the National League.

Looking for new ways of drawing customers, Chris decided that old Sportsman's Park was outdated. A new 10,000-seat stadium was built near a convenient trolley line. Chris hoped that access to mass transportation would lure the fans. However, the Browns became losers. Chris was unable to find a suitable replacement for manager Comiskey. Between 1892 and 1896, Von der Ahe convened a "reign of terror." Between 1894 and 1896, the Boss ran through a dozen managers; the eight he used in 1895 is a record that not even George Steinbrenner could assault.

AMONG THE MANAGERS was George Miller, known as "Calliope" because of his booming voice. When not hung over, he was at least an able hitter and catcher. Calliope's tenure was briefly broken in August, 1894, when the Phillies came to town. At the time Chris's secretary George Munson was out of town promoting a melodrama written by Al Spink. Harry Martin, the Browns' official scorer, was left to fill in as interim secretary, while continuing to score. When the Phillies scored eight runs in one inning, four of which were unearned on an errant throw by Calliope, Von der Ahe telephoned Martin in the press box and demanded to see him forthwith. Martin appeared in Chris's office.

"Why," demanded Chris, "didn't you go down there and kick the manager out of the game? Should I do everything around here — Is it up to me to manage those lousy low-lifers?"

"But I am only the official scorer, Mr. Von der Ahe," replied Harry, "I am no manager."

"Well then, from now on you are the manager too. You go down there and tell that Calliope feller [sic], that good-for-nothing bum to get the hell out of my park and you sit there on the bench and tell 'em what to do."

Martin had no choice but to relieve Miller of his duties. Calliope, slightly hung over as Martin recalled, was quite happy to give his gear to someone else. Martin sat quietly on the bench and watched Philadelphia score some more unanswered runs. The next day, however, Chris and

Calliope made up, and Harry gratefully returned to the press box.

Chris believed he was a good judge of baseball talent. Browns scout Billy Gleason brought in a young man named McGraw for a tryout with the Browns. Chris took one look at the skinny kid and without seeing him work out snorted, "that little feller, take him over to the Fairgrounds track and make a hoss yockey [sic] out of him!" Gleason sold the "little feller" to Baltimore, and John McGraw enjoyed a ten-year career as a third baseman for the Orioles followed by thirty years as one of the most successful managers of all time. Another example of Chris's mismanagement occurred in 1894 when he ordered Martin to trade shortstop Frank Shugart to Louisville. In return, Chris wanted an outfielder named Tom Brown. Martin drafted a telegram spelling out the deal in plain language, but it was vetoed by the Boss. Chris told Martin to write in a more obfuscated manner. The trade somehow went through. In 1895, Brown hit an unimpressive .217 before being traded to Washington where he hit .233. Shugart, who was batting .436 for the Browns, dropped to all of .374 with Louisville.

It was during this time that baseball evolved more and more into the game we know today. Overhand pitching became routine by 1890, diamonds were laid out by geometric principles in 1893, and the pitcher's mound was set at the present 60' 6". In 1896 efforts were made to codify scorekeeping. The immigrant-baiting Sporting News, which was antagonistic towards Von der Ahe throughout the 1890's as his entrepreneurial schemes subordinated his baseball interests, asked Chris's opinion of uniformity in scorekeeping. The recorded reply can only be taken as an attempt to discredit Chris as a baseball magnate:

"Vot [sic] do I think of uniformity in scorekeeping? Now vot do reporters want with uniforms on? Are they stuck on the dames and do they want to show off? Let the players wear uniforms, but not the reporters."

The Browns lost game after game, and Chris lost money to rainouts. Complaining of so many rainouts at a league meeting, Chris allegedly suggested that in all fairness, rainy days should be distributed more evenly throughout the league. Selling his highest-paid players to make up these losses, he reinvested not in players but promotions. To Von der Ahe, money was invested to draw patrons who sought diversions other than baseball. In fairness, his thinking was not unique. In an era in which people sought various forms of entertainment, a baseball magnate had to find ways to ensure that his customers would not seek their pleasures elsewhere. The choice was either to field a competitive club or resort to the extremes Chris did. His first such investment was the building of a "stadium club"

under the grandstands at new Sportsman's Park. The clubhouse motif, which has since been copied by modern owners as a luxury premium, was simply a shaded area protected from stray balls by a screened fence and was open to all on a first-come, first-serve basis. In the relative comfort of the shade, a fan could watch the game and eat and drink to his heart's content. The clubhouse idea seemed to work well, and beer sales increased. Harry Martin recalled, however, that when Chris discovered that the Cincinnati club's beer sales were greater, he took measures to expand his bar.

Another innovation was the installation of a shoot-the-chute in center field. After an elevator trip to the top of the water slide, the passenger was strapped in a boat by a nautically-clad attendant. As the passengers were about to take their plunge, they would be sent off by a women's silver cornet band that Chris hired for general entertainment. The Sporting News satirized the shoot-the-chute with a cartoon in which Chris was portrayed as a ship's captain with the boat taking its plunge. The cartoon was an apt analogy to the sinking fortunes of the Browns.

ANOTHER ATTRACTION CHRIS BROUGHT to Sportsman's Park was a Wild West show featuring fifty Indians and forty cowboys and cowgirls. The Indians were full-blooded Sioux whom the Boss rented from the government at the rate of $12 a month each. When doubts of the Indians' authenticity reached Chris's ears, he was furious, "I should pay an actor feller [sic] $50 a month when I can get squaws, bucks and a real Indian chief [Sitting Bull] at $12 a head?" After the 1895 season, Chris took his show on a southern tour but was crestfallen when it did not produce the desired profit. Undeterred, Von der Ahe continued to expand his ballpark enterprise and billed it as "the Coney Island of the West."

In 1896 Chris began building his most controversial enterprise: a one-third mile race track inside Sportsman's Park. The track was leased with concession rights to race promoter Fred Foster for two years. Von der Ahe expected to collect $20,000 over two years. The Sporting News, which held up baseball as a public icon, decried the electrically-illuminated pony track as an assault on baseball's integrity. League officials warned Chris that he violated Section 3 of the league's constitution. Chris replied that the specifics of the rule applied only to baseball. The league had no reply to that.

Critics clamored for Von der Ahe's removal from the game. The Sporting News advocated that the league protect itself from Chris, whom they called "Von der 'Ha-ha'" and referred to as a "maggot" as opposed to a "magnate." The Sporting News claimed that the league's toleration of Chris and his gambling associates would result in baseball's reputation being tarnished. Additionally, The Sporting News propagated the myth that baseball was still in the realm of upper-class entertainment, and that by ousting Von der Ahe and his cronies, the game would somehow be wrested from its democratized status and returned to its proper place in society. Von der Ahe ignored the bad press. The Coney Island venture demanded all of his attention, and the quality of baseball sank to ridiculous depths. In less than a decade, the mighty Browns fell from contender to doormat. The pony track, shoot-the-chute's water hazard, and fly-by-night sideshows took their toll on the condition of the playing field. Scorers had difficulty determining hits from errors because the pock-marked infield fell into disrepair. Losing interest in baseball, Von der Ahe concentrated only in making money to pay his mounting debts.

Von der Ahe's profligate lifestyle led to his eventual failure. The Sporting News painted a picture of Chris with a peasant demeanor and dressed in outrageously flashy clothes who thought of himself as a veritable Apollo, but in reality attracted women because of his fabulous wealth. It's true that Chris was adulterous. In 1896 his wife Emma sued for divorce while he carried on an affair with the housemaid, Anne Kaiser, to whom he had proposed. In August, Chris reneged on this promise and married Della Welles, a golddigger. Kaiser sued Chris for breach of promise but settled out of court. The marriage to Della was a disaster. In December, 1897, Chris filed for divorce citing Della as neglectful of her duties and physically abusive, as well as running "up large bills for things she does not need."

Chris's misfortunes came to a head in February, 1898, as the result of a suit originally filed against him in 1890. Mark Baldwin, a Pittsburgh club executive, had come to St. Louis in the midst of the Players' war and tried to steal Chris's star players. Chris had Baldwin arrested for conspiracy. When charges were thrown out of court, Baldwin sued Von der Ahe for false arrest and asked for $10,000 in damages. Baldwin was awarded $2,500 four years later, but could not collect because Chris avoided going to Pittsburgh. W. A. Nimick, who posted bond for Chris, wanted his money back and hired a private detective to seize Von der Ahe. Chris was lured into a trap by the detective, handcuffed, and taken to the Allegheny County jail where he sat for several days unkempt and humiliated until his lawyers could bail him out. The league stepped in on Chris's behalf and paid his debt. In return, Von der Ahe was required to retire from baseball. He complied and tried to sell the Browns, but couldn't get a clean bill of sale because of his debts. The club was put in a receivership by the courts and later put up for auction. The league moved to protect itself from an undesirable purchaser by declaring that ownership of the Browns' assets did not necessarily include league membership.

Mired in debt and out of baseball, Von der Ahe filed for bankruptcy in 1899. The onetime czar of the American Association left baseball a pariah. He returned to his old saloon but business was no longer booming. Chris was forced to rely on the benevolence of his old captain, Charles Comiskey, who had become a magnate in the fledging American League. In 1908, a benefit exhibition between St. Louis' two major league clubs helped build Chris a nest egg in the face of declining health.

After a long illness, Chris died on June 5, 1913, of dropsy and cirrhosis of the liver. Thanks to Comiskey, Chris was given a dignified burial in keeping with his once lofty status. Comiskey eulogized Chris as "the grandest figure baseball has ever known."

HOW SHOULD Chris be appraised? Harold Seymour called Chris "quixotic." Lee Allen suggested he "resembled something out of Rabelais," and David Quentin Voigt said he was "part-genius, part-clown." All these assessments capture the essence of a "character." But there was more to Chris than that. Unlike his conservative rivals, who saw baseball as a purely "American" institution to be enjoyed by the upper classes, Chris and his American Association colleagues were instrumental in democratizing the game. With the introduction of beer concessions, they succeeded in showing up the puritanical National League owners.

But success and respectability often have limits in high-risk enterprises. Successful in undercutting the National League monopoly for a few years, Chris could not adjust to the second Association war. His sideshow attractions dismayed the other owners, and they helped force him out of baseball.

But Von der Ahe was the prototype for other owner-promoters who changed the face of baseball. Larry MacPhail introduced night baseball to the major leagues. Although considered a novelty fifty years ago, it is standard practice today. Bill Veeck imitated Chris with schemes like exploding scoreboards that were designed to create maximum publicity and bolster attendance. The strategy worked for years. Charlie Finley introduced colorful uniforms of the 1970's and early 1980's reminiscent of nineteenth-century styles.

Today, even corporate owners follow Chris's example, albeit more conservatively. To lure fans, they offer cheap premiums like can wraps, socks, wrist bands, vinyl warm-up jackets, and special-honoree promotions. These Barnumesque trappings are minor but integral aspects of baseball today. They are also the legacy of Chris Von der Ahe, baseball's pioneering huckster.

Last Hurrah For The Seals

JOHN D. HIBNER

ON SEPTEMBER 15, 1957, the San Francisco Seals played their last home game. The news had broken that the major-league Giants would be replacing them in 1958, but no one was celebrating on this particular afternoon. Instead, San Franciscans were reminiscing about the fifty-five-year history of Seals baseball — a history complete with stars like Lefty O'Doul, Willie Kamm, Vince, Dominic, and Joe DiMaggio, and a tradition of colorful and plentiful crowds at Seals Stadium, where a minor-league attendance record of 670,560 was set in 1946 that lasted thirty-six seasons.

There was no getting around it: September 15 would be a wake. But in typical San Francisco style, Seal supporters made it a "joyous wake."

Before the last date of the season, scheduled for September 15, the Seals had won the pennant. They played the Sacramento Solons in a doubleheader that day before a good crowd of 15,484. Governor and Mrs. Goodwin Knight were honored, and many described it as a "joyous wake and a lot of fun." Both teams went through the motions in the first game, and nobody really cared who won. Then the second game started and the fun began.

The fans were surprised when Seals manager Joe (Flash) Gordon started the second game at his familiar old position of second base. At first, Sacramento Manager Tommy Heath protested to the umpires, claiming that Gordon wasn't on the official roster. Soon Heath withdrew his protest by announcing over the loudspeaker: "With him at second, we can't lose." The Solons scored four runs in the first off little Albie Pearson, now hurling, though he was the Seals starting centerfielder. But the Seals came right back in the bottom of the first inning to get two runs back.

As the Solons came to bat in the top of the second, Gordon took the mound, with Pearson moving to second base. Gordon threw a strike, but Umpire Chris Pelekoudas called "ball one." Gordon raced off the mound, ranting and raving about the call. Pelekoudas responded that maybe Gordon could do better at calling balls and strikes himself. Where upon the umpire took off his jacket, grabbed Gordon's glove, and walked to the mound.

Gordon went behind the plate, and Pelekoudas fired a ball right over. "Slow-wow-ball," yelled Gordon. One pitch was enough, and each went back to his normal position. Sacramento scored three runs and took a 7-2 lead.

Pearson played five different positions that day and was the losing pitcher. He allowed four runs on two hits,

walked four men, and served up a home run ball. But for the last six or seven innings the stadium was a big party. Fans filtered down to the field for a handshake or autograph. As often as not there were more or less than nine men on a side. Everyone wanted to laugh about the proceedings, but there was still some sadness in the air — soon an era would come to an end.

A very emotional event occurred late in the game, with the Solons ahead 13-6. First baseman Sal Taormina went to the public-address system and spoke about "Cap" Wright, a Seals coach who was dying of cancer. Donations would be accepted, he said, and each player had already donated a day's pay to the cause.

The game was stopped, and all the members of both teams, still in spikes, climbed the stadium stairs and passed their caps. After twenty minutes, PA announcer Jack Rice called out over the loudspeaker: "Has everyone been reached out there!!"

"No!!" the crowd shouted back. "No!!"

The managers and players continued circulating. Among them were some local worthies: Grady Hatton, Marty Keough, Ken Aspromonte. Eddie (Pumpsie) Green, Leo Kiely, Leo Righetti, trainer Leo (Doc) Hughes, Coach Riverboat Smith, and of course Gordon, Heath, and Pearson.

Approximately $7,000 was raised for the ailing coach, a substantial fund, but more important a very symbolic gesture from the fans. The players then went back to the diamond to finish up the seven-inning game. The Seals went into the bottom of the seventh behind 14-6, and did manage to score one run. A pop foul ball ended the game, and an era of baseball history in the "City" had come to an end.

The 15,484 fans stood and applauded the team for at least five minutes.

On April 18, 1958, the San Francisco Giants opened the first regular season against the new team in Southern California — the Los Angeles Dodgers. They played in the Memorial Coliseum, which had been converted into a baseball facility at the cost of $300,000. A crowd of 78,672 saw the game — and saw the Dodgers defeat the Giants 6-5.

A new era in San Francisco baseball had begun. But no one will ever forget the Seals. Especially the way they left.

John C. Hibner writes a sports-trivia column for a Sacramento, California newspaper and is director of Hibner's Sports Library.

The Other George Davis

JOSEPH M. OVERFIELD

Least known of the three major leaguers by that name, he pitched a no-hitter for the Miracle Braves and had an equally fascinating life outside of baseball.

THERE ARE THREE GEORGE DAVISES in the Macmillan Encyclopedia. Best known is George Stacey Davis, a shortstop for 20 seasons with a .297 lifetime average. This George Davis, much in the public eye for many years, literally disappeared late in his life, and it was not known when and where he died until the late Lee Allen discovered he had passed away in obscurity in a Philadelphia mental hospital in 1940.

George (Kiddo) Davis was a good-field, little-hit centerfielder who played for five clubs in eight seasons in the majors.

The last of the triumvirate was George Allen Davis Jr., whose major league record shows seven wins and ten losses for the years 1912 to 1915. Astronomer, lawyer, no-hit pitcher for the Miracle Braves, he may have been the most interesting George Davis of all.

The "Other George Davis" was born March 9, 1890, in Lancaster, New York, just east of Buffalo. His father, George A. Davis Sr., was a lawyer, a man of some affluence and at one time a member of the New York State Senate. Young George graduated from St. John's (later Manlius) Military Academy, near Syracuse, and entered Williams College in Williamstown, Massachusetts, in 1908. The transition from the strict discipline of the military school to the freer and easier atmosphere of college was a problem, if we are to judge from a sketch of Davis in the 1912 Williams Class Book: "How George occupied himself his freshman year is more or less a mystery, and the class almost lost him. At any rate, he got eligible at Easter in time for baseball. Four of Champ's [he had three other nicknames — Iron, Joe, and Jarge] roommates have resigned from the college and the other two are feeling nervous, but we attribute all this to chance."

Once past his freshman year, Davis began to shine in the classroom, on the diamond, and in the gym. The Class Book continues: "After smiting Latin-I, his work rose steadily to Phi Beta Kappa rank, but lack of hours made him ineligible for the Gargoyle." Davis, a righthander, pitched brilliantly and was captain his senior year. He had an intimidating fastball, a blazing curve and many strike-

George A. Davis, Jr.

outs. (His best was 20 against Wesleyan in 1910; he also had 18 against Trinity and 15 against both Princeton and Dartmouth.) He is also credited with beating Yale after the Elis had won 19 in a row.

Although just 5 feet, 10 inches and 165 pounds, he was considered the strongest man on campus, having set a Williams weightlifting record that stood for years. To improve his dexterity he participated in fencing. When he graduated in 1912, he was vice president of his class.

While he pitched for Williams, coached by former major-league pitcher Andy Coakley, Davis's work caught

Joseph M. Overfield, an old friend of George Davis, is a semi-retired businessman, historian for the Buffalo Bisons of the American Association, and author of "The 100 Years of Buffalo Baseball."

the eye of Doc Barrett, trainer for the New York High-landers, who worked in the Williams athletic department in the off-season. Barrett tipped off his bosses, who sent Arthur Irwin to look him over. On July 12, 1912, Davis signed a $5,000 contract, most generous for those days.

Four days later he made his major-league debut, losing to the St. Louis Browns 3-1. According to one account, Davis displayed "a sweeping curve, a fast jump ball and worked almost exclusively without a windup." He finished the season with a 1-4 record and an ERA of 6.50 in 10 games for the last-place Highlanders.

In the spring of 1913, he joined the Highlanders' (now Yankees) spring training junket to Bermuda. Frank Chance, who had succeeded Harry Wolverton as manager of the hapless Yankees, was pleased with the Williams graduate in the early drills, but was infuriated when Davis said he was going back to the mainland to get married. This defection sealed his doom with the Yankees, who ticketed him for Jersey City of the International League. Davis, who by now had enrolled in Harvard Law School, agreed to go, but grudgingly, saying he did not like the minors and did not have to play ball for a living.

Davis was 10-16 for the Skeeters, who were as pathetic as the '12 Highlanders had been. They finished last, after having lost 19 in a row in one stretch. According to the 1914 Reach Guide, Davis fanned 199 in 208 innings, but exhibited the wildness that plagued him throughout his career, walking 98, hitting eight, and unleashing 15 wild pitches. In late August, the Yankees, more concerned about his wildness than impressed with his strikeouts, released him to Rochester, also of the International League. John Ganzel, the Hustlers' manager, boosted Davis to skipper George Stallings of the Boston Braves, with whom Rochester had a close relationship. Before Davis made a single pitch for Rochester, he was on his way to Boston, where he appeared in two late-season games with no decisions.

BECAUSE OF OBLIGATIONS at law school, Davis reported to the Braves late in 1914. The first thing Stallings told him was to work on a spitball. For most of the season, he was used in mop-up roles. After one sharp relief performance, reporters nudged Stallings about giving Davis a start. Stallings said he was waiting for the right moment. That moment came on September 9, in the second game of a doubleheader against the Phillies. This was far from a meaningless game. After losing the first game to Grover Cleveland Alexander, the Braves, who had emerged from last place on July 19 in their "miracle" run for the flag, were now in first place but just a game ahead of the Giants.

The Braves scored twice off Ben Tincup in the second

and added two more in the fourth. Reliever Eppa Rixey yielded a fifth run in the seventh and Joe Oeschger gave up two more in the last of the eighth. Meanwhile, George A. Davis Jr., the Harvard law student, using the spitball Stallings had urged him to learn, shut out the Phillies without a hit or a run. His one rough moment came in the fifth, when he walked the first three batters. He worked his way out of that jam by fanning Ed Burns and forcing pinch hitter Gavvy Cravath to hit into a double play. In later years, whenever Davis talked about his "Pitchers' Hall of Fame" performance, he always took pains to point out he was 3 for 4 at bat that day. What he did not say was that those were the only hits he had all year.

Mac Davis, writer, broadcaster, and inventor of many baseball myths, once told the dramatic story of the Davis no-hitter. His punch line was that it was the last game Davis ever won. Actually, he won two games in '14 and then won three in '15. Davis did not see the action in the '14 Series. The Braves swept the Philadelphia Athletics, four games to none, using just three pitchers in the process, Dick Rudolph, Bill James, and George Tyler. The New York Times, after a 1950 survey, called the Braves' victory the greatest upset in sports history.

In 1915 the Braves were unable to repeat their miracle and finished second. As for Davis, who once more report-ed late because of law school, he had 10 starts and wound up 3-3 with an ERA of 3.80. For all practical purposes, this was the end of the baseball line for Davis. He made two appearances for Providence of the International League in '16 and then was released by the Braves. A compilation of his record in his Cooperstown file credits him with a 13-15 mark for Columbus in '16, but this record actually belongs to Frank (Dixie) Davis.

Meanwhile, Davis gained his degree from Harvard and became a lawyer. How he ranked in his class is not known, but it is certain he was the strongest man on campus, just as he had been at Williams. In 1914 he set a strength mark of 1,427.6 points, breaking a record set earlier by legend-ary football star Huntington (Tack) Hartwick. A year later, Davis broke his own record, totaling 1,693 points.

Why was his baseball career so short — over at 26? Perhaps the jump from campus to big leagues was just too much for him. His lack of honing in the minors and his missing of spring training each year probably were factors. There is also the suspicion that his heart was not com-pletely in baseball and that he was eager to get on to other things. If he had any hopes of a comeback after his release by the Braves, they were dashed by the onset of World War I. Early in 1918 he reported to Fort Lee, Virginia, and in ninety days he was a second lieutenant. During his train-ing he was outstanding in bayonet drills, probably because of his great strength and the dexterity he had learned in fencing. Before long he was in charge of bayonet training for replacement troops who came through Fort Lee. He was discharged a captain on January 14, 1919, having seen no overseas duty.

His Army service behind him and his baseball career over, Davis settled in Buffalo with his wife, the former Georgianna Jones. His profession was the law, but it never seemed to challenge him intellectually. In the early 1920s he began to take graduate courses in philosophy and comparative religion at the University of Buffalo. He was greatly challenged there by a Professor Boynton who encouraged him to acquaint himself with the sciences in order to better understand the philosophers. This led him to astronomy and opened new horizons that were to radically change his life. He avidly pursued his new interest in the arts, taking some courses at the University of Buffalo, but for the most part educating himself through reading and study. As he began to accumulate an astronomy library that was to grow to 1,500 volumes, he soon learned that many of the books were written in strange languages. To meet this challenge, he taught himself Sanskrit, Greek, Latin (his nemesis as a Williams freshman), Arabic, Persian, German, and French. He never claimed fluency in all of them, but did master them sufficiently to understand the astronomy texts. He even delved into the arcane world of Egyptian hieroglyphics. For thirty years he conducted astronomy classes at the Buffalo Museum of Science, where he was also a trustee. He lectured at the University of Buffalo and wrote widely on the subject. His paper, "The Pronunciation, Derivation and Meanings of Star Names," published in "Popular Astronomy," is considered definitive in its field. He was a member of the American Astronomical Society, a fellow of the Royal Astronomical Society of England, and an honorary member of the Canadian Astronomical Society.

He also found time for public service and was a member-at-large of the Buffalo Common Council from 1928 to 1934. In 1934 he unsuccessfully sought the Republican nomination for mayor, then threw his support to the Democrat, who was elected. He had a great love of books and, in a natural course of events, he was appointed to the Erie County Library Board (later Buffalo and Erie County Library Board), where he served 14 years.

In the Davis scheme of things, the law always seemed to be of secondary importance. At first he practiced with his father and later formed his own partnership. In 1929, with egregiously bad timing, he gave up law to join a brokerage firm. Eventually he returned to the law, specializing in real estate. For many years he was associated with Hodgson, Russ, Andrews, Woods and Goodyear, one of Buffalo's largest and most prestigious firms, which traced its beginnings to the law offices of Buffalo's two-time president, Grover Cleveland.

On January 1, 1961, shortly before his seventy-first birthday, Davis retired from the law firm. In an interview with the Buffalo Courier-Express, he said he planned to concentrate on his magnum opus, a two-volume work on the origins and history of the constellations. "I'll probably be working on it for the rest of my life," he told the interviewer. Unfortunately, what was left of his life was much too short to complete his project. On June 4, 1961, George A. Davis Jr., student, athlete, major-league pitcher, lawyer, soldier, astronomer, bibliophile, linguist, teacher, author, and public servant, went to the basement of his Buffalo home and hanged himself. He left his second wife, Grace O. Butler Davis (his first wife had died in 1952), a son, and two daughters.

POSTSCRIPT

What caused George Davis to end his life? No public explanation was ever given, nor have any former associates been able to give me a reason. The one member of the family I was able to talk to (a son-in-law) told me the family was not even told it was a suicide. One must look closely at his personality to try to find a reason. He was an intensely proud man, almost to the point of arrogance. He had spent most of his life in a profession he did not particularly like. He had wanted to be a doctor, but his father had persuaded him to follow his own profession, the law. Academia probably would have been a better choice. He was also an impatient man who did not suffer fools lightly. More than once, he stormed out of Erie County Hall when he thought other lawyers involved in a real estate closing were wasting his time with trivialities. He was known to respond waspishly to students in his astronomy class who asked "silly" questions. On the other hand, he often exhibited great patience with young lawyers who came under his wing, and it is told he delighted in playing mentor to neighborhood youngsters who came to his yard to view the wonders of the heavens through his telescope.

Davis had hoped to become full-time curator of astronomy at the Museum of Science after he retired from the law firm, but the job went to another man. He was not a partner in the law firm, so when he retired he apparently had to rely solely on his income from Social Security. He had accumulated very little of this world's goods, except for his library, which was eventually sold to the Museum of Science. According to his son-in-law, Davis had inherited a substantial sum from his father, but lost it all in the crash. The appraisal of his estate in the Surrogate's office of Erie County lists two bank accounts, both only in the hundreds of dollars; three small insurance policies and no real estate.

It is the guess here that George Davis could not face a future of impecunity and found escape through suicide.

Hall-Of-Fame Managers, Hall-Of-Fame Nicknames

JAMES K. SKIPPER, JR.

A MANAGER DOESN'T NEED A nickname to make the Hall, but it helps. Fully fourteen of the 16 Cooperstown skippers had calling cards. See if you can guess the people from their nicknames:

The Old Roman. When his White Sox won their first pennant in 1901, journalist Hugh Keogh began referring to their owner, who had managed in four leagues, as "The Old Roman." Thomas Shea, author of a 1946 book on baseball nicknames, suggests that the nickname was a composite of his characteristics — breeding, a patrician bearing, shrewdness, and a noble mane of white hair that crowned a classical profile. (Charles Comiskey)

The Old Fox. The name was probably given him by an opponent. It derives not from his wiliness as a manager and executive, but from his days as a pitcher, when he was guilty of much chicanery. "For a little fellow he was pretty good," umpire Bill Bryan observed. "He used to stand out there on the rubber and spend minutes knocking the ball against his spikes, pretending there was dirt on them, and meanwhile scuffing the cover of the ball." (Clark Griffith)

The Tall Tactician. The 6'1", 170-pound Athletics manager, a master of baseball strategy, was an unforgettable sight for more than half a century — sitting on the bench in suit, tie, and straw hat, and directing his players by waving a score card. (Connie Mack)

Little Napoleon. The nickname referred to the Giant skipper's height (5'7") and authoritarian and military style of managing. (John McGraw)

The Mahatma. The Browns and Cardinals manager always thought he had something important to say. He liked to lecture players individually and collectively, using catchy phrases and parables that often were over their heads. As a Dodger executive in the 1940s, he reminded sportswriters of India's orator-turned-statesman, Mahatma Gandhi, and they began to refer to him in print as "The Mahatma." (Branch Rickey)

Uncle Robbie. Managing the Dodgers from 1914 to 1931, the portly ex-catcher was a lax disciplinarian. This, combined with a fatherly attitude toward his players, not only won him respect and admiration, but also the nickname "Uncle Robbie." (Wilbert Robinson)

Cousin Ed. An ironic nickname for a man who liked to pick fights, "Cousin Ed" derives from "Cousin Egbert," a name given the 1920s-era Yankee general manager by sportswriter W.O. McGeehan. (Edward Barrow)

Bucky. The player-manager of Washington's 1924-25 championship teams, he was first called "Bucky" as a kid basketball player. "I had a couple of players on my back in a rough game," he related. "When I shook them off and shot a basket [a friend named Gary Schmeelk] said I bucked like a tough little bronco." (Stanley Harris)

The Mighty Mite. The 5'6½" Yankee skipper more than earned the name for controlling such strong-willed players as Babe Ruth, Joe Bush, and Jumpin' Joe Dugan. (Miller Huggins)

Marse Joe. Managing the Cubs in the 1920s, he was given the nickname by Chicago sportswriters. "Marse" is a variation of "Massa," a term for "master" once used by slaves. The manager may have first been called "Marse Joe" when he fired Grover Cleveland Alexander for breaking curfew regulations. (Joe McCarthy)

Deacon. The only manager to direct three teams (St. Louis, Cincinnati, and Pittsburgh) to pennants, this soft-spoken man was, in fact, a deacon in the Methodist Church. (William McKechnie)

Casey. He was born and raised in Kansas City, Missouri. According to one of several explanations for his nickname, he arrived in minor-league Kankakee in 1910 with "K.C." on his bags and introduced himself by saying "I'm from K.C." (Charles Stengel)

Señor. His managerial skills with the Indians (1954) and White Sox (1959) earned him the respectful "Señor," which is Spanish for "Mister." (Alfonso Lopez)

Smokey. As a kid on a grade-school baseball team, the legendary Dodger skipper threw a live fastball. The kids said he put plenty of "smoke" on the ball. (Walter Alston)

The other Hall-of-Fame managers, nineteenth-century greats George and Harry Wright, had no distinctive nicknames.

James K. (Skip) Skipper, Jr. is chairman of the sociology department at the University of North Carolina at Greensboro.

Critters, Flora, And Occupations: Minor-League Team Nicknames

DAVID PIETRUSZA

WHILE WE ARE aware that colorful monikers of baseball players have all but vanished, we sometimes forget that this is also true for team nicknames. For example, the *noms de guerre* of minor-league teams just ain't what they used to be.

In decades gone by, local outfits were free to let their imaginations run wild, and the results were out of this world. When I studied this, I found basically three broad species of *Nicknamus Baseballus*: critters, flora, and occupations. Other genuses, such as ethnics and sock colors and even theology and owners, were also catalogued.

Let's go first to the animal world. Who couldn't find a warm spot in their heart for the Galveston Sandcrabs, the Evansville River Rats, the Wilson Bugs, the Perth Blue Cats, the Tarboro Serpents, the Grand Rapids Wolverines, the Jersey City Skeeters, or the Temple Boll Weevils?

There were less malevolent breeds found, too. The Union City Greyhounds, Columbus Foxes, Ada Herefords, San Francisco Seals, Newark Bears, Hutchinson Elks, Orlando Bulldogs, Cedar Rapids Rabbits, Smiths Falls Beavers. In a class by itself was Schenectady's "Frog Alley Bunch" of the 1902 New York State League.

And let's not forget our fine feathered friends. Nothing as prosaic as Cardinals, Orioles, or Blue Jays in this aviary. Take the Leavenworth Woodpeckers for a starter. What about the Henryetta Hens, Dayton Ducks, Aberdeen Pheasants, Sioux Falls Canaries, Miami Beach Flamingos, Owls of the Two Laredos, New Orleans Pelicans, Columbia Gamecocks, Rayne Rice Birds, and that quintessential minor-league team, the Toledo Mud Hens?

And dare we slight that old chlorophyl crowd, the plant kingdom, in favor of more mobile forms of life? (Mobile, did someone say Mobile? What about the Mobile Sea Gulls or the Mobile Bears?) Opposition fans loved roasting the Idaho Falls Russets but weren't above picking (on) the Suffolk Goobers, Selma Cloverleafs, Hammond Berries, Palatka Azaleas, Oakland Acorns, Toronto Maple Leafs, and for the historically minded, York White Roses and Lancaster Red Roses.

What gives more pride to a community (and a stranger name to a ballclub) than a favorite local product or occupation? "We make stuff around here and we're darn proud of it!" virtually shout the uniform shirtfronts. Mull over the fine wares of the Amsterdam Rugmakers, Oswego Starchmakers, Troy Collar and Cuff Makers, Bassett Furnituremakers, Petersburg Trunkmakers, and Brockton Shoemakers. But wait, we've just begun: The Pueblo Steel Workers, Des Moines Undertakers, Mayfield Clothiers, Peoria Distillers, Oil City Refiners, Borger Gassers, Wausau Lumberjacks, Providence Clam Diggers, Welch Miners and the Blackstone Barristers. Who can ever forget the Kalamazoo Celery Pickers?

The races of mankind? Why not? We have many fine entries. Besides the overdone, and rather generic, "Indians," consider the Dublin Irish, Terre Haute Hottentots, Memphis Egyptians ("Keep your eye on the ball, and walk like an Egyptian!"), Canton Chinamen, Baton Rouge Cajuns, Pawhuska Osages, Syracuse Onandagas, Edmonton Eskimos, Havana Cubans, and Laredo Apaches.

Theology? Ponder the Salem or Wichita Witches, Des Moines Demons, and Macon Brigands taking on the Los Angeles Seraphs, Lufkin Angels, and St. Paul Saints.

Tired of mundane Red Sox and White Sox? Here's a veritable hosiery store of attire, including the Dublin Green Sox, Abilene Blue Sox, Amarillo Gold Sox, Reno Silver Sox, and the cryptically named Miami Sun Sox and Colorado Springs Sky Sox.

Think Charles O. Finley was egotistical? All he ever named after himself was the A's mule. Consider the Omaha Rourkes, Auburn Boulies, Springfield Dunnmen, Duncan Uttmen, and Flint Halligans.

And not just teams had nicknames. Whole leagues did: Pony (Pennsylvania-Ontario-New-York), Kitty (Kentucky-Illinois-Tennessee), Mint (Michigan-Ontario), Three Eye (Illinois-Iowa-Indiana), Sally (South Atlantic), and, my personal favorite, Mink (the long-gone Missouri-Iowa-Nebraska-Kansas League).

Then there was the just plain inexplicable — the Regina Bonepilers, Yakima Pippins, Wilmington Blue Rocks, Norfolk Mary Janes, Longview Cannibals, Lincoln Treeplanters, Houston Babies, and Springfield Foot Trackers. And the winner in the least imaginative category is . . . the Bangor Bangors.

David Pietrusza is working on a book about the Canadian-American League.

Virginia-North Carolina League: A Fascinating Failure

JIM SUMNER

Most professional baseball is minor league. Most minor leagues struggle. In this classic case, even a league in Bull Durham country failed in its first attempt.

IN VIRGINIA AND NORTH CAROLINA, as in most of the South, professional baseball in this century has meant minor-league baseball. On several occasions the two neighboring states have combined for successful interstate leagues. The Piedmont League, founded in 1920, was one of the best known minor-league associations before its demise after the 1955 season. The present Carolina League, founded in 1945, has attained a reputation as one of the country's premier Class A leagues. Other leagues like the Bi-State League and the Virginia League have combined franchises from both states. In retrospect this seems like a logical, even inevitable way to go. The two states share a common border, a common history, and long-standing economic and social ties. However, Virginia-North Carolina leagues were not necessarily favored by the baseball gods. The first such attempt in 1901 was a dismal failure. It was also a fascinating failure, one that illustrates many of the problems of turn-of-the-century minor-league ball.

The two states approached the 1901 league from different directions. Richmond, Virginia, had a brief fling in the big leagues, in the 1884 American Association, and the Virginia League had completed some respectable seasons. The 1900 Virginia League, with teams in Hampton, Newport News, Norfolk, Petersburg, Portsmouth, and Richmond, was one of these relatively successful seasons. Future Hall-of-Fame pitcher Christy Mathewson ran up a 20-2 record that year for Norfolk to give the league a special flavor.

Baseball in North Carolina, on the other hand, was a matter of amateur and semipro teams, usually unaffiliated. The semipro North Carolina league of 1900, with teams in Charlotte, Durham, Raleigh, Tarboro, Statesville, and Wilmington, lasted barely a month before going under. Given these different histories, it's somewhat surprising that Virginia cranks (as fans were called then) would be interested in a broader league. However, several of the 1900 Virginia franchises were weak, and the larger cities in North Carolina appeared to be more attractive propositions.

Discussions for the formation of the Virginia-North Carolina League began in January of 1901. From the beginning, the Virginia cities of Newport News, Norfolk, Portsmouth, and Richmond, and the North Carolina capital of Raleigh appeared to be solid for the league. Getting other North Carolina cities in the circuit, however, was more problematical. Charlotte, Durham, Greensboro, and Wilmington were all ardently wooed for the association. Danville, Virginia, was also considered. At various times plans for a ten-team league and an eight-team league were announced. The league was formally organized on February 18 at a meeting at Norfolk's Monticello Hotel. Norfolk businessman W.H. Cunningham was elected president. A month later, league secretary E.H. Doran was still looking for cities to complete the league. In the borderline cities only the Wilmington Athletic Association was able to raise enough money to fully commit to the project. Thus the league started play with six teams, four from Virginia and only two from North Carolina. A schedule was drawn up running from April 15 to September 21. General admission was set at 25 cents, with an extra dime necessary to gain a seat in the grandstands.

Perhaps the most interesting member of the league was Newport News player-manager Ed Ashenback. Invariably described as "a jolly baseball man," the irrepressible Ashenback won the affection of teammates, opponents, um-

Jim Sumner is historian for the North Carolina State Historical Preservation Office.

pires, even opposing fans. The exuberant exterior hid an astute baseball mind. Although only twenty-eight at the beginning of the 1901 season, the Cincinnati native had more than a decade of minor league experience in such circuits as the Tri-State League, the Pennsylvania State League, the Southern League, the Texas League, and the Interstate League. In 1900 he managed the Hampton club to second place in the Virginia League.

Ashenback's polar opposite was Raleigh player-manager George (King) Kelly (not to be confused with Hall of Famers King Kelly or George Kelly). A former baseball and football star at Georgetown, Kelly, like Ashenback, was an experienced and talented baseball man. Unlike the jovial Ashenback, however, Kelly was something of a hothead, with an unfortunate propensity for abusing umpires and playing games under protest.

THE LEAGUE also had some intriguing players. Wilmington pitcher Henry Burke (Cy) Voorhees was a graduate of Syracuse University and a former college teacher in Virginia. In the latter part of the 1901 season Voorhees would inherit $60,000 from a rich aunt. Whereupon he announced that he would now fulfill his life's ambitions: a tour of Europe followed by a course in vocal music. There were also some first-rate players. Raleigh featured former National League pitcher Otis Stocksdale and three future big leaguers, pitcher-outfielder Joe Stanley, third baseman Jake Atz, and pitcher Frank Smith. Smith would have a particularly successful career in the majors, winning 138 games in 11 seasons, and throwing two no-hitters. Other star players included speedy Wilmington second baseman Daniel (Davey) Crockett, slugging Portsmouth outfielder Buck Weaver (not the Black Sox' Buck Weaver), Newport News shortstop Fred Valdolz and pitcher Eddie High, and Norfolk outfielder Bill Spratt. Norfolk catcher Duff Lehman had big-league tools but was hampered by a nervous disorder that caused spasmodic twitches and jumps.

Norfolk jumped out of the blocks quickly, winning its first seven contests before being challenged by Raleigh, Wilmington, and Newport News. By May 10 the standings showed Norfolk with a 12-7 record, followed by Raleigh at 13-8, Wilmington, 11-9, and Newport News, 10-9. Portsmouth and Richmond brought up the rear. Although some games were horror shows, such as a May 14 Wilmington 15-9 win over Raleigh — a game marred by nine errors — many more games were close, well-played contests. League cranks were gearing up for what figured to be an exciting summer of baseball.

Unfortunately for the league, developments off the field were not as auspicious. Early games were plagued by rain and other bad weather, including a cyclone at Newport News on May 1. As a result, attendance was diminished in the season's crucial early segment. In fact, serious attendance problems developed at Portsmouth less than a month into the season. On May 2 the club was turned over to the league, renamed Orphans and slated for eventual relocation.

The league also suffered from a common problem of minor leagues during this period, inconsistent and controversial umpiring. The league employed a single umpire per game, at a salary of $7. This created obvious problems any time there were baserunners. The umpiring crew, which included former National League pitcher Harry Staley, was subjected to almost daily abuse, usually verbal, but occasionally physical. Raleigh manager Kelly was a notable offender, but he was hardly alone. One particularly serious incident occurred on April 27 in Raleigh when Richmond catcher Ganz threw the ball at Raleigh's Jake Atz following a close play at the plate. The ensuing brawl involved players from both teams, fans, and eventually the police. Raleigh won the game, 14-13, undoubtedly giving the fans their 25 cents worth.

The league's most serious problem, however, was bad timing. In 1901 the American League first challenged the senior National League for baseball supremacy. A casualty of this war was the National Agreement, which theoretically guaranteed the sanctity of player contracts. In the autumn of 1901 this would lead to the formation of the National Association of Professional Baseball Leagues. That development was too late for the Virginia-North Carolina League, whose better players were constantly signed by teams from the National League, the American League, and various wealthier minor leagues, especially the Southern League. You really couldn't tell the players without a scorecard.

AT LEAST THE PENNANT RACE was close. Norfolk dropped out of first in mid-May, replaced at various times by Raleigh or Wilmington. By the end of May Newport News was challenging for first, while Norfolk had dropped to fourth. On June 1 the New Orleans team of the Southern League purchased the contract of Norfolk's Ed Gilligan and announced that it was after several other league stars. This was the beginning of a season-long incursion by New Orleans into the younger league. Newport News was forced to pay extra money to pitcher Eddie High to keep him away from the Crescent City, a move that accelerated the demise of the franchise. By mid-June Newport News was ready to join the hapless Portsmouth Orphans on the sidelines. On June 21 it was announced that the Portsmouth team would be transferred to Charlotte, North Carolina, and the Newport News team to Tarboro, North Carolina. The league was now composed of four North Carolina cities and only two Virginia cities. A split season was hastily declared. Wilmington was the first-half champion, with a 35-23 record, followed by Newport News, 32-24; Norfolk, 32-24; Raleigh, 29-28; Portsmouth, 24-32; and Richmond, 17-38. If all went well, the second-half winner would meet Wilmington for the postseason championship.

UNFORTUNATELY, THINGS DIDN'T go well. On the last day of the first half-season, the league lost two of its best players. Newport News/Tarboro pitcher Eddie Osteen jumped to the Southern League, while the same team sold High's contract to New Orleans for $700. Later in June, New Orleans purchased the contract of star Wilmington pitcher R.M. Stafford for $300, while teammate Cy Voorhees jumped to independent Atlantic City. Thus the first-half champions were crippled early in the second season. The other league teams were continually forced to fend off repeated raid attempts. The magnetic manager Ashenback elected not to accompany Newport News to its new home. The umpiring problems also continued with Tarboro forfeiting a game to Richmond because of what Tarboro perceived as bad calls. By the second week of July the two remaining Virginia cities had decided they had seen enough and dropped out.

The league entered its third incarnation, as a four-team association. The abortive second-season games were discarded. With no Virginia teams left, the league officials from that state resigned. Raleigh businessman Sherwood Higgs was elected president, a schedule was drawn up for a third season, and play resumed on July 8. Raleigh, which had suffered relatively little player attrition, jumped out in front early. On July 29 Tarboro manager Henry Bryan, Ashenback's replacement, had Barley Kain, manager of a Darlington, South Carolina, team, arrested for allegedly inducing his catcher Reddy Foster to jump to the South Carolina nine. The next week Raleigh manager Kelly unsuccessfully attempted to have a man named George Leidy arrested for enticing his stars Smith and Atz to jump ship. Nothing came of these legal proceedings. Late in the season it was discovered that league umpire Ed Clark was scouting players for the Southern League.

Despite the distractions Raleigh continued to play well, and was never really challenged. On August 9 the Cardinals were 18-9 and were the only team over .500. The games had deteriorated badly by this point, with fighting and wrangling a common occurrence. On August 17 Charlotte forfeited a doubleheader to Tarboro, claiming

bias and incompetence on the part of umpire Paul Russell. (Interestingly enough, after the games were declared forfeited, the two teams played a pair of five-inning exhibitions to raise money.) The league gave up the ghost after this sorry display, almost a month before the scheduled conclusion.

Although the Charlotte and Tarboro teams disbanded shortly thereafter, the league unwisely tried to conduct a championship series between first-half champion Wilmington and second-half champion Raleigh. Incredibly, league officials planned an eleven-game series. The first five games were scheduled in Raleigh, the next five in Wilmington, and the final game at an undetermined site. Predictably, this series was also a disaster. Wilmington was weakened by the loss of key players, including recently departed star Davey Crocket, who had jumped to the Detroit Tigers, while Raleigh played without Atz and Stanley, who had also recently jumped ship.

ON AUGUST 20 Raleigh won the first game of the series 4-0, in only sixty-eight minutes, behind a Frank Smith five-hitter. Raleigh followed with a disputed 6-3 win in game two. The game was played on a wet field and was started too close to sunset, prompting a Wilmington protest. After a rainout, Raleigh won the third game 1-0 with Smith hurling his second shutout. This game was marred by a major brawl in the eighth inning involving both teams, umpire Harry Mace, and fans. The last game of the series, on August 24, was also won by Raleigh, 6-2. More rain was followed by squabbles over finances, umpiring, and the disputed second game. The series was never finished. Raleigh, having won all four games played, claimed the league championship.

The league's litany of problems is only too familiar to students of minor-league ball: uncertain finances, player raiding, chaotic umpiring, and a small fan base, plus the 1901 war between the American and National leagues. Yet Virginia and North Carolina minor-league enthusiasts persevered. The North Carolina State League in 1902 and another attempt at a Virginia-North Carolina league in 1905 shared the same fate as the 1901 league. Beginning in 1906, however, the Virginia League, which occasionally included North Carolina cities, began a run of prosperity. In 1908 the Eastern Carolina Association and the Carolina Association, with teams in North and South Carolina, became the first two leagues in the Tar Heel state to finish a season. Eventually the two states became hotbeds of minor-league ball, but only after a difficult apprenticeship.

Runs Tallied

BARRY CODELL

The homer hitter is the only player who scores or drives in a run without the assistance of a teammate. This new statistic gives the circuit clout full recognition.

RUNS TALLIED ("RT") is a simple measure of offensive production ("tally" was Henry Chadwick's term in the first box score). The team with the most runs tallied invariably wins the game; the player who tallies most for his team has been most valuable toward this victory.

Runs Tallied reinstates the primacy of the home run — the only scoring a player accomplishes without the aid of a teammate. It is based on the premise that all other runs are collaborative efforts. Virtually all team runs, aside from home runs, are a combination of a run scored and a run batted in (except for defensive lapses ["DL's"] or double play grounders ["GIDP's"], which score those runs not batted in). The batters or baserunners contributing to these runs are equally important; no run can exist without both of them. So a "non-homer" team run is generally ½ R and ½ RBI (occasionally ½ R and ½ DL), while a home run is one full run tallied.

The ultimate offensive payoff for team and individual is in Runs Tallied, as is shown by the following formula:

$$[(R - HR) \div 2] + [(RBI - HR) \div 2] + HR = RT$$

This formula separates the contributory tallies (runs and RBI) from the solo tally (home runs). This formula can be further reduced to

$$\frac{R + RBI}{2} = RT$$

Note that this simplified formula gives a credit of one RT for a home run, since a home run produces both a R and a RBI for the player. In other words, the simple averaging of runs and RBI results in Runs Tallied (RT). No computer — not even a calculator — is needed here.

The essence of RT is that home runs are already given their true doubled value when runs and runs batted in are added. The well-known "strength" of Runs Produced (subtracting homers or R + RBI − HR = RP) is actually its fatal weakness. Let's go to two examples to see this:

the 1988 statistics of Kirby Puckett and Jose Canseco, and the all-time bests of Lou Gehrig and Babe Ruth.

	G	R	RBI	HR	RP	RT
Puckett	158	109	121	24	206	115
Canseco	158	120	124	42	202	122

Canseco's 1988 supremacy is reaffirmed by the RT. His singluar 40/40 season added up to 0.77 Runs Tallied per Game — the best in the majors.

Interesting applications of the RT could include RT/ Team, RT/Game, RT/Plate Appearance, but what is undeniable is this: However gaudy the hitting or baserunning, if a player does not tally runs, it's all window dressing. For the score, after all, is the essential stat.

Gehrig's famous 301 Runs Produced (1931) get knocked down a peg by Babe Ruth (who else?) and his all-time single-season (1921) RT:

	G	R	RBI	HR	RP	RT
Gehrig	155	163	184	46	301	173.5
Ruth	152	177	171	59	289	174

Ruth's 1.14 Runs Tallied per Game is also an all-time best, but Gehrig's 0.89 RT/G reigns supreme career-wise. New Hall of Famers Johnny Bench (0.56 RT/G) and Carl Yastrzemski (0.55 RT/G) and all-time hit leader, Pete Rose (0.49 RT/G!) are surprisingly low in this latter category.

The comparisons, as with all statistics, are endless (see accompanying charts). Perhaps they will be done by a new generation of statisticians, without PC's, armed only with baseball cards and minds, following this simple commandment: Average those runs and RBI! It's all right there — in RT.

Barry Codell is a nursing home director in Chicago, winner of the Governor's Award for Innovation in Gerontology, and the inventor of the base-out percentage ("BRJ," 1979).

Runs Tallied Per Game
1988 Leaders (90 or More RT)

Player, Team	Games	Runs	RBI	RT	RT/G
1. Canseco, OKA	158	120	124	122	0.77
2. Puckett, MNA	158	109	121	115	0.74
3. Evans, BSA	149	96	111	103.5	0.69
4. Winfield, NYA	149	96	107	101.5	0.68
5. Henderson, NYA	146	100	94	97	0.66
6. Strawberry, NYN	153	101	101	101	0.66
7. Van Slyke, PIN	154	101	100	100.5	0.65
8. Clark, SFN	162	102	109	105.5	0.65
9. Greenwell, BSA	158	86	119	102.5	0.65
10. Burks, BSA	144	93	92	92.5	0.64
11. Mattingly, NYA	144	94	88	91	0.63
12. Tartabull, KCA	146	80	102	91	0.62
13. McReynolds, NYN	147	82	99	90.5	0.62
14. Brett, KCA	157	90	103	96.5	0.61
15. Galarraga, MNN	157	99	92	95.5	0.61
16. Gibson, LAN	150	106	76	91	0.61

Runs Tallied Per Game
1988 Career Leaders (1,000 or More RT)

Player, Team	Games	Runs	RBI	RT	RT/G
1. Rice, BSA	2033	1227	1423	1325	0.65
2. Schmidt, PAN	2362	1487	1567	1520	0.64
3. Murray, LAN	1820	1048	1190	1119	0.61
4. Brett, KCA	2013	1233	1231	1232	0.61
5. Winfield, NYA	2269	1314	1438	1376	0.61
6. Murphy, ATN	1675	1005	1004	1004.5	0.60
7. Dawson, CHN	1753	996	1054	1025	0.58
8. Lynn, DTA	1762	1001	1042	1021.5	0.58
9. Parker, OKA	2033	1098	1245	1171.5	0.58
10. Dw. Evans, BSA	2236	1287	1183	1240	0.55
11. Fisk, CHA	2038	1108	1098	1103	0.54
12. Yount, MLA	2131	1234	1021	1127.5	0.53
13. Carter, NYN	1958	941	1128	1034.5	0.53
14. Da. Evans, ATN	2580	1313	1315	1314	0.51
15. Bell, TXA	2371	1147	1103	1125	0.48
16. Buckner, KCA	2416	1066	1189	1127.5	0.47

Runs Tallied Per Game
Past Career Leaders (1,000 or More RT)

Player	Games	Runs	RBI	RT	RT/G
1. Lou Gehrig	2164	1888	1991	1939.5	0.89
2. Babe Ruth	2503	2174	2209	2191.5	0.88
3. Joe DiMaggio	1736	1390	1537	1463.5	0.84
4. Hank Greenberg	1394	1051	1276	1163.5	0.83
5. Ted Williams	2292	1798	1839	1819.5	0.79
6. Jimmie Foxx	2317	1751	1921	1836	0.79
7. Al Simmons	2215	1507	1827	1667	0.75
8. Earl Averill	1669	1224	1165	1194.5	0.72
9. Roger Hornsby	2259	1579	1579	1579	0.70
10. Ty Cobb	3033	2244	1954	2104	0.69
11. Charlie Gehringer	2323	1773	1427	1610	0.69
12. Hank Aaron	3298	2174	2297	2235	0.68
13. Goose Goslin	2287	1483	1609	1546	0.68
14. Mel Ott	2732	1859	1860	1859.5	0.68
15. Chuck Klein	1753	1168	1201	1184.5	0.68
16. Mickey Mantle	2401	1677	1509	1593	0.66

HARRY HEITMAN DESERVES RESPECT

Harry Heitman pitched in one major league game in 1918, and although he died in 1959, his name is still the subject of ridicule each year on the anniversary of his debut. Last year the entry on Heitman in "The Date in Baseball" read:

"July 27, 1918 — Brooklyn Dodger rookie Henry Heitman completed the shortest career in major league history. He faced four Cardinals and gave up four hits; he never played pro ball again."

It is true that Harry gave up hits to the first four batters he faced and never pitched again in the majors. However, the statement that he never played pro ball again is erroneous. Heitman was a fine minor-league player before and after his one game in the majors. A Brooklyn lad, he was taken south by the Dodgers in 1918. Sent to Rochester in the International League for seasoning, he won 17 games and lost only six, with a league leading ERA of 1.32, and was hitting .336 in 47 games before he left the club in July to join the Navy. He was stationed in Brooklyn and played that one game with the Dodgers while on leave from his Navy duties. After his discharge in 1919, Heitman returned to Rochester. He spent many years in the International League with both Rochester and Buffalo, playing the outfield and pitching, and later played first base and the outfield in both the Eastern and New England leagues.
— Al Kermisch

BAT, ALMOST SIX FEET LONG, USED IN N.L. GAME

In 1894 the regulation length of a bat was 42 inches, just as it is today. In a game played at the Polo Grounds on August 22 of that year, a Chicago player actually used a bat that was almost six feet long. A theatrical man named Frank McKee, manager of the Madison Square Theatre, presented Chicago's Jimmy Ryan with a bat five feet, ten inches long and five inches in diameter at the thickest part.

When Bill Lange, who had been struck out twice by pitcher Jouett Meekin, came to bat in the eighth inning, he surprised the players, spectators, and umpires by carrying the oversized bat with him. He pleaded with umpire John McQuaid to let him try it just once. Neither McQuaid nor the Giants, who were six runs ahead, objected, and the crowd howled happily. A big roar went up when Lange hit an easy grounder to first baseman Jack Doyle, who fumbled the ball for an error. Next batter Charlie Irwin also wanted to use the big bat, but Manager John Ward of the Giants objected and the umpire had the oversized lumber returned to the bench. New York won the game 8-5.
— Al Kermisch

Demise Of The Triple

THOMAS COLLELO

A thing of beauty and suspense, the triple may be the most exciting twelve seconds in sport. Unfortunately, it's rapidly disappearing from the baseball box score.

WITH THE EXCEPTION OF the almost extinct inside-the-park home run, the triple is rarest of hits. This was not always so. For more than fifty years after the founding of the major leagues, the home run was the rarest hit, followed by the triple, double, and single. The logic behind this was obvious: The farther a batter struck the ball, the more bases he could reach.

Even such changes as overhand pitching and enclosed ballparks did nothing to affect the natural order of hits. From 1901 to 1929 the average distribution was: 76.9 percent for singles, 15.2 percent for doubles, 5.3 percent for triples, and 2.7 percent for homers. In the pre-Ruthian years, there were roughly three to four times as many triples as homers. Furthermore, the overwhelming majority of everyday players who ended their careers before 1930 had more three-base hits than home runs. This list includes Home Run Baker, Honus Wagner, Ty Cobb, Joe Jackson, Eddie Collins, Tris Speaker, George Sisler, and Sam Crawford; the latter holds the career record for triples with 312.

The heyday of the three-base hit was the nineteen-teens. The newly built concrete-and-steel parks had huge outfields and distant fences, with foul lines often in the 370-foot range and with center-field fences more than 450 feet away. Although a new ball was used after 1910, it was dead by modern standards and often doctored by the pitchers, so outfielders played shallow. Balls hit over their heads or line drives in the gaps (especially in the early innings before the ball got soft) could roll to the deepest part of the park. With pitching dominant and low scores common, the strategy of the times was that it was often worth the risk of stretching a double in order to get one base closer to home. In 1912 Owen Wilson set the single-season record with 36 triples and helped the Pirates establish the team record of 129.

The emergence of the home run in the 1920s was the death knell of the three-base hit. This event was no accident, but a conscious effort by the team owners noting the correlation between the increase in home runs and the rise in attendance. The baseball establishment assisted the triples-to-homer shift in two significant ways. First, the architecture of the ballparks was changed. The outfield fences were moved in, shortening the distance for a home run and reducing the length of outfielders' throws to third. The second alteration was the ball. In the 1920s it was given a more resilient center and many more new balls were used per game. When the "rabbit ball" was introduced in 1930, batting averages and home runs skyrocketed.

By 1920 the ratio of triples to home runs had dropped from three or four to one to only two to one. By the late 1920s triples and home runs were virtually even. In 1929 home runs surpassed triples for the first time. Over the years the gap has widened. In the late 1940s there were about 2.5 home runs for every triple. A decade later that ratio was more than three to one, and by 1988 there were almost four round trippers for every three-base hit — a level of domination the triple never enjoyed over the homer.

A review of the career leaders for the four types of hits reveals that none is more biased by era than that for triples. The singles, doubles, and home run leader lists all show "ancients" interspersed with "moderns." Of the top fifty players on the triples list, however, only Stan Musial (twentieth place) and Roberto Clemente (twenty-eighth) played after World War II. Until 1945 it was fairly common

Tom Collelo is a Library of Congress research analyst specializing in Africa and the Middle East. Playing in an over-30 league, he has no triples.

for the triples leader to have 20 or more in a season. But since then, only Dale Mitchell, Willie Mays, George Brett, and Willie Wilson have reached that figure (and the latter two did it on artificial turf — but more on that later). At the other extreme, Del Unser won the 1969 American League triples crown with eight, and in four other years (excluding the 1981 strike season) players with nine triples have taken the top spot in the AL. In the National League the low points were 1962 and 1982. In 1962 Johnny Callison and Willie Davis tied for the triples lead with 10, and in 1982 Dickie Thon won the triples leadership with the same number. To put this kind of hitting into context, consider that the notoriously torpid Ernie Lombardi had nine triples in 1932.

SINCE THE BANNER YEAR of 1912, the frequency of three-base hits has fallen 64 percent, from 16.5 per 1,000 at bats to the 1988 figure of 5.9 per 1,000. Much of this slide was concentrated in the homer-happy 1930s, when the frequency of triples fell by four per 1,000 AB.

Upward and downward fluctuations have occurred over the years. However, major modifications in the game, such as expansion, the strike zone, and mound height changes of the late 1960s, and the introduction of the designated hitter in the American League have had only minor impact on the triple's demise. Other factors, including the building of uniform ballparks and the trend toward faster outfielders, probably have increased the decline of the triple. On the other hand, one development that has had a positive statistical effect has been the proliferation of ballparks with artificial turf. Because the ball moves faster on turf and can get through the outfielders more easily, the number of triples hit on turf from 1985 to 1988 exceeded the number hit on grass by an average of 2.6 per 1,000 at bats. Over the long run, however, this development has not stopped the triple from dropping further; it has merely cushioned its fall.

Even with the beginning of the 162-game schedule in 1961-62 and the increased use of artificial turf in the 1970s, one must retreat to the 1932 Senators to find the last team that hit as many as 100 triples in a season. At the other extreme, the Baltimore Orioles may have set the rock-bottom standard for three-base hits. In 1977-88 they finished last in the triples column seven times and next to last the other five times. In 1988 the Yankees, with 12 triples, broke the 1986 Orioles' record (13) for fewest triples in a season.

Based on at least 1,000 career at bats, all of the worst triples hitters played after 1945. Some notables in the triples Hall of Shame are Earl Averill (no triples in eight big-league seasons), Terry Crowley (1 triple in fifteen

seasons), Cookie Rojas (621 at bats in 1968 without a three-base hit), and Darrell Evans (1 triple in his last 2,449 at bats).

BY AND LARGE, CATCHERS form the bulk of bad triples hitters. Of those players with at least 1,000 at bats and a triples-per-1,000 ratio of less than 2.0, almost two-thirds have been catchers. Recently, however, the number of non-catchers on the list has been growing. To put the 2.0 ratio into perspective, again consider that Ernie Lombardi registered a career ratio of 4.6 triples per 1,000 AB. In contrast, Jose Canseco, the modern-day personification of speed and power, had a triples per 1,000 at bat ratio of 2.07 after three full seasons.

Despite these trends, the data seem to indicate that even in a boom year for extra-base hits, triples seem destined to remain an insignificant offensive statistic. In 1986 triples constituted 2.31 percent of all hits, the lowest ratio ever. In the extra-base-hit boom year of 1987, this figure barely increased to 2.36 percent, and by 1988 it was 2.32 — nearly back to the record low. If the pattern continues — and there is nothing to suggest that it won't — one of the most exciting plays of the game, the three-base hit, will be relegated to baseball's statistical scrapheap.

GAME-WINNING HOMERS AGAINST OLD CLUB IN DAY AFTER TRADE

WOODIE HELD was sitting on the Baltimore bench during the first months of the 1967 season. But at the June 15 trading deadline, he was sent to the California Angels. The Angels had just arrived in Baltimore, and the next day, June 16, they played a doubleheader against the Orioles. Their starting shortstop, Jim Fregosi, was hurt early in the opener, and Held was brought into the game. Woodie hit a tie-breaking home run in the ninth inning to give the Angels a 2-1 victory over his old teammates. He started the second game and began the scoring with a two-run homer in the third inning. The Angels built the lead to 5-0 and finally won 5-3. So Woodie Held hit not one but two game-winning home runs against the Baltimore Orioles on the very next day after they traded him away.

— Robert L. Tiemann

No Score, Big Score

EMIL H. ROTHE

ON SEPTEMBER 11, 1946, Cincinnati and the Dodgers played 19 innings at Ebbets Field without a run being scored by either side: the longest 0-0 game ever played in the major leagues.

Johnny Vander Meer pitched the first 15 innings of the scoreless game for the Reds, striking out 14 and allowing only seven hits. Harry Gumbert relieved Vandy and allowed one hit in four innings. Four pitchers worked for the Dodgers. Hal Gregg started and lasted through 10, Hugh Casey added five innings, Art Herring put in three more, and Hank Behrman pitched the final inning before darkness halted proceedings.

There were several scoring opportunities for the Reds, but both Pete Reiser and Dixie Walker nipped Cincinnati runners at home. Walker's throw was especially crucial. It came in the 19th. With Red runners Dain Clay on second and Lonnie Frey at first, Bert Haas singled to right. Clay tried to score, but Walker threw to Bruce Edwards to cut him down. In the fifth Eddie Lukon tried to stretch a triple; he was nailed, Reiser to Pee Wee Reese to Edwards.

The Brooklyn-Cincinnati scoreless tie broke the former record of 18 innings established on July 16, 1909 by Washington and Detroit.

A vastly different type of baseball was played in Cleveland's League Park on July 10, 1932. After 17 innings it was also a tie—a 17-17 tie! In the top of the 18th Jimmie Foxx carried the winner across the plate. Jimmie had a busy day because he also contributed three homers.

Cleveland accumulated 33 hits, a modern-day best for one club in one game. The combined total of 58 hits is a major-league record. The nine hits—seven singles and two doubles—by Johnny Burnett, Cleveland's shortstop, is the most ever collected by a single player in one game of any length. Ed Rommel's 29 hits allowed is the most ever surrendered since the turn of the century. And he was the winning pitcher!

Cincinnati	AB	R	H	E		Brooklyn	AB	R	H	E
Clay cf	5	0	1	0		Stanky 2b	7	0	0	0
Zientara 3b	7	0	1	0		Reese ss	8	0	2	0
Frey 2b	6	0	1	0		Reiser lf-cf	7	0	1	0
Haas 1b	8	0	2	0		Walker rf	8	0	1	0
West lf	8	0	0	0		Furillo cf	6	0	0	0
Mueller c	6	0	0	0		Galan lf	1	0	0	0
Lukon rf	7	0	1	0		Lavagetto 3b	7	0	3	0
Corbitt ss	7	0	3	2		Edwards c	6	0	0	0
Vander Meer p	6	0	1	0		Schultz 1b	6	0	1	0
Gumbert p	1	0	0	0		Stevens 1b	1	0	0	0
						Gregg p	3	0	0	1
						Casey p	1	0	0	0
						Medwick ph	1	0	0	0
						Herring p	0	0	0	0
						Whitman ph	1	0	0	0
						Behrman p	0	0	0	0
	61	0	10	2			63	0	8	1

Cincinnati— 000 000 000 000 000 000 0—0
Brooklyn— 000 000 000 000 000 000 0—0

Two base hit—Lavagetto; **Three base hit**—Lukon
Sacrifice hits—Reiser, Clay, Zientara and Casey
Double plays—Frey, Corbitt and Haas; Reese, Stanky and Schultz; Stanky and Schultz; and Schultz and Reese
Bases on balls—Gregg 2, Herring 1, Behrman 2, Vander Meer 2
Struck out—Vander Meer 14, Gumbert 2, Gregg 6, Casey 2, Herring 1, Behrman 1
Hits off—Vander Meer 7 in 15 innings, Gumbert 1 in 4, Gregg 5 in 10, Casey 2 in 5, Herring 2 in 3, Behrman 1 in 1
Umpires—Barr, Conlan and Boggess
Time—4:40; **Att.**—14,538

Philadelphia	AB	R	H	E		Cleveland	AB	R	H	E
Haas rf	9	3	2	0		Porter rf	10	3	3	0
Cramer cf	8	2	2	0		Burnett ss	11	4	9	1
Dykes 3b	10	2	3	0		Averill cf	9	3	5	0
Simmons lf	9	4	5	0		Vosmik lf	10	2	2	0
Foxx 1b	9	4	6	0		Morgan 1b	11	1	5	1
McNair ss	10	0	2	0		Myatt c	7	2	1	0
Heving c	4	0	0	0		Cissell 2b	9	1	4	2
Majeski c	5	0	0	0		Kamm 3b	7	1	2	0
Williams 2b	8	1	2	0		Brown p	4	0	2	1
Krausse p	1	0	0	0		Hudlin p	0	0	0	0
Rommel p	7	2	3	1		Ferrell p	5	0	0	0
	80	18	25	1			83	17	33	5

Cincinnati— 201 201 702 000 000 201 -18
Brooklyn— 303 011 601 000 000 200 -17

Runs batted in—Porter 2, Burnett 2, Averill 4, Vosmik, Morgan 4, Cissell 3, Cramer, Dykes 4, Simmons 2, Foxx 8, Rommel, McNair
Two base hits—Burnett 2, Myatt, Cissell, Vosmik, Morgan 2, Haas, Dykes, Kamm, Porter, McNair, Foxx
Three base hit—Williams; **Home runs**—Foxx 3, Averill; **Stolen base**—Cissell
Sacrifice hits—Kamm, Ferrell
Double plays—Williams, McNair and Foxx; Burnett, Cissell and Morgan; Kamm, Cissell and Morgan; Williams, Madjeski and Foxx
Bases on balls—Krausse 1, Brown 1, Hudlin 2, Ferrell 4, Rommel 9
Struck out—Brown 3, Ferrell 7, Rommel 7
Hits off—Krausse 4 in 1 inning, Rommel 29 in 17 innings, Brown 13 in 6⅔ innings, Hudlin 0 (pitched to 2 batters), Ferrell 12 in 11⅓ innings
Wild pitches—Rommel 2
Winning pitcher—Rommel; **Losing pitcher**—Ferrell
Umpires—Hildebrand and Owens; **Time**—4:05; **Att.**—10,000

Emil H. Rothe, a retired teacher and assistant principal, is a frequent contributor to "BRJ."

Jack the Giant Killer

A.D. SUEHSDORF

JACK PFIESTER was known as "Jack the Giant Killer" for his successful pitching against John McGraw's team in the great days of its rivalry with the Cubs. But just how successful was he? How frequently, in fact, were the Giants slain? The answer is not easy to come by. Although Jack and his presumably apt nickname appear in many standard sources, no one undertakes to substantiate this interesting claim.

Actually, Jack's mastery of the Giants was asserted soon after he joined the Cubs. He had had two minimal seasons at Pittsburgh with no starts against New York. In Chicago, after one no-decision game, he trounced the Giants four straight times in the seasons of 1906-07. Ultimately, his record against them was 15-5 for a winning percentage of .750. Against the rest of the National League his career percentage was .590.

Jack was a capable lefthander with a good move to first that held runners close. He had a 20-win season as a rookie with the Cubs (1906), and in 1907, when he was 14-9, he led the league with a 1.15 earned run average that stands as the fifth best single-season mark ever. Overall, he was 71-44, with a career earned run average of 2.04. He appeared in four World Series, winning one game and losing three.

As can be seen from the seasonal statistics below (developed from National League records and the Tattersall box-score collection at Cooperstown), Jack faced the Giants most frequently during the memorable pennant race of 1908. He was credited with one victory in July for relieving Ed Reulbach, although Orval Overall pitched the ninth when the Cubs scored the winning run. By today's rule Orvie would be the winner. In August Jack also was credited with a shutout victory, although rain shortened the game to six innings.

In two vitally important games, however, the magic failed to work. On September 23, Jack started against Mathewson in the famous "Merkle game." If Fred had not failed to touch second, Jack would have been the loser. And facing Mathewson in the resultant playoff on October 8, Jack was shelled in the first inning. He would have suffered a second loss if Three Finger Brown had not pitched superb relief and won.

Even so, Jack went on to enjoy the 1909 and 1910 seasons as a Giant killer. After fifteen triumphs, he lost for the fifth time in May, 1911. It was Jack's final appearance in the major leagues.

JACK "THE GIANT KILLER" PFIESTER
Pitching Record Against New York Giants
Compiled by Bill Deane and William Vaules,
National Baseball Library

DATE	IP	H	R	BB	SO	W-L
5/22/06	4	4	2	1	4	
6/7/06	7	3	0	6	2	W
8/20/06	9	6	0	1	2	W
8/17/07	4	3	0	0	0	W
8/20/07	9	7	2	2	4	W
5/25/08	2.1	4	4	2	1	
5/27/08	8	4	1	4	5	L
6/19/08	8	10	6	2	0	L
7/15/08	4.2	7	4	2	0	
7/18/08	6	3	2	3	4	W
8/11/08	6	2	0	2	1	W
8/27/08	9	9	1	2	3	W
8/30/08	9	5	1	2	3	W
9/23/08	9	6	1	2	0	
10/8/08	.2	1	1	2	1	
5/14/09	9	4	0	1	3	W
6/10/09	9	8	0	1	7	W
8/12/09	5	7	2	0	2	L
8/30/09	11	6	0	3	3	W
9/17/09	8	8	4	1	2	L
9/19/09	7	4	0	0	2	
9/20/09	5	5	2	1	0	W
5/9/10	9	3	0	1	2	W
6/10/10	2.1	6	5	3	0	
7/9/10	7	4	1	0	0	
8/3/10	9	7	0	2	2	W
9/22/10	9	10	1	3	1	W
5/10/11	2.1	6	6	1	1	L

Summary

YEAR	G	IP	W	L	PCT.	SO	BB	H	R	SHO
1906	3	20	2	0	1.000	8	8	13	2	1
1907	2	13	2	0	1.000	4	2	10	2	0
1908	10	62.2	4	2	.667	18	23	51	21	1
1909	7	54	4	2	.667	19	7	42	8	3
1910	5	36.1	3	0	1.000	5	9	30	7	2
1911	1	2.1	0	1	.000	1	1	6	6	0
TOTAL	28	188.1	15	5	.750	55	50	153	46	7

A.D. Suehsdorf, retired editor of Ridge Press, is the author of "The Great American Baseball Scrapbook."

Hall-of-Fame Teams: A Study in Paradox

JEREMY GILLER and HENRY BERMAN

The more Hall of Famers a team owns, the more championships it wins, right? Research suggests a far different picture. For one thing, those Famers may be finished.

ALTHOUGH MUCH IS WRITTEN about Hall of Fame players, little is written about the teams they have played on together. Fans who know the answer to questions like, "Which teams have won (or lost) the most games?" or "Which teams have hit the most home runs?" don't know which teams had the most Hall-of-Fame players and how well those teams did. This article will answer these questions, and discuss some of the interesting teams that we studied in the process of doing this analysis. It also will show that, with extraordinarily few exceptions, the teams with the most future Hall of Famers were not successful teams. They were rarely championship teams, and seldom even won pennants; a number finished in the second division.

We gathered our data by studying all National and American League teams from 1901 to the present; although a case can be made for including teams before 1901, we felt we had more consistency by restricting our study to the "modern baseball era." The last teams with Hall of Famers, through 1988, were the 1983 Red Sox and Reds (Carl Yastrzemski and Johnny Bench), preceded by the 1982 Pirates (Willie Stargell), the 1980 Giants (Willie McCovey), and the 1979 Yankees (Catfish Hunter). Hall of Famers who played after 1969 were so few that we ended our study that year, although at the end of the article we will look at some of the great teams of the 1970s, to see how many future Hall of Famers they may have had.

Seventy-eight times a team has had five Hall of Famers for at least part of the season. Four of these had eight such players: the 1930-33 Yankees. A look at these four teams demonstrates two points: The first, not surprisingly, is the Hall's preponderance of players from the late 1920s and early 1930s, presumably because of that era's inflated batting averages. The other, very surprisingly, is the lack of direct correlation between having many Hall of Famers and outstanding success. Although 1930-1933 fall within the Yankee dynasty years (1921-1964), the Yanks won only one pennant during those years (1932). Their world championship teams of 1936 through 1939, in contrast, had "only" five Hall of Famers.

Seven teams had seven Hall of Famers: the 1927 and 1929 Giants; the 1933 Cardinals; the 1934 Pirates; the 1927 and 1928 Athletics; and the 1928 Yankees. The two principles mentioned above apply: All of these teams are in that same era, and the Giants, in particular, show a pattern they continued into the 1960s of having a large number of Hall of Famers with little to show for it.

Of the sixteen teams with six Hall of Famers, all but two—the 1912 Athletics and the 1956 Dodgers—played from 1923 to 1934. True to form, those Athletics did not win the pennant, and the 1956 Dodgers, although pennant-winners, did not win the World Series; it was their predecessors, in 1955, with five Hall of Famers, who had broken the Dodger drought.

If we need further evidence of these patterns, we need look no further than the Reds of 1932-1935. Each of these teams had four Hall of Famers. Yet in the first three of those years, the Reds finished last; in 1935 they finally escaped the cellar, to reach sixth place. Indeed, except for the Black Sox' opponents, the only Cincinnati team to win the World Series in the era under consideration was the 1940 Reds—with only one Hall of Famer. To understand how unusual that is, consider that only two other

Jeremy Giller is a student at Lexington (Mass.) High School. Henry Berman is president of Group Health Northwest, a health maintenance organization in Spokane, Washington.

teams (excluding the 1943-45 wartime championship teams) ever won the World Series with only one Hall of Famer: the 1960 Pirates (which will no longer be the case once Bill Mazeroski is awarded his rightful place in Cooperstown), and the 1906 White Sox—the famous "Hitless Wonders."

Overall, of the forty National League teams with five or more Hall of Famers, fifteen won pennants, and five of those won the World Series. The American League teams were a bit more successful: Of 38 such teams, 13 won pennants, and 10 of those won the World Series. The latter in large part owed to the success of those 1936-39 Yankees. To learn more about these teams, and about their relative lack of success despite their superstars, we did a more detailed study of the teams.

We originally decided that to construct the data base for our more thorough analysis, we would define a "Hall-of-Fame team" as one with four or more Hall of Famers. That left us with the heavy bias toward the 1920s and '30s that we have discussed.

Number of "Hall-of-Fame teams"

Decade	National League	American League
1901-09	9	6
1910-19	7	10
1920-29	27	24
1930-39	34	24
1940-49	7	9
1950-59	10	11
1960-69	2	0

Rather than assume that the players were actually that much better from 1920 to 1939, we decided that it made more sense for us to adjust our criterion to reflect the obvious bias that has been shown to the players of that era, when a .300 hitter was only an average player. To do that, we looked at how our data would come out if we kept the same criterion for "Hall-of-Fame teams" of 1920-1939, but made the criterion for before and after those years three or more Hall of Famers. This made our table look like this:

Number of "Hall-of-Fame teams" (adjusted)

Decade	National League	American League
1901-09	20	23
1910-19	21	24
1920-29	27	24
1930-39	34	24
1940-49	23	15
1950-59	19	20
1960-69	22	10

This adjustment gives us a reasonably equal distribution of "Hall-of-Fame teams" by decade, which is consistent with our intuitive sense that there should be about the same number of Hall of Famers in one decade as another. From here on, we will use this as our data base, since it corrects for the bias toward the two "hitting decades."

Top Hall-of-Fame teams by decade

To study further this phenomenon of "Hall-of-Fame teams" not being as successful as we had expected, we developed a list of the top Hall-of-Fame teams of each decade. Since a number of future Hall of Famers who played in the '60s have yet to be voted into the Hall, we ended this study in 1959. The list looks like this:

Decade	National League	American League
1900	1904 Giants (5)*	1907-08 Athletics (5)
1910	1917 Phillies (5)	1912 Athletics (6)
1920	1927, 1929 Giants (7)	1927-28 Athletics 1928 Yankees** (7)
1930	1933 Cardinals 1934 Pirates (7)	1930, 31, 32**, 33 Yankees (8)
1940	1948 Dodgers (5)	1940-41 Red Sox 1949 Indians (5)
1950	1956 Dodgers (6)*	Nine Yankee teams 1950, 1955 Indians (4)

*pennant winner only
**world champion

Not counting the cluster of Yankee teams from 1950 to 1959, there are twenty-three teams on this list. Of those, only the 1928 and 1932 Yankees were world champions; the 1956 Dodgers were pennant winners and World Series losers; and the 1904 Giants were pennant winners who refused to play in a World Series. Let's look in more detail at some of these unsuccessful "Hall-of-Fame teams."

1906-1914 Athletics

Player	'06	'07	'08	'09	'10	'11	'12	'13	'13
Bender	y	y	y	y	y	y	y	y	y
Plank	y	y	y	y	y	y	y	y	y
E. Collins	y	y	y	y	y	y	y	y	y
Waddell	y	y	n	n	n	n	n	n	n
J. Collins	n	y	y	n	n	n	n	n	n
Baker	n	n	y	y	y	y	y	y	y
Coveleski	n	n	n	n	n	n	y	n	n
Pennock	n	n	n	n	n	n	y	y	y
Total	4	5	5	4	4	4	6	5	5
Standings	4th	2nd	6th	2nd	1st	1st	3rd	1st	1st

y = yes (played on team that year); n = no

A closer look at the players' stats shows that Pennock and Coveleski both broke in with the Athletics, contributing little to the 1912-14 teams, but much to their subsequent teams. Waddell won 19 games in 1907, but was sold to the Browns in February of 1908; he won 19 again in 1908, but was out of baseball two years later. Jimmy Collins joined the Athletics at the end of his career, contributing little in 1908. Baker was a rookie with 31 at bats in 1908; once he got going, in 1909, and in concert with the nucleus of Bender, Plank, and Eddie Collins, the Athletics finished first four times, second once, and third once in six years.

The next teams we will examine, however, show a much different pattern:

1923-1932 Giants

Player	'23	'24	'25	'26	'27	'28	'29	'30	'31	'32
Bancroft	y	n	n	n	n	n	n	y	n	n
Kelly	y	y	y	n	n	n	n	n	n	n
Youngs	y	y	y	y	n	n	n	n	n	n
Frisch	y	y	y	y	n	n	n	n	n	n
Jackson	y	y	y	y	y	y	y	y	y	y
Terry	y	y	y	y	y	y	y	y	y	y
Lindstrom	n	y	y	y	y	y	y	y	y	y
Ott	n	n	n	y	y	y	y	y	y	y
Grimes	n	n	n	n	y	n	n	n	n	n
Hornsby	n	n	n	n	y	n	n	n	n	n
Roush	n	n	n	n	y	y	y	n	n	n
Hubbell	n	n	n	n	n	y	y	y	y	y
Schalk	n	n	n	n	n	n	y	n	n	n
Hoyt	n	n	n	n	n	n	n	n	n	y
Total	6	6	6	6	7	6	7	6	5	6
Standings	1st	1st	2nd	5th	3rd	2nd	3rd	3rd	2nd	6th

Although the Giants won the pennant the first two of these years, they did not win the World Series, which they had won in 1921 and 1922 with fewer Hall of Famers. After that, there were no more pennants until 1933, when they were down to four Hall of Famers (Jackson, Terry, Ott, and Hubbell). Although several of the players the Giants had added to this nucleus were winding down their careers—Bancroft, Schalk, Hoyt—two, Grimes and Hornsby, clearly were not.

Hornsby, after hitting .361 with 26 home runs, 133 runs scored, and 125 RBIs in his year with the Giants (1927), was traded to the Braves for Shanty Hogan and Jimmy Welsh. Both Hogan and Welsh were .300 hitters, but in an era when that was commonplace; together the next year they drove in 125 runs and scored the same number, in 887 at bats. Hornsby, in contrast, hit .387 in 1928 and .380 in 1929 for the Cubs, with 39 HRs, 149 RBIs, and 156 runs scored. Grimes, after winning 19 games for the Giants in 1927, was traded to the Pirates for Vic Aldridge, a pitcher the same age who had won 15 games in 1927. Aldridge won four games in 1928 (ERA 4.83), while Grimes won 25 games for the Pirates, with an ERA of 2.99.

This was just the first group of unsuccessful "Hall-of-Fame teams" that the Giants produced: The Giants of 1943 and those of 1964 and 1965 also had many Hall of Famers with no pennants. The 1943 Giants still had Hubbell, and had added Johnny Mize, Joe Medwick, and Ernie Lombardi, but finished last. Poor Lombardi: He was a member of those 1932-34 Reds teams with four Hall of Famers that finished last three consecutive years. (On the other hand, in a nice touch of poetic justice, he was the only Hall of Famer on the 1940 Reds.) And the Giants of 1964-65, by now in San Francisco, added first Duke

Snider and then Warren Spahn to their Hall-of-Fame triumvirate (1960-1972) of Willie Mays, Willie Mc-Covey, and Juan Marichal, only to finish fourth and second.

1925-1932 Athletics

Player	'25	'26	'27	'28	'29	'30	'31	'32
Simmons	y	y	y	y	y	y	y	y
Foxx	y	y	y	y	y	y	y	y
Cochrane	y	y	y	y	y	y	y	y
Grove	y	y	y	y	y	y	y	y
Cobb	n	n	y	y	n	n	n	n
E. Collins	n	n	y	y	n	n	n	n
Wheat	n	n	y	n	n	n	n	n
Speaker	n	n	n	y	n	n	n	n
Hoyt	n	n	n	n	n	n	y	n
Total	4	4	7	7	5	5	5	4
Standings	2nd	3rd	2nd	2nd	1st	1st	1st	2nd

Although the Athletics were a very successful team through these years, their only pennants came after their complement of Hall of Famers had been reduced from seven to five. Cobb, forty when he joined the team, in 1927, hit .357 with 104 runs scored and 93 RBIs; his last year in baseball, 1928, he kept his average up, at .323, but his production fell to 54 runs and 40 RBIs. Wheat in 1927 and Speaker in 1928 finished their careers with the A's, contributing little. Hoyt, on the other hand, won 10 games in half a season for the 1931 A's, and went on pitching reasonably productively for another half a decade, for three other teams.

1926-1934 Yankees

Player	'26	'27	'28	'29	'30	'31	'32	'33	'34
Combs	y	y	y	y	y	y	y	y	y
Gehrig	y	y	y	y	y	y	y	y	y
Hoyt	y	y	y	y	y	n	n	n	n
Pennock	y	y	y	y	y	y	y	y	n
Ruth	y	y	y	y	y	y	y	y	n
Coveleski	n	n	y	n	n	n	n	n	n
Dickey	n	n	y	y	y	y	y	y	y
Gomez	n	n	n	n	y	y	y	y	y
Ruffing	n	n	n	n	y	y	y	y	y
Sewell	n	n	n	n	y	y	y	y	n
Grimes	n	n	n	n	n	n	n	n	y
Total	5	5	7	6	8	8	8	8	6
Standings	1st	1st	1st	2nd	3rd	2nd	1st	2nd	2nd

The Yankees were certainly a strong team these years, but for the most part these were not their glory years. And, in particular, the "all-time Hall-of-Fame teams," with eight such stars, won only one pennant in the four years from 1930 to 1933. Admittedly, Gomez pitched only 60 innings in his rookie year, but he won 21 in 1931. Sewell was winding down his career, but he scored 102, 95 and 87 runs in each of his years with the Yankees to make a reasonable contribution. It almost seems as if there is a limit to how many Hall of Famers can be on a given team if it is to be successful. The 1936-1939 Yankees, winning four consecutive world championships while losing a total of three World Series games, had gotten down to a streamlined five: Gehrig, Dickey, Gomez, Ruffing, and DiMaggio.

1926-1934 Cardinals

Player	'26	'27	'28	'29	'30	'31	'32	'33	'34
Haines	y	y	y	y	y	y	y	y	y
Bottomley	y	y	y	y	y	y	y	n	n
Hafey	y	y	y	y	y	y	n	n	n
Alexander	y	y	y	n	n	n	n	n	n
Hornsby	y	n	n	n	n	n	n	y	n
Frisch	n	y	y	y	y	y	y	y	y
Maranville	n	y	y	n	n	n	n	n	n
Dean	n	n	n	n	y	n	y	y	y
Grimes	n	n	n	n	y	y	y	y	y
Medwick	n	n	n	n	n	n	y	y	y
Vance	n	n	n	n	n	n	n	y	y
Total	5	6	6	5	6	5	5	7	6
Standings	1st	2nd	1st	4th	1st	1st	7th	5th	1st

These Cardinals were another successful team, but not in 1932 or 1933, even though the latter year found an NL-record-tying seven Hall of Famers. Hornsby played only 46 games for the Cards in 1933, but hit .325; Vance, winding down his career, pitched 99 innings, and was 6-2 that year. Grimes pitched in just four games that year and four more the next. In truth, only Dean, Frisch, and Medwick were at the Hall-of-Fame level in 1933, so the figures in a sense misrepresent how many Hall-of-Fame performances were delivered. Nevertheless, the pattern continues: Teams do not have their most successful results with the most Hall of Famers.

1933-1939 Pirates

Player	'33	'34	'35	'36	'37	'38	'39
Hoyt	y	y	y	y	y	n	n
Lindstrom	y	y	n	n	n	n	n
Traynor	y	y	y	n	y	n	n
L. Waner	y	y	y	y	y	y	y
P. Waner	y	y	y	y	y	y	y
Vaughan	y	y	y	y	y	y	y
Grimes	n	y	n	n	n	n	n
Manush	n	n	n	n	n	y	y
Klein	n	n	n	n	n	n	y
Total	6	7	5	4	5	4	5
Standings	2nd	5th	4th	4th	3rd	2nd	6th

The Pirates of this era were not a very successful team; in particular, adding Lindstrom, a very marginal Hall of Famer, in 1933; Grimes, in 1934; and Manush, in 1938, did nothing for the team. The latter two retired after playing a handful of games, while Lindstrom contributed two ordinary years before winding down with the Cubs (1935) and the Dodgers (1936). The only reason Klein is in the Hall of Fame is his outstanding seasons from 1929 through 1933. During those five years, he averaged 224 hits, 46 doubles, 36 home runs, 132 runs scored and 139 RBIs, while hitting between .337 and .386 and slugging between .584 and .687. The rest of his career, which

dragged on to 1944, was only average; the 1939 Pirates had him for 85 games during a season in which he hit 12 home runs with 56 RBIs.

The other interesting observation to emerge from studying these teams is that Lloyd Waner was no Hall-of-Fame player. After an excellent first three years (1927-1929), he never again scored 100 runs or drove in more than 57. During his career, which looks more like an infielder's, the outfielder had only 28 home runs. And he didn't make up for it anywhere else offensively: he stole only 67 bases lifetime, and never walked more than 40 times in a season. His outstanding achievement was that he rarely struck out: 173 times in 7,772 at bats! And he had a remarkable statistic his rookie year: He scored 133 runs, while driving in only 27. It is hard to imagine that "feat" has ever been duplicated.

1936-1942 Red Sox

Player	'36	'37	'38	'39	'40	'41	'42
Cronin	y	y	y	y	y	y	y
Grove	y	y	y	y	y	y	n
Foxx	y	y	y	y	y	y	y
Ferrell	y	y	n	n	n	n	n
Manush	y	n	n	n	n	n	n
Doerr	n	y	y	y	y	y	y
Williams	n	n	n	y	y	y	y
Total	5	5	4	5	5	5	4
Standings	6th	5th	2nd	2nd	4th	2nd	2nd

It is not surprising that one of the franchises that led a decade in non-winning Hall-of-Fame teams would be the Red Sox, who seem never to have shaken the bad luck that started when they sold Babe Ruth. Admittedly, Lefty Grove was at the end of his glorious career by 1940 and 1941; but in 1939 he went 15-4, and led the league with an ERA of 2.54. Williams was a mere rookie that year, so hit only .327, with 31 home runs, 131 runs scored, and 145 RBIs! Foxx led the league in homers and slugging percentage that year, while hitting .360; Doerr hit .318, and Cronin .308, with 97 runs and 107 RBIs. Yet the Sox finished second—to the Yankees.

We all know that the dominant team in baseball from 1948 to 1956 was the Yankees, with seven pennants and six world championships, and an average of 97 wins a year. But which team during those years won one world championship, never winning fewer than 88 games, and averaging 94 wins a season? The answer is not the Dodgers, who won only 84 games in 1948, but the Indians, a great team that had the misfortune to compete with the Yankees year after year. From 1951 to 1956, the Indians finished second five times and first once, winning 111 games in 1954.

Once again we see that the pattern holds: The two pennant-winning teams did not have the most Hall of Famers for the franchise. Admittedly, Kiner joined the

1948-1956 Indians

Player	'48	'49	'50	'51	'52	'53	'54	'55	'56
Boudreau	y	y	y	n	n	n	n	n	n
Feller	y	y	y	y	y	y	y	y	y
Lemon	y	y	y	y	y	y	y	y	y
Paige	y	y	n	n	n	n	n	n	n
Wynn	n	y	y	y	y	y	y	y	y
Kiner	n	n	n	n	n	n	n	y	n
Total	4	5	4	3	3	3	3	4	3
Standings	1st	3rd	4th	2nd	2nd	2nd	1st	2nd	2nd

team for his last year. However, he was not unproductive: In 321 at bats, he hit 18 home runs, with 56 runs scored, 54 RBIs and 65 walks. Paige was forty-two (at least) when he joined the Indians, and pitched only 155 innings in the two years, but was reasonably effective. Boudreau, too, was at the end of his career, with productivity dropping sharply after his 1948 MVP season. But the Indians of those years also had Larry Doby, who drove in over 100 runs four times between 1950 and 1954; Mike Garcia, who won 79 games from 1951 to 1954; Al Rosen, who drove in over 100 runs every year from 1950 through 1954; and Bobby Avila, who averaged .307 during those five years. The same problem plagued these Indians as the 1936-42 Red Sox and 1925-32 Athletics: the New York Yankees.

1948-1958 Dodgers

Player	'48	'49	'50	'51	'52	'53	'54	'55	'56	'57	'58
Reese	y	y	y	y	y	y	y	y	y	y	y
Robinson	y	y	y	y	y	y	y	y	y	n	n
Snider	y	y	y	y	y	y	y	y	y	y	y
Campanella	y	y	y	y	y	y	y	y	y	y	n
Vaughan	y	n	n	n	n	n	n	n	n	n	n
Koufax	n	n	n	n	n	n	n	y	y	y	y
Drysdale	n	n	n	n	n	n	n	n	y	y	y
Total	5	4	4	4	4	4	4	5	6	5	4
Standings	3rd	1st	2nd	2nd	1st	1st	2nd	1st	1st	3rd	7th

With the exception of Vaughan, finishing his career in 1948, of these exceptional teams we find no has-beens coming on to finish their careers; Campanella and Snider made peripheral contributions in 1948, but for the next eight years, until Robinson retired, the Dodgers had a core of four Hall of Famers playing together during their prime years. Koufax pitched only 41, 58, and 104 innings in 1955, '56, and '57, and Drysdale only 99 innings in 1956. Don Newcombe, however, was a Hall-of-Fame-caliber pitcher from 1949 through 1956, winning 112 and losing 48, while missing 1952 and 1953 in the military. But even here, with a team that won five pennants, and lost the 1950 and 1951 pennants on the last day of the season, their only team with six Hall of Famers was not their only championship team, in 1955, but rather their 1956 team.

The Yankees here follow a similar pattern to the Dodgers, with whom they are forever twinned for this era (the

1949-1959 Yankees

Player	'49	'50	'51	'52	'53	'54	'55	'56	'57	'58	'59
DiMaggio	y	y	y	n	n	n	n	n	n	n	n
Berra	y	y	y	y	y	y	y	y	y	y	y
Mize	y	y	y	y	n	n	n	n	n	n	n
Ford	n	y	n	n	y	y	y	y	y	y	y
Mantle	n	n	y	y	y	y	y	y	y	y	y
Slaughter	n	n	n	n	n	y	y	y	y	y	y
Total	3	4	4	3	4	4	4	4	4	4	4
Standings	1st	1st	1st	1st	1st	2nd	1st	1st	1st	1st	3rd

two played against each other six times from 1947 to 1956, the Dodgers winning only in 1955). Berra, Ford, and Mantle played together for more than a decade—through 1963. Hall of Famers Mize, then Slaughter, played productively in support roles to round out the team. Why were these Yankees able consistently to turn back the challenges of the Indians, in their own league, and the Dodgers, come October? Possibly it was because the Indians' Hall-of-Fame teams consisted almost exclusively of pitchers, and the Dodgers almost exclusively of hitters. Perhaps Whitey Ford, with his record of 207-83 from 1953 to 1964, was the real key to the extraordinary success of these teams; only the Yankees had Hall-of-Fame hitting, pitching, and fielding those years, and only these Yankees have been able to break out of the pattern of having their "Hall of Fame teams" be losers.

THERE IS ONE ADDITIONAL pattern that can be discerned by a careful examination of the most successful "Hall-of-Fame" teams—the presence of a Hall-of-Fame catcher. Using Bill James' rankings in the updated "Historical Baseball Abstract," the top catchers in baseball history are Yogi Berra, Johnny Bench, Mickey Cochrane, Gary Carter, Carlton Fisk, Gabby Hartnett, Bill Dickey, Ernie Lombardi, and Roy Campanella. With the exception of Carter and Fisk, both of whom are still active, only Hartnett does not figure prominently on Hall-of-Fame teams. Bench, we will see, starred on the team that is apt to end up with the most Hall of Famers in the 1970s—the Big Red Machine. And one of the strongest teams of the 1980s, the New York Mets, did not win a pennant until they added Carter.

The 1960s and 1970s

It is too soon to come to conclusions about these decades; too many Hall of Famers are yet to be voted in. But we have already discussed the 1964 and 1965 Giants, losers despite four Hall of Famers. And suppose Ferguson Jenkins makes Cooperstown (284 wins, 4,499 innings pitched, 3,192 strikeouts, 49 shutouts, seven 20-win seasons, six in a row): that will make the 1970 Cubs a four-Hall-of-Famer team (with Banks, Williams, and Wilhelm in addition to Jenkins). If Ron Santo is added (.277 BA, .464 SA, 342 HRs, 1,331 RBIs), that would make five for this second-place team. On the other hand, another team that could have five—the 1967 Cardinals—were world champions. That team had Lou Brock and Bob Gibson, already in the Hall; Steve Carlton, a shoo-in once eligible; Orlando Cepeda, with 379 home runs, a .297 BA, and a .499 SA; plus Roger Maris. Of course, if Cepeda makes the Hall, he would join his 1964 and 1965 Giant teammates; when Gaylord Perry is voted in, that would give those Giant teams, which finished fourth and second, six Hall of Famers.

It does appear that the 1970s may break the pattern of the best teams not having the most Hall of Famers. That decade was dominated by two teams: the Oakland A's in the American League, who won five straight divisional championships from 1971 to 1975, and three consecutive world championships, from 1972 to 1974; and the Cincinnati Reds in the National League, who won six divisional championships, four pennants and two world championships. Let's see how these teams might chart out:

1970-1976 A's

Player	'70	'71	'72	'73	'74	'75	'76
Hunter	y	y	y	y	y	n	n
Jackson	y	y	y	y	y	y	n
Fingers	y	y	y	y	y	y	y
Williams	n	n	n	n	n	y	y
McCovey	n	n	n	n	n	n	y
Campaneris	y	y	y	y	y	y	y
Total	4	4	4	4	4	4	4
Standings	2nd	1st	1st	1st	1st	1st	2nd

Hunter, Williams, and McCovey are already in the Hall; Jackson and Fingers will probably be admitted. Campaneris may well be elected: He played shortstop on the best team of the early '70s, had 2,249 hits, and stole 649 bases while leading the league six times. In addition, he was remarkably consistent, getting between 135 and 177 hits every year from 1965 to 1977.

1970-1979 Reds

Player	'70	'71	'72	'73	'74	'75	'76	'77	'78	'79
Rose	y	y	y	y	y	y	y	y	y	n
Bench	y	y	y	y	y	y	y	y	y	y
Perez	y	y	y	y	y	y	y	n	n	n
Concepcion	y	y	y	y	y	y	y	y	y	y
Morgan	n	n	y	y	y	y	y	y	y	y
Seaver	n	n	n	n	n	n	n	y	y	y
Total	4	4	5	5	5	5	5	5	5	5
Standings	1st	4th	1st	1st	2nd	1st	1st	2nd	2nd	1st

This impressive team was pulled together when future Hall of Famer Joe Morgan joined Rose, Bench, and Perez. Concepcion seems likely to be elected for similar reasons

to Campaneris: shortstop on the best team of the decade; .268 hitter with 2,326 hits; between 1973 and 1979, hit between .271 and .301 each year; stealing between 19 and 41 bases. These teams are reminiscent of the Dodgers of the 1950s: Hall of Famers galore in the field but none on the mound, until Seaver joined the team—just as Perez left.

The 1980s

The team with the most potential Hall of Famers right now would seem to be the New York Mets; according to "The 1988 Bill James Baseball Abstract," both Carter and Hernandez could be elected on the basis of present credentials, which they added to in 1988. Gooden at age twenty-three was already "building credentials" and Strawberry, at twenty-six, was "working on it." Ron Darling, now twenty-eight, is 73-41; Early Wynn was only 72-87 at that point in his career. From 1984 through 1988, the Mets were the only team in baseball to win at least 90 games each year; however, through 1988, they have only their 1986 world championship and 1988 division crown to show for it—and were within one strike of not having the World Series victory.

Why do so few teams with many Hall of Famers win the world championship—or even the pennant? There could be many explanations, but the most likely is a lack of team chemistry. A team with six or seven great stars could also be a team with six or seven great egos; perhaps the individuals can't work with each other for the benefit of the team. (The phenomenon does not seem unique to baseball: "Dream backfields" of Earl Campbell and George Rogers, or Tony Dorsett and Herschel Walker, or "Hall-of-Fame" combinations of Wilt Chamberlain, Elgin Baylor, and Jerry West, or Ralph Sampson and Akeem Olajuwon have also proved not to work out.) Or perhaps the rest of the players wait around for the superstars to carry the team. Or some of the Famers are aborning or over the hill. Without recounting every case history, it's safe to say that the splendid work old Johnny Mize did for the 1949-53 Yankees and Enos Slaughter for the 1954-59 Yankees were the exceptions rather than the rule.

In any case, we feel the facts clearly speak for themselves: maximizing the number of future Hall of Famers on a team is not the key to success. If any specific strategies can be learned from our study, they are the following: Do not add a future Hall of Famer at the end of his career; and find yourself a catcher with great potential. The Mets of the 1980s did do the latter, and to date have not made the mistake of doing the former.

Bill Terry As Pitcher

ROBERT C. McCONNELL

Bill Terry was a Hall-of-Fame first baseman and player-manager. He was also a sensational lefthanded pitcher — at least, for one Class-D season in Georgia.

BILL TERRY IS PROBABLY BEST KNOWN as the last National League player to hit .400 (.401 in 1930). He had a lifetime batting average of .341 over 14 seasons and had enough extra-base hits to give him a .506 career slugging average. Less well-known is that Terry was an excellent first baseman. He led the NL five times in putouts, five times in assists, and three times in fielding percentage. As a player-manager he led the New York Giants to three pennants and one world championship.

Almost completely forgotten is Terry's record as a minor-league pitcher. A native of Georgia, he started with Dothan in the Class-D Georgia State League in 1915. The slender six-footer was only sixteen but looked older. He pitched three games for Dothan, losing two and getting a "no-decision." In one outing the young lefthander walked 10 batters. He was cut in mid-May, and there was no published news about him until the June 21 Griffin Daily News said that "Harry Mathews, of the Newnan club, has signed Lefty Terry, who failed to make good with Dothan in the Georgia State League. Terry is just a kid, but it is said that he has the goods all right. He was released down there over the manager's protest."

Newnan, a town of about 5,500, was in the six-team Class-D Georgia-Alabama League. The other clubs were located at Griffin, LaGrange, and Rome, Georgia; and Anniston and Talladega, Alabama. Newnan did not have a newspaper. Fortunately, the Griffin Daily News provided some information and the Birmingham Age-Herald carried box scores of all league games during the short summer season.

In spite of the lack of publicity, Terry's 1915 pitching stint with Newnan bordered on the sensational. (He batted only .143 in 28 at bats. At Dothan he had two hits in 10 at bats.) Bill pitched in his first game on June 16, beating Talladega and allowing only five hits and one run. He was then put in the starting rotation and on June 21 defeated Rome, allowing two runs on six hits and no walks.

Terry then reeled off three consecutive shutouts. The second was a no-hitter against Anniston on June 30. The

Bill Terry

third was a 13-inning 1-0 victory over Rome in which he yielded only four hits and one walk. After winning his first six starts, Terry went down to his only defeat, dropping a 2-1 decision to Talledega on July 10.

Bill pitched in the last game of the season on July 14. It would be a fitting climax to this story to say that the pennant was on the line. However, Newnan had a one-game lead over Talladega going into the final day and even with a loss could clinch the pennant by percentage points.

Bob McConnell is a retired engineer and a charter member of SABR.

Nevertheless, the young southpaw came through with a sparkling 1-0 win over LaGrange.

Terry's game-by-game record is carried in the accompanying chart. Each of his eight games was complete and four were shutouts. He never allowed more than two runs in a game, including his one loss. On a 9-inning game basis he gave up 0.8 runs, 4.9 hits, 1.9 walks, and struck out 4.0 batters. He obviously was not a strikeout pitcher. What was surprising in light of his wildness at Dothan was that he had such good control, particularly for a sixteen-year-old.

Terry's Pitching For Newnan in 1915

Date	Opponent	H/A	IP	W	L	H	R	BB	SO
June 16	Talladega	Home	9	1		5	1	3	3
June 21	Rome	Away	9	1		6	2	0	1
June 26	Griffin	Home	9	1		5	0	2	7
June 30	Anniston	Away	9	1		0	0	2	2
July 3	Rome	Home	13	1		4	0	1	3
July 7 (2)	LaGrange	Away	9	1		8	2	2	6
July 10	Talladega	Away	8		1	8	2	2	4
July 14	LaGrange	Home	9	1		5	0	4	7
Totals		8 Games	75	7	1	41	7	16	33

Terry returned to Newnan at the beginning of the 1916 season. He didn't dominate as he had the year before, but his record was good enough (11 wins and 8 losses) for him to be sold July 20 to Shreveport in the Texas League. He was 6-2 there with a 1.07 ERA. Spending the 1917 season at Shreveport, he won 14 and lost 11. By this time he was playing part-time in the outfield and pinch hitting. However, his batting average in 95 games was only .231. It was time to make a decision about his career.

Although only eighteen years old, Bill married a Memphis girl and went to work for Standard Oil in Memphis. For the next four years, 1918-21, he played semipro ball on the strong company team and developed a basis for the future nickname of Memphis Bill. His diamond performance came to the attention of Tom Watkins, owner of the Memphis Southern Association team, who recommended him to manager John McGraw of the New York Giants. McGraw, more impressed with Terry's hitting than his pitching, assigned him to Toledo in the American Association.

Bill spent the 1922 and 1923 seasons with Toledo. In the first season he pitched in 26 games with a 9-9 won-lost record, played first base in 48, and batted .336. He gave away his toe-plate and in 1923 hit a resounding .377. The Giants called him up at the end of the season, and he never looked back.

With his pitching career over — he never even made a token mound appearance in the majors — William H.

Terry removed any possibility that he might be confused with William J. (Adonis) Terry, a well-known nineteenth-century hurler. Bill Terry the younger went on to a Hall-of-Fame career as a superb hitting and fielding first baseman. Once he became an established star, he dismissed his early pitching effort as "nothing to write home about." But Memphis Bill didn't have to be apologetic about his 47-33 mound record. In fact, he could be justly proud of his spectacular performance with Newnan in 1915 when he was only sixteen. Bill Terry died recently. His pitching record should not die with him.

BAN JOHNSON PREFERRED ERA OVER WON-LOST RECORDS

The American League did not adopt earned run averages until 1913. League president Ban Johnson was so enthusiastic about earned run averages that he dropped won-lost records from the official averages, saying they were not necessary. Johnson's decision was not a popular one. Thanks to the editors of both the Reach and Spalding guides, the unofficial won-lost records were published each year until 1920, when Johnson finally relented and gave approval for both ERA and won-lost records to be part of the official averages.

Imagine what National League won-lost records would have looked like if a plan proposed by league president John Heydler had been adopted in 1922. The following item from the Chicago Herald and Examiner of May 14, 1922 denotes the plan he proposed to amend the scoring rules:

"John Heydler, president of the National League, is in favor of changing baseball scoring rules to permit more fairness to be shown toward pitchers in crediting them with defeats or victories.

"He thinks it advisable to amend the scoring rules so that a pitcher can be credited with half a victory or half a defeat in games where two or more pitchers share in winning or losing."

— Al Kermisch

TWO TRIVIA QUESTIONS

Who holds the National league record for total bases in a game by a pitcher?

Braves knuckleballer Jim Tobin, who homered three times for 12 total bases against the Cubs on May 12, 1942.

Who allowed Stan Musial's first hit?

Jim Tobin, as a Pirate, on Sept. 17, 1941. Pitching most of his career for second-division teams, he led the National League twice in complete games and once in innings pitched, threw a no-hitter, and went 105-112 in 1937-45.

— José Jiménez Jr.

Vic Willis:
Turn-of-the-Century Great
STEPHEN CUNERD

He ranked with contemporary pitching stars like Iron Man McGinnity, Three Finger Brown, Jack Chesbro, and Rube Waddell. So why isn't Vic Willis in the Hall?

TURN-OF-THE-CENTURY BASEBALL: It was a time of uniforms with baggy pants and no number. A time when players used gloves with no padding that they left in the field between innings. A time of ballparks with no lights. The parks were in the middle of the city because that's where the fans were, and where the parks could be reached by public transportation such as trolleys. The games were all played on natural grass and without the help of electronic scoreboards and video replays.

It was, for all that, a time similar to today, because the nation was filled with baseball fans who loved the game and regularly followed their favorite teams and players. They watched their local team in person when it played at home, followed the newspaper reports of road games and pennant races, and collected baseball cards of the stars of the day.

Baseball at the turn of the century was a game dominated by the pitchers. The mound had been moved back to its present distance of 60 feet 6 inches. The great pitchers threw overhand, and many were experimenting with the curveball and other unusual deliveries. In the 1880s, each team only had two or three pitchers. By 1900, most teams used three or four starters so that a pitcher could rest between starts, and carried several other pitchers as well. Team batting averages were low, and there were few really great hitters. In the American League, Nap Lajoie was the premier hitter, and would be joined later in the decade by Ty Cobb and Tris Speaker. Honus Wagner of the Pirates dominated the National League hitting scene, along with teammates Ginger Beaumont and Fred Clarke. It was a dead-ball era, home runs were scarce, runs were scored by grouping hits and stealing bases, and defense was becoming increasingly important.

Mostly, however, the turn of the century was a time for great pitchers. The 1890s featured Cy Young, Kid Nichols,

and fireballing Amos Rusie. The 1900s would bring Christy Mathewson, Eddie Plank, Joe McGinnity, Rube Waddell, Mordecai Brown, and Addie Joss, all Hall of Famers. One great turn-of-the-century pitcher, however, has thus far been bypassed in the Hall-of-Fame voting. Vic Willis is still waiting to join the honored greats at Cooperstown.

Willis, who was born in Wilmington, Delaware, in 1876 and pitched in Harrisburg and Syracuse before making it to the majors with Boston in 1898, is like so many of his contemporaries, mostly a name in the record books. There is virtually no one still living who saw him pitch and only a few who have talked to someone who has. Those who saw him, though, remember one of the National League's truly great turn-of-the-century hurlers. They remember his pitching duels against Mordecai Brown of the Cubs and Joe McGinnity of the Giants. They remember a big righthander with a great curveball who is still waiting outside the door at Cooperstown.

Victor Gazaway Willis, 6'2" and 185 pounds, worked for the Boston Beaneaters, Pittsburgh Pirates, and St. Louis Cardinals from 1898 to 1910. He spent his first eight seasons in Boston, then four in Pittsburgh before wrapping up an outstanding career with one year in St. Louis. Physically, he would remind modern fans of Robin Roberts or Tom Seaver, powerful righthanders who tend to dominate a game, especially after the first few innings. Willis was known for both a powerful curveball and a habit of completing everything he started. In his 13 major league seasons, Willis won 248 games, including 20 or more in eight different seasons. He hurled 50 career shutouts, pitched a no-hitter against Washington in 1899, and three one-hitters later in his career. In the 1902 season, Willis won 27 games and led the league in strikeouts, innings

Stephen Cunerd is wage-and-salary manager for a Philadelphia-area hospital.

pitched, and complete games. His 45 complete games represent a modern NL record that still is standing 86 years after he accomplished the feat.

Willis joined the Boston team as a twenty-two-year-old rookie in 1898. The Beaneaters were a hard team to break into at this time, because they had just won the NL pennant in 1897 and had been a strong team throughout the 1890s. The team featured several future Hall of Famers, Jimmy Collins, Hugh Duffy, Billy Hamilton, and Kid Nichols. Willis replaced an aging Jack Stivetts in the Boston rotation and proceeded to win 24 games while losing only 13. Boston repeated as NL champs and, if they had been giving such awards, Willis would have handily won Rookie of the Year honors.

At this time in baseball's history, a major change was taking place in the type of player making a career out of baseball and in the team image that was being presented to the fans. Frank Selee, who managed the Boston team, believed strongly that the game had developed an image that was much too rowdy. As a result, he deliberately recruited players who would fit a more gentlemanly image. He believed that this was not only the right approach, but also one that would increase fan interest in the game.

Vic Willis fit right in with Selee's approach. He was described in the Boston newspapers of his time as a gentleman both on and off the field. His loyalty was such that, when many players jumped to the new American League for more money, he stayed with the Boston club. By 1906, he was the National League pitcher with the longest continuous service in the league.

In 1899, in only his second season, Willis established himself as the premier pitcher in baseball, winning 27 while losing only 8. His ERA (2.50) was second to Al Orth's by only .01. He led the league in shutouts and in fewest hits allowed per nine innings. Boston won 95 games but finished second to a Brooklyn team featuring future Hall of Famers Willie Keeler and Joe Kelley. In that season, Willis pitched his no-hitter, besting Washington in August.

After winning 51 games in 1898 and '99, Willis struggled in 1900 through one of his few off-seasons, as his victory total dropped to 10, against 17 losses.

BOSTON AT THIS POINT was a team on the decline. By 1901, Collins and Duffy had jumped to the new American League and Hamilton was well past his prime. Accordingly, there was little support for the pitching staff. First baseman Fred Tenney, a defensive standout, was also one of the few consistent hitters remaining in the Boston lineup. Despite playing for a weak team, however, Willis continued to be a big winner during the first several years of the century. In 1901, he posted his third 20-win

season, and led the league in several categories defining pitching excellence. He allowed the fewest baserunners per nine innings, and led the league in shutouts.

In 1902, Willis put up durability marks that are still standing. He worked 411 innings, joining Joe McGinnity as the only modern NL hurlers to exceed 400 innings in a season. It was during this year that Willis completed 45 of his 46 starts, winning 27 of them. He posted an ERA of 2.20, pitched four shutouts and led the league with 225 strikeouts. Imagine the salary this performance would draw in the 1980s market!

For the next three years, Boston was an extremely weak-hitting team and pitchers struggled to get every victory. The team never finished higher than sixth place, and could get no closer than 32 games out of first place. But in spite of limited support, Willis continued to be an effective pitcher. In 1903, he won 12 games. In 1904, although leading the NL in losses with 25, he had a fine ERA, posted 18 wins, finished second to Christy Mathewson in strikeouts, and tied for the league lead in complete games.

In 1905, he set the modern National League record for losses in a season with 29. As many baseball analysts have observed, it takes an outstanding pitcher to lose 20 games in a season because no manager is going to keep pitching him otherwise. During that season, Willis was second in the league in innings pitched and complete games, and four of his 11 victories were shutouts.

After the 1905 season, Willis was traded to Pittsburgh for third baseman Dave Brain, outfielder Del Howard, and pitcher Vive Lindaman. This was one of the early examples of a trading principle that has been true down through the years: trading quantity for quality. There have been numerous examples of teams that packaged several good players to a weak team to obtain the star who would make a difference for a pennant contender. This was true for the Pirates at this time. They had been chasing the Cubs and Giants for several years since their flags in the early 1900s. Willis was the key addition who kept them in pennant contention for the rest of the decade and brought them a world championship in 1909.

Willis pitched in Pittsburgh for four years, winning 20 or more games in every season and posting a total record of 90-47 as a Pirate. In addition, he pitched 23 shutouts. Only Hall of Famers Mordecai (Three Finger) Brown and Christy Mathewson were pitching at a comparable level. In 1906, Willis's first year in Pittsburgh, he was 22-13 with a 1.73 ERA and did not allow a home run in the entire season. In 1907, he won 21 more, and in 1908, with the Pirates in the battle for the pennant right up to the last day of the season, Willis won 24 more. Then in 1909, Willis was a 23-game winner again, as the Pirates swept to the NL crown and won the World Series, beating Detroit.

Vic Willis (back row, third from left) and his Boston teammates in 1902.

THE 1909 PIRATES were a great team, featuring Hall of Famers Honus Wagner, who batted .339 to win his fourth consecutive batting title, and Fred Clarke, who played left field and managed the team to a 110-42 record. As the Pirate ace, Willis also had the honor of pitching the first game played in the new Pirate stadium, Forbes Field. Over 30,000 fans were on hand June 30 to see the Pirates play the Cubs. During this outstanding 1909 season, Willis also put together a personal 11-game winning streak.

After the 1909 season, Willis was sold to St. Louis, where he wrapped up his career a year later. Without Willis, the Pirates dropped to third in 1910 and didn't win another pennant until 1925. During his 13-year career, Willis was a major factor in championships for both Boston and Pittsburgh and is remembered as one of the great pitchers for both franchises.

Willis was a contemporary of several Hall-of-Fame pitchers, and the table compares his career statistics to theirs. It is of particular significance to compare Willis to this group because they played in the same era, against some of the same competition, and under the same playing conditions. Slight variations in these statistics will exist, since scoring rules differed from those in effect today. However, the conclusion seems obvious. If these men are worthy Hall of Famers — and most baseball experts

believe they are — then Vic Willis belongs in there with them. Willis posted more wins, more 20-win seasons, more innings pitched, and more complete games than all of them. Even though he played a significant portion of his career for weak teams, Willis posted a fine ERA and is among the all-time leaders in careers shutouts.

This is not an attempt to discredit any of the players already enshrined at Cooperstown, only an effort to indicate that Willis belongs with them. Willis has more career victories than twenty-two of the pitchers already elected. He has a better earned run average than twenty-eight of them and more shutouts than thirty-three of them.

In addition to the statistical case for Vic Willis's election to the Hall of Fame, there is now a moral case as well. Willis is the only player in baseball history to receive 75 percent of the vote in a Hall of Fame election and not be enshrined at Cooperstown. In the 1986 Veterans Committee election, Bobby Doerr, Ernie Lombardi, and Willis all received 75 percent or more of the votes cast. Since the Veterans Committee has a rule limiting the number of electees in any year to two, only Doerr and Lombardi made it into the Hall that year.

In the 1987 election balloting, the committee had difficulty agreeing and elected only one person, Ray Dandridge. No one was elected by the committee in 1988, and in 1989 the honors went to Red Schoendienst and Al Barlick.

But the fact remains: The statistical evidence and the moral principle both argue for the election of Vic Willis.

	W-L	ERA	SO	IP	CG	Sho	20-win Seasons
Willis	248-206*	2.63	1651	3996	388	50	8
Bender	208-127	2.46	1711	3017	257	41	2
Brown	229-131	2.03	1375	3172	271	56	6
Chesbro	196-131	2.68	1265	2897	261	35	5
Marquard	205-177	3.08	1593	3307	197	30	3
McGinnity	247-145	2.66	1068	3455	314	32	7
Waddell	191-141	2.16	2316	2961	261	50	4
Walsh	194-130	1.82	1736	2964	250	58	4

*The authorities vary slightly on Willis's exact won-lost record. The figures given in this article are believed to be correct.

200-Homer Teams:
An Analysis

ED GOLDSTEIN

Baseball teams didn't slug 200 homers in a single season until 1947; they've been doing it pretty regularly ever since. But does all that power guarantee a title?

FEW ASPECTS OF BASEBALL capture the imagination as forcefully as the home run. The pages in record books devoted to home-run hitting outnumber those of any other hit many times over. While the number 50 signifies the single-season slugger par excellence, the team that reaches 200 home runs is equally distinguished.

Nineteen-eighty-seven marked a watershed year in home-run hitting. Both leagues, arguably aided by a hyperthyroid baseball, and/or internally altered bats, shattered league home-run records. For the first time no fewer than five teams hit over 200 home runs apiece, and six others smashed 190 or more. This new extreme in team prowess begs an inquiry on teams that have accomplished this feat — who they were, how they did it and how significant the accomplishment was.

All teams that have hit 200 or more home runs are listed in the accompanying table, with the pennant winner of that season if different. All date from the post-World War II era, starting with the 1947 Giants.

Considering that 182 homers was the team record before 1947, it is astonishing that that year's Giants belted almost 40 more, upping the record to 221. In the next decade they were joined by three other National League clubs, the 1953 and 1955 Dodgers and the 1956 Reds, the latter of which tied the Giants' record of 221.

The American League did not produce a 200-homer club until 1961, and then produced four consecutive seasons in which a team hit that many. The 1961 Yankees shattered the Giants' and Reds' record by establishing the current standard of 240. There followed the Tigers of 1962 and the only back-to-back 200-homer team, the 1963-64 Twins, who slugged 446 home runs in two years. The 1962

Giants hit 204 home runs, while the 1966 Braves closed the decade of the 1960s with 207.

In the 1970s the 1970 Red Sox, 1973 Braves and 1977 Red Sox joined the list. The 1980s have proven the busiest 200-homer decade, with the 1980 and 1982 Brewers, 1985 and 1987 Orioles, 1985 and 1987 Tigers and 1987 Blue Jays, Cubs and Giants.

To sum up, the Giants and Tigers have performed the feat three times each, while the Dodgers, Twins, Braves, Red Sox, Brewers, and Orioles appear on the list twice. The Yankees, Reds, Cubs and Blue Jays did it once each.

While the thought of a 200-homer team conjures up visions of an entire roster bulging with sluggers, the fact is that the bulk of the slugging is done by a select few. On no club did the top three home-run hitters account for less than 38.5 percent of the club's production, ranging to a high of 60.1 percent. The average percent of homers hit by the top three sluggers on all 200 home runs clubs is 49.7. We also see that most of these clubs were accompanied by at least one hitter who produced 20 or more homers in addition, further concentrating the power. On the record-holding 1961 Yankees, Berra's 22 homers and Howard and Blanchard's 21 apiece mean that 207 of the 240 homers were produced by six men, 86.2 percent of the total, and the sixteenth best team total of all time from just those six.

Most 200-homer teams consistently field the same lineup. And most of these clubs repeat the accomplishment, though not necessarily in the short span of time that the Tigers and Giants did. While you must have the personnel to do the job, it would seem that having a park

Ed Goldstein is a computer analyst in Palos Verde, California, and secretary of SABR's Allan Roth chapter.

conducive to slugging doesn't hurt. However, home and road figures belie that assumption. Six of the twenty-two 200-homer teams hit more road than home four-baggers, and in most of the other cases the differential between home and road totals is around 20. As we get further into the era of the all-purpose stadium, the ability to tailor a lineup to a ballpark will become more difficult to achieve. It would appear that even when this was possible, loading up for your home field didn't produce that many more home runs.

There are those who would mark the expansion era as the beginning of the decline in the science of pitching, or at least as the age when the percentage of competent hurlers in the major leagues dropped steadily. Whether this is true or not, it is undeniable that eighteen of the twenty-two 200-homer performances came in the post-expansion era. Expansion also brought with it a longer schedule, as Ford Frick was quick to remind Roger Maris and the world in 1961. Considering a 200-homer team produces at a pace of about 1.25 homers a game in a 162-game schedule, we can assume that any team hitting fewer than 209 homers in that span would not have hit 200 homers in the old 154-game scheme. Seven of the eighteen post-expansion teams fall into this category.

While the year 1947 is significant for this study as the first appearance of a 200-homer team, it is better known as the year that baseball's racial barriers were dropped. Could the emergence of the black and Hispanic major leaguer have played a part in the growth of team home-run production? As we have noted, the ability to achieve 200 home runs in a season depends to a great extent upon the production of the three or four top home-run producers on the club. Of the sixty-six individuals we find in the table as top producers for 200-homer clubs, twenty-five are either black or Hispanic, a total of almost 38 percent. This figure is disproportionate to the general population, and would seem to indicate a definite contribution by these groups.

Almost all baseball fans, even those who swear that the 1-0 pitcher's duel is the greatest spectacle in sports, are turned on by powerful offense. Take many of the greatest games in baseball history, and they'll turn on a famous home run hit at a crucial moment. Logic dictates, therefore, that the team crushing 200 or more homers in a season must have extraordinary success.

The facts speak otherwise. Of the twenty-two teams that have hit 200 or more home runs in a season to date, only seven won their league or division. Of these, only two went on to be world champions.

Of the fifteen non-champions, one finished last, two next to last, and only two second. Why doesn't enormous home-run production correlate with victory?

In two notable cases, the answer is one-dimensional

Frank Robinson and Boog Powell

ballclubs. The 1947 Giants and 1973 Braves, knowing they had little else to offer, purposely stocked their teams with sluggers to create excitement amid the losses. In most cases, however, the clubs that hit 200 home runs, expecting to succeed in this fashion, simply were not able to keep up with a somewhat less powerful club that outpitched them. In every case, when the 200-homer team did not win the pennant, the team that did had an earned run average lower not only than that of the 200 home-run team, but of the league average as well. Only the 1987 Blue Jays had an ERA lower than that of the pennant winner.

It is still surprising to see the number of 200-homer clubs that had an ERA lower than that of the league average. However, the pennant winner was always lower still. Additionally, while the pennant winners did not join the exclusive 200 club, they most often had power. The 1962-4 Yankees followed their 240-homer season with years of 199, 188, and 162 respectively. The table shows several other 150+ years for other pennant-winning teams as well. One can almost imagine the Yankees conning the rest of the league with their home-run propaganda, suckering other clubs into thinking they could win with power alone, while the string of Yankee pennants was nurtured on pitching, defense, and balanced hitting.

Only the 1947 Dodgers and 1987 Cardinals were relatively weak in this department — the latter outscoring both 200-homer National League teams that year with half the power, and a third of that coming from just one player.

Considerations of performance aside, major league baseball remains a business, and the bottom line for any general manager is money passing through the ticket windows. Does hitting 200 home runs bring more people to the ballpark? Fifteen of the twenty-two 200-homer teams saw attendance rises of 13,000 to more than 1,000,000 fans. Most of these clubs were either pennant

winners, in the race, or improving their position in the standings. The 1963-4 Twins saw their attendance drop both seasons, a total of almost a quarter million in two years, as they fell further back from the pennant winners. The 1970 Red Sox, well behind the rampaging Orioles of that year, lost 240,000 in attendance in a single year. The lesson to general managers is that the fans will pay for visceral thrills for just so long. Over a long schedule, a team has to win to draw crowds.

Finally, it would be remiss to leave this subject without a tip of the cap to the only two 200-homer teams outscored by their opponents — the 1987 Cubs and Orioles. Their performances prove that it don't mean a thing if all you can do is swing.

Comparison of 200-Homer Teams to First-Place Finishers

Team	HR	Home HR	Road HR	BA	Runs	Opp Runs	ERA	Lg ERA	Pos	Top Three Home Run Hitters			Others w/ Many HRs	Pct Of Hrs By Top 3
1947 Giants	221	131	90	.271	831	761	4.44	4.07	4th	Mize 51	Marshall 36	Cooper 35	1 + 20	55.2%
1947 Dodgers	83			.272	774	668	3.82		1st	Reese 12	Robinson 12			
1953 Dodgers	208	110	98	.285	955	689	4.10	4.29	1st	Snider 42	Campanella 41	Hodges 31	1 + 20	59.6%
1955 Dodgers	201	119	82	.271	857	650	3.68	4.04	1st	Snider 42	Campanella 31	Hodges 27	1 + 20	49.7%
1956 Reds	221	128	93	.268	775	658	3.85	3.77	3rd	Robinson 38	Post 36	Kluszewski 35	2 + 20	49.3%
1956 Dodgers	179			.258	720	601	3.57		1st	Snider 43	Hodges 32	Furillo 21	1 + 20	
1961 Yankees	240	112	128	.263	827	612	3.46	3.87	1st	Maris 61	Mantle 54	Skowron 28	3 + 20	59.5%
1962 Giants	204	109	95	.278	878	690	3.79	3.94	1st	Mays 49	Cepeda 35	Alou 25	1 + 20	53.4%
1962 Tigers	209	117	92	.248	758	692	3.81	3.97	4th	Cash 39	Colavito 37	Kaline 29	1 + 20	50.2%
1962 Yankees	199			.267	817	680	3.70		1st	Maris 33	Mantle 30	Skowron 27	2 + 20	
1963 Twins	225	112	113	.255	767	602	3.28	3.63	3rd	Killebrew 45	Allison 35	Hall 33	1 + 20	50.2%
1963 Yankees	188			.252	714	547	3.07		1st	Howard 28	Pepitone 27	Tresh 25	1 + 20	
1964 Twins	221	115	106	.252	737	678	3.57	3.63	6th	Killebrew 49	Allison 32	Oliva 32	3 + 20	51.1%
1964 Yankees	162			.253	730	577	3.15		1st	Mantle 35	Pepitone 28	Maris 26		
1966 Braves	207	119	88	.263	782	683	3.68	3.61	5th	Aaron 44	Torre 36	Alou 31	1 + 20	53.6%
1966 Dodgers	108			.256	606	490	2.62		1st	Lefebvre 24	Johnson 17			
1970 Red Sox	203	117	86	.262	786	722	3.90	3.72	3rd	Yastrzemski 40	Conigliaro 36	Petrocelli 29	1 + 20	51.7%
1970 Orioles	179			.257	792	574	3.15		1st	Powell 35	F. Robinson 25			
1973 Braves	206	118	88	.266	799	774	4.25	3.67	5th	Johnson 43	Evans 41	Aaron 40	1 + 20	60.1%
1973 Reds	137			.254	741	621	3.43		1st	Perez 27	Morgan 26	Bench 25		
1977 Red Sox	213	124	89	.281	859	712	4.16	4.07	2nd	Rice 39	Scott 33	Hobson 30	2 + 20	47.9%
1977 Yankees	184			.281	831	651	3.61		1st	Nettles 37	Jackson 32			
1980 Brewers	203	90	113	.275	811	682	3.71	4.03	3rd	Oglivie 41	Thomas 38	Cooper 25	1 + 20	51.2%
1980 Yankees	189			.267	820	662	3.58		1st	Jackson 41	Nettles 16			
1982 Brewers	216	89	127	.279	891	717	3.98	4.07	1st	Thomas 39	Oglivie 34	Cooper 32	2 + 20	48.6%
1985 Orioles	214	103	111	.263	818	764	4.38	4.15	4th	Murray 31	Young 28	Ripken 26	1 + 20	39.7%
1985 Tigers	202	108	94	.253	729	688	3.78		3rd	Evans 40	Gibson 29	Parish 28	1 + 20	48.0%
1985 Blue Jays	158			.269	759	588	3.31		1st	Bell 28	Barfield 27			
1987 Cubs	209	114	95	.264	720	801	4.55	4.08	6th	Dawson 49	Durham 27	Moreland 27		49.2%
1987 Cardinals	94			.263	798	693	3.91		1st	Clark 35				
1987 Giants	205	118	87	.260	783	669	3.68	4.08	1st	Clark 35	Davis 24	Maldonado 20		38.5%
1987 Tigers	225	125	100	.272	896	735	4.02	4.46	1st	Evans 34	Nokes 32	Trammell 28	2 + 20	41.7%
1987 Blue Jays	215	101	114	.269	845	655	3.74		2nd	Bell 47	Barfield 28	Moseby 26	1 + 20	46.9%
1987 Orioles	211	110	101	.258	729	880	5.01		6th	Sheets 31	Murray 30	C. Ripken 27	1 + 20	41.7%

The Great American Baseball Trivia Sting

ROBERT E. SHIPLEY

How to make friends, influence people, suffer no bores, and learn important baseball facts without ever having to look them up. An unusual statistic unveiled.

THE OBJECTIVE: To set up and execute a well-deserved sting operation against the perfectly obnoxious baseball trivia bore of your choice.

The Mark: Any insufferable acquaintance who insists on torturing the entire world with constant, meaningless baseball minutiae. I am not talking about the average enthusiastic baseball fan, but about the person who seems to gain feelings of superiority by learning and then expounding on every boring and trivial detail of the game. You know the type well. His/her last conversation with you probably began with "What was the highest fielding average ever achieved by a third baseman using a Wilson glove?" For the purposes of this demonstration we will refer to the deserving mark as "Insufferable." We will also assume that the individual is male, even though this is not a prerequisite.

The Set-Up: You approach Insufferable with a sporting proposition to prove that, contrary to his own opinion, anyone can learn to become a baseball trivia expert with a minimum amount of effort. After deciding on an appropriate wager — perhaps for Insufferable to avoid all talk of trivia for a month — you suggest the following rules:

1. Only one question will be used to decide the bet. (As you will see, you can liberalize this rule later to your own advantage.)

2. The subject of the question will be limited to guessing the pennant winner for any major league pennant race since 1876.

3. Insufferable gets to select the contestant.

4. You will be allowed one minute before the contest to pass your secret formula for trivia success along to the contestant.

5. The contestant will be allowed to ask two questions (clues) and will be given two chances to guess the pennant winner based on the answers to the clues. Obviously, the clues cannot be any variation of: "Which teams were in the World Series that year?" or "Which team had the best won-lost record?", etc.

The Sting: You arrive at the appointed time to discover that Insufferable has selected his cousin Larchmont as the contestant. Although you fully expected Insufferable to choose, perhaps, a five-year-old child or someone in a coma, the selection of Larchmont does appear to go beyond the bounds of fair play. Insufferable is justifiably smug — secure in the knowledge that Larchmont once thought the Bronx Bombers were a group of terrorists from New York City. Your work is cut out for you.

Larchmont sits as if in a trance, preoccupied with adjusting his favorite red paisley bow tie and picking dried spaghetti sauce off his Madras shirt. With great trepidation you take him aside to whisper your secret instructions. He seems to understand, but who knows?

The game begins. Opening his Total Baseball with a Cheshire grin, Insufferable decides to go for a merciless kill. "Larchmont, old buddy, name the pennant winner in the Union Association in 1884."

Eyes rolling toward the ceiling, Larchmont slowly forms the first question that you imparted to him. "Which team led the league in runs scored that year?"

The grin quickly disappears from Insufferable's face. In barely audible tones he replies, "St. Louis."

Robert E. Shipley is a systems analyst for the Department of Defense in Philadelphia.

"Then St. Louis was the pennant winner," Larchmont says matter-of-factly.

Insufferable's silence tells the whole story. Larchmont claps his hands in glee, knocking his glass of iced tea into his shoe. He seems not to notice.

With growing rage, Insufferable demands another chance — double or nothing. Graciously, you consent.

No fool, Insufferable searches for a pennant winner that did not lead the league in runs scored. The silence is broken only by the sound of flipping pages and of Larchmont absent-mindedly squishing iced tea in and out of his toes.

Finally: "Which team won the National League pennant in 1966?"

Without hesitation Larchmont counters, "Which team led the league in runs scored?"

"Atlanta."

"Then Atlanta was the winner."

"Wrong! Wrong! Wrong!" Insufferable shouts in triumph.

"He gets another clue," you remind.

"No problem," Insufferable replies, his confidence restored.

Larchmont pauses to remember the second question. Finally he blurts out, "Which team gave up the fewest runs in the league that year?"

Insufferable answers by slamming the book shut and storming from the room.

Opening the discarded volume to officially confirm the outcome, you tell the confused cousin, "Los Angeles, Larchmont. Los Angeles gave up the fewest runs."

"Then, Los Angeles was the pennant winner."

"Precisely."

Why The Sting Works: While not 100 percent foolproof, the league leaders in runs scored and least runs allowed (opponent runs) are the two most powerful historical predictors of pennant success. Between 1876 and 1987, 50.2 percent of all pennant races were won by the team that led the league in runs scored. Thus the contestant has a one-in-two chance of deriving the right answer after the first clue. In 79 percent of the pennant races during the same period, the pennant winner either was first in runs scored or in least runs allowed. Hence, in eight out of ten contests, the contestant will be able to guess the pennant winner after two clues.

As shown in the table below, your chances for success improve the more unscrupulous Insufferable is. For example, he is more likely to pick pennant races in the more distant past to avoid lucky guesses based on general knowledge of current events. Unfortunately for him, these two predictors were even more powerful before 1980. (While not shown, these predictors succeed only 37.5

percent of the time from 1980-1987.) Or, if Insufferable tries to confuse the issue by turning to one of the past major leagues other than the National and American Leagues (i.e., Union Association, American Association, Player's League, or the Federal League) your chances for success are improved to no worse than 86 percent (92 percent for the 19th century).

Percentage of Pennant Races in Which Winners Led Their League in Runs Scored or Least Runs Allowed 1876-1987

	NL	AL	Other	Composite
1876-1987	77	82	86	79
1876-1900	79	—	92	83
1876-1910	82	100	92	87
1876-1920	82	95	86	86
1876-1930	83	97	86	88
1876-1940	81	95	86	86
1876-1950	82	92	86	86
1876-1960	82	88	86	85
1876-1970	81	86	86	83
1876-1980	80	86	86	83

This table also suggests refinements to the sting which you may want to attempt to improve your chances of success. For example, if Insufferable is agreeable, you could limit your universe to pre-1940 American League pennants, thus giving yourself no less than a 95 percent chance of success.

Of course, you could even try to limit the contest to pre-1910 American League pennants, where the chance of success is 100 percent. But I am sure you would not want to take advantage — good sport that you are!

A RED-LETTER BAT DAY FOR LEFTY GOMEZ

Lefty Gomez was a star pitcher with the New York Yankees from 1930 through 1942, but his .147 batting was another matter. In his final year with the Yanks, however, Gomez had one great batting day. Beating Washington 16-1 and allowing only four hits on May 28, 1942, Lefty equalled the Senators' hit total with four singles in five times at bat, scored three runs and batted in two. He singled in the second, third, seventh, and eighth innings. The only time he was retired was in the fifth, when he was thrown out by pitcher Walter Masterson. A few weeks earlier, he had singled off Bobo Newsom for his only other hit of '42. After his four-hit game, Lefty never registered another hit in the majors.

— Al Kermisch

The Statistical Mirage of Clutch Hitting

HAROLD BROOKS

Do clutch hitters exist? Not according to the most popular yardstick used to define them, says the author. Clutch hitting, he concludes, is "a mirage at best."

IS THERE SUCH A thing as a clutch hitter? This question has been the subject of endless discussion through the years. Until recently, the evidence on the subject was purely anecdotal and often based on single or very limited numbers of events (Carlton Fisk is a great clutch hitter because of one at bat in the 1975 World Series). As a result, most people would have answered the question "yes." Recently, however, a little more data has been collected and more rigorous tests of the question have been attempted. In 1977, in "Baseball Research Journal," Dick Cramer concluded that clutch hitters definitely do not exist. Bill James and Pete Palmer supported this conclusion, although more cautiously, calling clutch hitting a "shadow" and an "optical illusion," respectively.

In "The 1985 Elias Baseball Analyst," the opposite conclusion is reached. They claimed that Cramer's conclusion was wrong because the definition he used was improper. They defined the best clutch hitter as the man whose total batting average improved the most in late-inning pressure situations. (A late-inning pressure situation is one occurring in the seventh inning or later, with the batter's team either tied or trailing by three runs or less, four runs if the bases are loaded.) Since the first publication of this idea, each successive "Analyst" has continued to stress the existence of clutch hitting. These comments reached their peak with the statement in the Milwaukee Brewer comment in the "1988 Analyst" that "a small group of shrill pseudo-statisticians has used insufficient data and faulty methods to try to disprove the existence of the clutch hitter." However, using the published data in the "Analyst" for 1984 to 1987, the simple statistical analysis here shows that conclusion — that clutch hitters do exist — is blatantly untrue, at least according to the Elias definition. We cannot prove that clutch hitters do not exist, only that they do not exist as defined by Elias.

In 1985, Elias presented lists of the ten best and worst clutch hitters in each of 1983 and 1984 and then how those players had performed in the other year. They noted that the best in one year averaged out to being better than the norm in the other year, and the worst were worse than the norm in the other year. This procedure used only a small part of the available data, ignoring the vast majority of the players in between and how they performed. In 1988, they took players who had been above or below average each of two years and then saw how those players did in a third year. They found that the percentage of players in the "above both years" group who were above the next year was higher than the percentage of players who were mixed or below both years. This study neglected the degree to which players were above or below average. In other words, if a player was 1 point above his average in pressure situations each of the first two years and then was 1 point below in the third, this was a negative result for their hypothesis, while a player who was always above his average, but who went from 1 point above to 200 points above to 1 point above was a positive result, even though the former player was much more consistent in his clutch performance than the latter.

There are three basic methods we will use on the four years of data to look at this question. The first will be to compute correlations between the performances of players for each pair of years for each league. Secondly, we will consider the number of years a player performed better or worse in late-inning pressure situations than overall. Finally, we will look at the performance of those players who were substantially above or below their overall performance in late-inning pressure more than one time. For clutch hitting to be something more than a statistical

Harold Brooks is a Ph.D. candidate in atmospheric sciences at the University of Illinois.

artifact, we would expect (1) significant correlations in performance from year to year, (2) large numbers of players being either always "good" or "bad" clutch hitters, and (3) that those players who were the best or worst more than once would consistently be on the same side (i.e. better or worse) of their overall performance. We will limit the data set to those players who have individual boxes in the "Elias Analyst" and who have a minimum of either 25, 50 or 75 late-inning pressure at bats in a given year. (Assuming that the effect is real, one would expect that the signals from each of the three studies would increase as the number of at bats increases.) For year-to-year comparisons, we will further require the player to be in the same league both seasons.

Correlation coefficients tell how closely related two data sets are. They range in value from 1 to −1. A correlation coefficient near 1 indicates that when the value of a quantity from one of the sets is above its average, the corresponding value in the other set will be above its average. Similarly, when one value is below its average, the other will be below its average. Correlation coefficients do not imply cause-effect relationships. Instead, they do tell you, given the value from one data set, what kind of value you can expect in the other set. The larger the absolute value of the correlation coefficient the more likely you are to be able to predict the value from one set, given the corresponding value from the other set. For a correlation of exactly 0, the two sets are unrelated and there is no predictive value between them.

WE HAVE BROKEN the data down by league and computed the correlation coefficient for both the overall batting average and the Elias clutch rating (late-inning pressure minus overall average) for every possible pair of years, i.e., 1984-1985, 1984-1986, 1984-1987, 1985-1986, 1985-1987, and 1986-1987. Since we have six pairs of years and two leagues, we can compute twelve correlation coefficients using a cutoff of 25, 50 and 75 late-inning pressure at bats. We can then determine the degree of significance of each of these correlations. For the same correlation, the significance increases as the number of data points (players, in this case) increases. The level at which a correlation is significant tells us what chance there is that this is not a result of random chance. For example, there is a 99 percent chance that something at the 99 percent confidence level did not occur by chance, and thus we would feel pretty confident that is a real signal. For twelve correlations, we would expect one of them to be significant at the 11/12 (91.7%) confidence level just by random chance. Table 1 summarizes the results of the correlation calculations. It gives the number of players (n) involved in each pair of data sets (i.e. for AL

1984-1985, there are 127 players who had at least 25 late-inning pressure at bats each year, and 78 who had at least 50), the correlation coefficient (r) between the two data sets (i.e. −0.049 for the AL 1984-1985 with 25 pressure at bats), and the confidence level at which this correlation is significant (only confidence values greater than 90 percent are given).

TO PUT IT SUCCINCTLY, year to year values of the Elias "clutch" rating are uncorrelated. This is in contrast to overall batting average, which is highly correlated in all pairs of seasons. This latter conclusion is simply a reflection of the fact that people like Ty Cobb always hit for a high batting average and people like Mario Mendoza never do. In both the 25 and 75 at bat levels, there is the one correlation significant at the 91.7 percent level predicted by random chance, while at the 50 at bat level, there are only two. Of the 36 correlations for the clutch average, 16 are negative (all 36 are positive for overall average), and, in fact, the most significant correlation, between the American League in 1985 and 1986 for a minimum of 75 pressured at bats, is negative. If this were a true indicator of the situation, it would mean that rather than showing that good clutch hitters repeat their performance from year to year, good clutch hitters have a tendency to be bad clutch hitters the next year. The results of these correlation calculations imply that while an individual's batting average is somewhat predictable from year to year, clutch hitting (by the Elias definition) is not predictable.

Secondly, consider the number of players who always hit better or worse than expected (according to their overall batting average) in pressure situations and compare this to the number you would get from a purely random process. Since the average player does not hit at his overall average in pressure situations, we will compare a player's clutch rating to the average clutch rating for that year and league. If clutch hitting is random, after two years, you would expect a quarter of the players to be above average both years, a quarter below both years, and half would have one year below and one above. After three years, one-eighth of the players would be always above, three-eighths with two years above, three-eighths with one year above, and one-eighth with no years above. With the four years available for study from the "Analyst" numbers, we would expect one-sixteenth of the players at both four years and no years above, one-fourth at both three years and one year above, and three-eighths at two years above average.

Once we have counted up the number of players in each of the five categories (four years above through zero years above), we can compute the chances that any of those numbers of players would be in that category using the statistical process called a Monte Carlo simulation. Table 2 summarizes the results of these simulations. (The database is liminted to players who remained in the same league for all four seasons and who had the relevant number — 25, 50 or 75 — of pressured-at-bats.) The data is broken down by league and minimum pressured-at-bats. Each row of the table gives the number of players who had a certain number of years above average, the percentage of the total players that number represents and the random chance (from the Monte Carlo simulation) that you would have that many or more players in that category. (Probabilities of occurrence of at least 90 percent or at most 10 percent are in bold.) If the Elias clutch rating is not random, you would expect to see very small probabilities of occurrence of the values at four- and zero-years-above-average- and high probabilities at two years above. Instead, what you actually see in the major league totals at both 25 and 50 at bats is that the large number of people at two years above is very *unlikely*. We also see that there is only a small chance that you would see only two players above their expected value for all four years at the 50 at bat level. (The sample size at the 75 at bat level is small [thirteen players] and, as a results are not particularly meaningful there, but at the lower minimum-at-bat levels, the signal is clear.) [The percentage of players in the two-year category increases from 25 to 50 at bats.] This implies that, as you increase the significance of the data, allowing players to show their "true" clutch ability, the chances of anyone being always above or always below decreases. All of these results are directly opposite to what one would expect if the Elias conclusion was correct.

Finally, we look at the issue of the players who show strong tendencies one way or the other in more than one season. First, the mean and standard deviation of clutch rating for each season and league are computed. We then consider only those players who were either above or below the mean league-clutch-rating by more than one standard deviation in two or more different seasons. In other words, we are looking at players who were among the best or wrost performers more than once. One would expect, based on the Elias conclusion that a large majority of these players would be on the same side of the mean each time. Unfortunately, that is not true. Table 3 summarizes these results, giving the number of times a player is on the same side of mean both times and the number of times he is on each side once. (There are six players — Ed Romero, Dick Schofield, Rick Dempsey, Mariano Duncan, Dave Anderson, and Jerry Mumphrey — who were more than one standard deviation away from the mean three times, using the 25 at-bat cut-off. Each pair of years was treated separately, resulting in three pairs for each

player. Romero was the only one to be on the same side, above average, each of the three years. Only one player from each league made the 75 at bat cut-off. Steve Sax was above the mean both times and George Bell switched sides.) At both the 25 and 50 at bat levels, 48 percent of the pairs have one point on each side of the mean versus 50 percent by "chance." Once again, this is not what would be expected based on the Elias conclusion.

We have looked at the Elias definition of "clutch" hitting three different ways. In each case, the signal is clear that their definition is simply a statistical artifact with no predictive value, and that its distribution is random. We are then left with the question, "Why did Elias get the answer wrong in their 1985 article?" It appears that having reached a conclusion before looking at the data, they did not check their data very carefully or do any real analysis of it. The data was then described in an unusual fashion to uphold their conclusion. The hints that they are wrong are there from the original article. There, they looked at the clutch ratings over ten years of ten players traditionally viewed as strong clutch hitters. One (Eddie Murray) performed 25 points better in pressure situations, one (Carlton Fisk) was 17 points worse and the other eight were no more than 11 points away from their overall average. This appears to be symptomatic of regression towards the mean, in which, as the sample size increases (number of pressure-at-bats) the deviation of the sample from its true mean decreases. (Since that time, Murray's pressured batting average has dropped 11 points, while his overall average has dropped 2 points, and Fisk's pressured average has dropped 5 points, with the overall average dropping 12 points. Thus, both men have decreased their deviation from the mean.) In the Elias lists in the article of the best and worst clutch hitters of 1983 and 1984, 30 percent of the hitters change from "best to worst" in the other year. In 1988, Elias compiles lists of players who were either above or below in each of two years and then compare that to their performance in the third year, for each of four three-year periods, using a cut-off of 25 pressured at bats. Using these four trios of years, we can calculate how many players from that group were above in all three years, below in all three years, or calculate what combination of years above and years below they had. In all four cases, the number of players who were either always above average or below average was less than you would expect by random chance. (The fact that fewer than half of the "good" clutch hitters from the first two years repeated in the third year in three of the four trios was not commented upon in the article, nor was the fact that the difference in percentage above average the third year between the "good" and "bad" clutch hitters decreased in at least the 1984-1986 case when the minimum at bats were raised to 50 and changed sign when the minimum was 75, albeit with a sample of only twenty-six players.) The evidence was there when the articles were written and the evidence has grown since the first publication. We are forced to agree almost completely with the quote from the Milwaukee comment of the 1988 "Analyst." The only disagreement is about who is shrill and that the effort has been to prove, rather than to disprove, the existence of clutch hitting. Based upon the data published in the "Elias Baseball Analyst," the conclusion that the Elias definition of clutch hitting is irrelevant is inescapable. Clutch hitting, as presently defined, is a mirage at best.

TABLE 1
Elias "Clutch" Rating

Years	Min. 25 LIP At Bats			Min. 50 LIP At Bats			Min. 75 LIP At Bats		
	n	r	Signif-icance	n	r	Signif-icance	n	r	Signif-icance
AL 84-85	127	-0.049		78	0.106		21	0.240	
AL 84-86	113	-0.097		69	-0.104		14	-0.011	
AL 84-87	83	0.054		49	-0.029		12	0.221	
AL 85-86	122	0.075		79	-0.041		19	-0.533	(-)99.1
AL 85-87	90	0.041		59	-0.203	(-)93.8	9	-0.058	
AL 86-87	113	0.128	91.1	75	0.063		14	0.112	
NL 84-85	100	0.040		71	-0.081		26	0.016	
NL 84-86	86	0.068		61	0.191	92.9	20	0.393	95.6
NL 84-87	66	-0.162	(-)90.3	44	-0.055		14	-0.173	
NL 85-86	106	0.168	95.7	73	0.199	95.4	28	0.226	
NL 85-87	83	0.113		51	0.046		17	0.008	
NL 86-87	100	-0.002		66	-0.069		22	-0.087	

Overall Batting Average

Years	Min. 25 LIP At Bats			Min. 50 LIP At Bats			Min. 75 LIP At Bats		
	n	r	Signif-icance	n	r	Signif-icance	n	r	Signif-icance
AL 84-85	127	0.409	>99.99	78	0.355	99.9	21	0.402	96.4
AL 84-86	113	0.463	>99.9999	69	0.611	>99.9999	14	0.287	
AL 84-87	83	0.577	>99.9999	49	0.644	>99.9999	12	0.361	
AL 85-86	122	0.544	>99.999999	79	0.651	>99.999999	19	0.630	99.85
AL 85-87	90	0.377	99.9	59	0.595	>99.9999	9	0.759	99.2
AL 86-87	113	0.463	>99.9999	75	0.601	>99.9999	14	0.635	99.3
NL 84-85	100	0.239	99.1	71	0.345	99.85	26	0.224	96.2
NL 84-86	86	0.392	99.9	61	0.414	99.9	20	0.309	98.8
NL 84-87	66	0.277	98.8	44	0.329	98.5	14	0.215	
NL 85-86	106	0.173	96.2	73	0.296	99.4	28	0.309	94.4
NL 85-87	83	0.247	98.8	51	0.307	98.6	17	0.214	
NL 86-87	100	0.337	99.9	66	0.393	99.9	22	0.495	98.4

Legend: Correlation coefficients and levels of significance for each pair of years in the study and each league for the Elias "clutch" rating and overall batting average. The minimum number of late inning pressure (LIP) at bats required each year for a player to be in the data set is at the top of each trio of columns. The number of players in the sample is given by n, the correlation coefficient is r, and the significance level (if above 90 percent) are given for each combination.

TABLE 2

Minimum 25 LIP At Bats

Years Above	American			National			Majors		
	Batters	Percent	Chance	Batters	Percent	Chance	Batters	Percent	Chance
0	5	6.8	48.1	6	9.8	17.1	11	8.1	22.4
1	15	20.3	90.0	11	18.0	93.4	26	19.3	94.5
2	33	44.6	13.8	23	37.7	50.4	56	41.5	19.6
3	17	23.0	71.6	17	27.9	65.4	34	25.2	51.2
4	4	5.4	67.7	4	6.6	50.4	8	5.9	59.2
Total	74			61			135		

Minimum 50 LIP At Bats

Years Above	American			National			Majors		
	Batters	Percent	Chance	Batters	Percent	Chance	Batters	Percent	Chance
0	44	9.1	27.5	4	9.8	23.2	18	9.4	15.7
1	9	20.5	81.3	9	22.0	75.2	18	21.2	83.7
2	20	45.5	15.6	16	39.0	47.9	36	42.4	14.2
3	11	25.0	57.4	10	24.4	60.6	21	24.7	55.7
4	0	0.0	100.0	2	4.9	73.9	2	2.4	96.8
Total	44			41			85		

Minimum 75 LIP At Bats

Years Above	American			National			Majors		
	Batters	Percent	Chance	Batters	Percent	Chance	Batters	Percent	Chance
0	2	66.7	0.7	0	0.0	100.0	2	15.4	18.2
1	0	0.0	100.0	3	30.0	49.7	3	23.1	68.4
2	0	0.0	100.0	5	50.0	33.2	5	38.5	56.8
3	1	33.3	56.4	2	20.00	76.3	2	15.4	68.6
4	0	0.0	100.0	0	0.0	100.0	0.0	100.0	
Total	3			10			13		

Legend: Subdivision of data by number of batters whose clutch rating was above average all four years of the study, three years, two years, one year, and no years. Minimum LIP at bats is at top of each third. Percent is the percentage of the total number of batters in that subdivision (i.e., 5 AL batters with at least 25 LIP at bats were never above average out of the total of 74 players, 5/74 = 6.8 percent) and Chance is the random chance, based on a Monte Carlo simulation, that that many or more players would have been that many years above average, given the total number of players in the pool.

TABLE 3

Minimum 25 LIP At Bats

	American		National		Majors	
	Same	Different	Same	Different	Same	Different
Number	8	7	7	7	15	14
Percent	53.3	46.7	50.0	50.0	51.7	48.3

Legend: Table gives how many players who were more than one standard deviation away from the mean clutch rating more than once were either on the same or different sides of the mean each time. For instance, George Bell was one standard deviation above the mean in 1985 and one standard deviation below in 1986, so he counts as a different in the American totals, while Steve Sax was one standard deviation above in both 1984 and 1986, so he is a same in the National totals. Again, the minimum number of LIP at bats is at the top.

Simon Nicholls: Gentleman, Farmer, Ballplayer

CAMPBELL GIBSON

Was Simon Nicholls a typical turn-of-the-century player? Maybe not, but he certainly represented an overlooked contributor to the era: the well-mannered college grad.

If you take into account the proportion of the total population that went to college back in those days I think it's pretty clear that we had more than our share of college men in baseball. And it's also pretty clear that the usual picture you get of the old-time ballplayer as an illiterate rowdy contains an awful lot more fiction than it does fact.

—Harry Hooper, in The Glory of Their Times

TURN-OF-THE-CENTURY BALLPLAYERS were constantly fighting a reputation for fast living and coarse behavior. As Hooper states, this stereotype was overdrawn. Among the ranks were many college men—the best-known perhaps being that illustrious Bucknell product, Christy Mathewson—and many gentlemen.

One of the best combinations of degrees and decorum was a little-known infielder named Simon Burdette Nicholls. The first graduate of Maryland Agricultural College (later called the University of Maryland) to play in the majors, Nicholls was a farmer and family man. In fact, his concern for personal and community life may have cut short his big-league career.

Simon was born on July 17, 1882 near Germantown, Maryland, the son of George Nicholls, a farmer, and Courtney Burdette Nicholls, who died when Simon was five years old.

During his four years at college, Nicholls was the team's shortstop and star player, but despite his reputation on the ballfield it was not certain that he would play professionally, at least partly because of parental objection. When the 1903 class historian of the Maryland Agricultural College prepared a prophecy for the year 1935, it envisioned Simon as a gentleman farmer with ample time to take part in local politics.

In September, 1903 Nicholls was recruited by the Detroit Tigers, who were short of infielders and in the area to play the Washington Senators. He made his major league debut on September 18 in a doubleheader. In the first game, Simon had two hits and fielded well, but in the second game, after being picked off first base, he lost his composure and made three errors. The consensus of the Detroit and Washington papers was that he needed experience but had played quite well for a young man jumping from the amateur level to the major leagues.

In the following two years, Nicholls competed for several amateur and semi-professional teams, two of which won championships. In 1904, he played for the town of Ridgely on Maryland's Eastern Shore. Ridgely had only about 800 residents, but the team recruited widely and won the Maryland "amateur" championship, although several of the team's players were paid. The most notable attribute of the 1904 Ridgely team was that it included five future major leaguers: Sam Frock (P), Bill Kellogg (1B), Buck Herzog (2B), Frank Baker (3B), and Simon Nicholls (SS).

The following year Nicholls played for Piedmont, West Virginia, which finished first in the Cumberland Valley League. At Piedmont, Simon's play impressed Charlie Babb, and shortly after Babb was signed to manage Memphis in the Southern Association in 1906, he signed Simon to play shortstop. Nicholls' fine play in spring training drew attention, and John McGraw, manager of the New York Giants, offered to purchase him but was turned down.

Campbell Gibson is a Census Bureau demographer and a distant relative of Simon Nicholls. The author thanks Jim Flack and Bob Davids for their encouragement.

Simon Nicholls

The 1906 season was a very successful one for Nicholls and the Memphis team, which finished second. Simon played every inning of the club's 142 league games. He hit .260, well above the league average of .230, and was a standout defensively. Near the end of the campaign, Connie Mack, manager of the Philadelphia Athletics, purchased Nicholls for $2,500, and Simon joined the A's for the last few games of the major-league season.

The Athletics' starting infield for 1907 was set with veterans Danny Murphy (2B), Jack Knight (3B), and Monte Cross (SS), so Nicholls was a utility infielder. In June, Murphy suffered a sprained ankle, and Nicholls was inserted in the infield. Mack then traded Knight (and $7,500) to Boston for third baseman Jimmy Collins. With Nicholls playing second base and Collins and Cross at their regular positions, the A's won 15 of their next 20 games to move into pennant contention. Simon contributed to this spurt with a 20-game hitting streak during which he hit .413 and moved to the top of the American League batting race. His hitting dropped off, but when Murphy returned to the lineup in July, Mack moved Nicholls to shortstop in place of the aging Cross.

The American League pennant race in 1907 was one of the best in history, and in early September, only two

games separated the top four teams. First Cleveland and then Chicago dropped back, and prior to the opening of a three-game series between Detroit and the Athletics in Philadelphia on Friday, September 27, the A's trailed the Tigers by just one-half game.

In the first game, the Athletics left 12 men on base and lost 5 to 4. Saturday's game was rained out, and because Sunday baseball was not then legal in Pennsylvania, a doubleheader was scheduled for Monday. As it turned out, only one game was played, and it was a classic, as described by baseball historian John Thorn in "Baseball's 10 Greatest Games."

Before a crowd of about 24,000 (including about 6,000 standing in the outfield), the Athletics built up a 7 to 1 lead; the Tigers, however, scored four runs in the seventh inning with the aid of errors by Rube Oldring and Nicholls. And with the A's leading 8 to 6, Ty Cobb hit a dramatic two-run home run in the ninth inning to tie the game. After Detroit scored in the eleventh inning, Nicholls doubled and later scored to tie the game at 9 to 9. In the fourteenth inning, the A's Harry Davis led off with what appeared to be a ground-rule double into the center-field crowd. After a prolonged argument and melee on the field and disagreement between the two umpires, Davis was ruled out because of interference by a policeman with centerfielder Sam Crawford when he tried to catch Davis's long drive. Murphy's ensuing single, which would have scored Davis with the winning run, went for naught. After 17 innings, the game was called on account of darkness, and the A's, who were hoping to win a doubleheader and regain first place, ended the day one and a half games behnd Detroit.

The Athletics won five of their remaining seven games, but it was not enough. The Tigers, inspired by escaping Philadelphia without a loss, won their next five games to clinch the pennant.

While the last series with Detroit and his costly error in the second game must have dampened Nicholls's feelings about the 1907 season, it was a successful one for both the Athletics, who had not been viewed as pennant contenders, and for Simon. He hit .302 in 126 games to finish fifth in the league behind Cobb, Crawford, George Stone, and Elmer Flick, and just ahead of the great Nap Lajoie. Simon had also been versatile in the field, playing shortstop, second base, and third base. If there had been Rookie of the Year awards in 1907, Nicholls would have been a prime candidate for American League honors.

Mack was optimistic about his club's chances in 1908; however, the Athletics were out of the pennant race by July. The team's hitting fell sharply, with Nicholls' average plummeting to .216. Simon's batting average was actually not so bad for a shortstop because the American

League average was only .239, but his fielding fell off as well.

While Nicholls's poor 1908 season raised some question about his future with the Athletics, it was all the more uncertain because of four young infielders whom Mack was grooming for stardom. By 1911, they would be known as the "$100,000 infield": Stuffy McInnis (1B, though originally a shortstop), Eddie Collins (2B), Frank (Home Run) Baker (3B), and Jack Barry (SS).

Nicholls was designated as a utility infielder for the Athletics in 1909, but Baker suffered a spike wound in an exhibition game, and Simon played third base on opening day, April 12, in Philadelphia against the Boston Red Sox. The game marked the opening of Shibe Park—the first of the new wave of steel-and-concrete stadiums—which was packed with an unprecedented 35,000 fans. This historic game turned out to be one of the best of Simon's career. In the first inning, he singled to register the first base hit in Shibe Park and then scored the first run. Altogether, Simon had a double, two singles, and a walk and scored four runs as the Athletics won 8 to 1.

For the season, Nicholls played in only 21 games and hit .211. Barry, the regular shortstop, hit only .215 and fielded poorly. Barry was only twenty-one years old, however, and Mack no doubt expected him to improve with age and experience.

In December, Mack traded Nicholls to Cleveland for outfielder Wilbur Goode. Simon reported to Cleveland's spring training camp in 1910, but never showed the form expected of him, partly owing to family concerns. In October 1908, Simon had married eighteen-year old Marie Conneen of Philadelphia, and in the following September, their first child, a daughter, was born. Travel between Philadelphia and the Nicholls's family farm in Maryland was relatively easy. Cleveland was several hundred miles northwest of the two focal points of their lives.

After appearing in just three games with Cleveland, Nicholls was sold farther west to Kansas City of the American Association in early May. He refused to report and returned home to Maryland.

The Baltimore Orioles (then in the Eastern League) got off to a poor start in 1910 because of a weak infield. Manager Jack Dunn purchased Nicholls from Kansas City, and with Simon at shortstop, the Baltimore *Sun* reported that the Oriole infield was 100 percent improved.

The Orioles finished in third place, and Simon hit .255, which was the highest among the league's shortstops. While he was no longer in the major leagues, playing regularly and close to home must have made the 1910 season especially satisfying. Dunn developed a strong friendship with Simon as well as respect for his

leadership on the field and named him the Orioles field captain for the 1911 season. In February, Simon and his family moved from the farm to a house on Cator Avenue in Baltimore.

On March 5, the Nicholls' second child, a son, was born, but what should have been a joyous occasion was tempered by the diagnosis received the previous day that Simon had typhoid fever. His case did not appear to be severe, but after a few days he developed pelvic peritonitis. An operation provided the only chance for his recovery. After surgery, hemorrhaging developed and all hope for Simon's recovery was lost. On the morning of March 12, George Nicholls saw his dying son for the last time, the dolorous scene being recounted in the Baltimore Sun:

About 11 o'clock Simon's father arrived at his son's bedside. Simon was breathing hard and was conscious.

"Hello, papa," said Simon just above a whisper, as he feebly clasped the white-haired, stately old gentleman's right hand between both of his.

Tears trickled down the furrowed cheeks of the father as he looked at his dying son, the pride of his heart.

The evening edition of the Baltimore *News* reported on the front page that the popular Oriole captain died about 1:45 that afternoon. Simon's wife, weak from childbirth and the tragedy, had not been able to see her dying husband, and Simon never saw his newborn son.

After funeral services were held at the Nicholls home, Dunn accompanied the body to Philadelphia. Simon was buried in Holy Cross Cemetery in Yeadon, just west of Philadelphia. The inscription on the tombstone reads: "My beloved husband, Simon B. Nichols, died March 12, 1911." Unfortunately, the much more common spelling of his surname accompanied him in perpetuity.

On April 11, the day before the opening of the American League season, the Philadelphia Athletics, now world champions, came to Baltimore to play the Orioles on "Nicholls Day." More than 5,000 fans turned out in tribute to the memory of the young Oriole captain, and $3,000 was raised for his widow.

Perhaps the finest tribute to Nicholls appeared the day after his death in the Baltimore News under the by-line of "Danny," a sportswriter whose surname is unknown:

In the game on the field he was a fighter, but of the right sort. He was always out to win, and did everything in his power to do it, but never stepped beyond the bounds of what would be considered proper by a thoroughbred gentleman.

Though the sport on the diamond was a big thing in the life of Simon Nicholls, he was a home man, not the make-believe sort, and that, after all, topped everything else.

Nic thought well enough of Baltimore to become a citizen. He belonged to us, and we should feel it a duty to see that the widow and youngsters will realize to the end of their days that his death was not the earthly end of just a ball player, but a man respected and honored by everyone who had the pleasure to know him as a friend either off or on the field.

The 1.000 Hitter and the Undefeated Pitcher

NORMAN L. MACHT

Two sons of famous major leaguers had mere cups of coffee in the bigs. But what a show they staged one afternoon in The Show: a 1-0 record and a 3.000 slugging average.

IT WAS ONE OF THOSE late-season games that meant nothing to the standings. The Chicago White Sox had clinched second place and the Kansas City Athletics were snugly seventh when they met at Comiskey Park on September 28 to close out the 1958 season.

But for two sons of former major league stars it was the biggest—and for one the only—appearance of their major league careers.

As a result Chuck Lindstrom, son of Hall of Famer Fred Lindstrom, made the record books as one of fifteen non-pitchers with a lifetime 1.000 batting average.

And Hal Trosky Jr., whose father was a .302 lifetime hitter in 11 seasons with the Indians and White Sox, finished the day as the winning pitcher in the only big-league decision of his career.

Both had been called up from the minors to finish out the season. Lindstrom, at twenty-two an all-star catcher with Davenport in the Three-I League, got in the game in the fourth inning. He walked his first time up. The next time, the KC catcher, Frank House, tipped him to look for a fastball. Lindstrom banged it against the left-field wall for a triple, driving in a run. He later scored.

He was on deck when the last out was made in the bottom of the eighth in the 11-4 White Sox victory, the biggest offensive outing in two months for the light-hitting Sox.

Lindstrom never batted in the big leagues again. His 3.000 lifetime slugging average is unsurpassed.

It was a day off for most of the regulars. Rookies and veteran benchwarmers were in the lineup for Chicago. Nellie Fox was the only regular starter on the field; one of the reserve infielders was hurt.

Stover McIlwain, a nineteen-year-old righthander, started for the Sox. He pitched four innings, gave up one

run and four hits, and struck out four. The score was 1-1 when Earl Battey pinch hit for him in the fourth. The Sox scored two runs. McIlwain went out with the lead, but he was one inning shy of earning the victory. It was the only game he ever started in the majors. After a few minor-league seasons he was stricken with cancer and died at twenty-six.

The call went out to the bullpen for Hal Trosky to come in for the fifth. He had been at Colorado Springs until three weeks before. This proved to be his second—and last—big-league game.

Three days earlier, Trosky had pitched a scoreless fifth inning in relief of Dick Donovan against the Tigers. Ray Boone grounded into a double play pinch hitting for him.

A 6-foot-3 inch righthander who had started out as a first baseman (his father started as a pitcher and switched to first), Trosky again pitched a scoreless fifth this day. Chicago scored three in the last of the fifth for a 6-1 lead.

Taking the mound for the sixth, Trosky looked around his infield and took comfort from the steadying presence of Fox. Then a rare series of events occurred. Three ground balls were hit to Fox. Two went through his legs and one bounced off his chest. All three were scored as hits. Trosky walked a couple, and Suitcase Simpson, who had hit Trosky hard in the minors, roped one into center field for the only solid hit of the inning, and three runs were in.

"When we got back to the dugout," Trosky recalls, "they were all kidding Fox. George Kell, Sherm Lollar, Earl Torgeson, all of them. Somebody said to him, 'Gee, you musta had a good week at the track to pay off the

---

Norman L. Macht, a writer, is chairman of SABR's oral-history committee.

scorer to call those base hits instead of errors.' Nellie laughed it off."

In the last of the sixth Jim Rivera batted for Trosky and struck out. Bob Shaw finished up. The win was credited to Trosky. He was twenty-two the next day. He never pitched another big-league inning.

What cut short the careers of Lindstrom and Trosky, despite their impressive debuts?

Lindstrom expected to make the team the next spring, 1959.

"I never got a chance to play," he says. "At the minor-league camp I hit nothing but frozen ropes, but didn't even make the AAA club. Finally, they sold me to San Diego in the PCL. Ralph Kiner was the general manager. They cut my pay in half, to $3,200, and gave me a ticket back to Class A. I took the ticket and swapped it for one going home and never looked back.

"I could have taken the pay cut if I'd had a decent shot at a higher league. I didn't like the treatment I was getting, didn't have the mental toughness to keep fighting back, so I decided, with all the negative aspects of the game, the travel, the hanging around all day waiting to play, who needed it?"

As for Trosky, he had been offered substantial bonuses by several teams as a youngster, but this was in the days when anything over $4,000 forced you to sit on the major-league roster for two years.

"The Cubs, Tigers, and Braves wanted to sign me, but players like Hank Aaron, Ed Mathews, Joe Adcock, Randy Jackson all advised me not to take the money and sit on the bench. Even some of the bonus babies who had done it said to me, don't do it. So I didn't.

"Chuck Comiskey was running the White Sox. I liked him. He was young, genuine, a guy who wanted to play himself and had empathy for young players. They had a good farm system. I signed with them."

Playing first base, he was injured in a collision with a baserunner. Something snapped in his left arm. He couldn't bend it and was out for the year.

S WITCHING TO THE MOUND, he had good spring trainings every year, never had a losing record, kept his ERA under 4.00, was a good fielder, started and relieved, but never made it to the big club, until that tail end of 1958.

After his brief stint with the White Sox, he started the 1959 season at Indianapolis and worked in each of the first 11 games.

"I never knew how I was going to be used. Then they sent me down to Memphis. Luke Appling was the manager. He was the only one who was consistent and up front with me. He told me how he intended to use me, so I knew what to expect."

Trosky was second in ERA in the Southern Association when he was recalled to Indianapolis. That's as far as he got.

His last year was 1960, at Nashville.

"Jim Turner, the Vols manager, told me if I'd been in the Yankees' organization I would have been in the big leagues two years ago. I was twenty-three, and I wanted out of the White Sox system. They'd had a shakeup and Chuck Comiskey was out. I didn't sign for 1961. I was contacted by fifteen other clubs, but the White Sox wouldn't sell or release me.

"A year and a half later they were offered what I thought was a generous amount for me. They turned it down. Every spring for three years scouts came around and wanted to see me throw. They still wanted me. After that I'd been out too long. Physically I could come back but I couldn't get mentally and emotionally ready again.

"I don't know what the club's thinking was. I guess somebody up there didn't like me. Finally, eleven years later, they sent me my release."

N EITHER PLAYER HAD FELT any pressure from his famous father. Writers made comparisons, but the players never imposed that burden on themselves. And neither one dwells on regrets about his big-league career.

"It was a neat experience, being up there with people I liked," says Trosky. "I wouldn't sell it for half a million dollars.

"Just the chance to be a teammate of Early Wynn's, no matter how briefly, made it all worthwhile. My dad had held him up as what a person should be, an example of pure dedication. And he was right.

"The day before I got my only victory, Wynn had gone after his 250th. But he lost, 2 to 1, to Howard Reed, a kid making his first big-league start. The next day here he was, thirty-eight years old, on the last day of the season, when nobody is going anywhere but home the next day, and he's out there before the game running wind sprints, foul line to center field and back, for twenty minutes. Every pitcher does it, dull and monotonous as it is, all season. But nobody was out there on the last day—except Gus. I know; he called me over to come out and pace him that day.

"He was the first example to follow I ever saw."

Today Lindstrom is the Parks and Recreation director in Lincoln, Illinois. He also sells outdoor lighting systems and Diamond Dry, a substance used to soak up excess water on playing fields. Trosky became a life-insurance agent while he was playing and continues in that field in Cedar Rapids, Iowa.

Twenty Years of Playoffs
And the Home-Field Advantage
PAUL HENSLER

Unique among major sports, baseball awards no home-field advantage to the team with the best regular-season record. An analysis of the results and a plea for change.

ONE OF THE THINGS that makes major-league baseball such a great pastime is that only winners play the postseason. Over a 162-game schedule, a team must be the best in its division before advancing to the League Championship Series.

Unlike basketball and hockey, whose teams play for six months to eliminate a handful of potential playoff entrants, or football, with its absolute tie-breaking system for teams with equal records, baseball has but one qualification: win your division.

But is there a chink in the armor? Whereas the NBA, NFL, and NHL have several inequities in their playoffs, they do reward their better teams with something that is not found in baseball — the home-field advantage for teams with the best regular-season records.

With only two teams from the National and American Leagues qualifying for the LCS, there is just a 50-50 chance that the team with the better regular-season record will have the home-field advantage for the LCS because of the alternating sequence currently in use. This method gives the NL East and AL West leaders the home-field advantage (HFA) one year and the NL West and AL East champs the HFA the following year.

After clubs have finished a grueling six-month schedule through a variety of seasonal weather, baseball should reward those with the better won-lost records with the home-field advantage in the LCS. Why should the 1973 Mets (82-79) have been given the HFA when their playoff opponent, the Reds (99-63) were far superior over the regular campaign? Yet thirteen years later, those same Mets (108-54 in 1986) would be on the short end against the Astros (96-66).

There is some good news for dominant teams: Of those that won one hundred or more games in the regular season but were not fortunate to have the HFA in LCS play, only two failed to advance to the World Series. Also, seven of eleven 100-game winners who did have the HFA won their

league's pennant. This is indicative of these teams' overall strengths and fine play against their LCS rival regardless of who had the HFA. The strongest single year for all playoff participants was 1977, with three clubs (New York Yankees, Royals, and Phillies) all winning at least 100 games and the Dodgers winning 98.

One Hundred Game Winners Without the HFA

Team	Season Record	Record vs. LCS Opponent	Home Record vs. LCS Opp.	Home Playoff Record	Won LCS
1969 Baltimore	109-53	8-4	5-1	2-0	Y
1975 Cincinnati	108-54	6-6	4-2	2-0	Y
1986 New York (N)	108-54	7-5	5-1	2-1	Y
1988 Oakland	104-58	9-3	6-0	2-0	Y
1979 Baltimore	102-57	9-3	5-1	2-0	Y
1976 Philadelphia	101-61	7-5	4-2	0-2	N
1985 St. Louis	101-61	5-7	3-3	3-0	Y
1971 Baltimore	101-57	7-4	3-2	2-0	Y
1977 New York (A)	100-62	5-5	4-1	1-1	Y
1988 New York (N)	100-60	10-1	4-1	1-2	N

One Hundred Game Winners With the HFA

Team	Season Record	Record vs. LCS Opponent	Home Record vs. LCS Opp.	Home Playoff Record	Won LCS
1970 Baltimore	108-54	5-7	2-4	1-0	Y
1984 Detroit	104-58	7-5	1-5	1-0	Y
1980 New York (A)	103-59	4-8	2-4	0-1	N
1970 Cincinnati	102-60	8-4	5-1	1-0	Y
1974 Los Angeles	102-60	4-8	4-2	1-1	Y
1977 Kansas City	102-60	5-5	4-1	1-2	N
1976 Cincinnati	102-60	5-7	3-3	1-0	Y
1977 Philadelphia	101-61	6-6	4-2	0-2	N
1971 Oakland	101-60	4-7	2-4	0-1	N
1978 New York (A)	100-63	5-6	3-3	2-0	Y
1969 New York (N)	100-62	8-4	4-2	1-0	Y

Paul Hensler is a computer programmer analyst for Travellers Insurance Company in Hartford, Connecticut.

The essential factor in determination of which club should have the HFA should be "Who had the better record during the regular season?" When necessary, tie-breaking criteria should be established by record versus the LCS opponent during the regular season and runs scored/runs allowed differentials. However, in twenty years of playoffs, no two opponents have ever entered league-championship play with identical records, thereby limiting the need for tie-breakers and facilitating the selection of the team worthy of the HFA.

For clubs that clearly dominated their playoff opponent during the regular campaign, some found that when October rolled around they did not repeat success. Only ten of seventeen* teams who had at least twice as many regular-season victories as losses against their LCS rival went on to win the pennant, and only three of these teams had the HFA. Noteworthy upset victims include the 1988 Mets, the 1983 Dodgers, and the 1971 Giants.

Best Season Series Record Versus LCS Opponent

Team	Season Record vs. LCS Opponent	Home Record vs. LCS Opponent	Had HFA	Won LCS
1983 Los Angeles	11-1	6-0	N	N
1988 New York (N)	10-1	4-1	N	N
1979 Baltimore	9-3	5-1	N	Y
1988 Oakland	9-3	6-0	N	Y
1971 San Francisco	9-3	5-1	N	N
1980 Philadelphia	9-3	5-1	N	Y
1969 Baltimore	8-4	5-1	N	Y
1970 Cincinnati	8-4	5-1	Y	Y
1987 Detroit	8-4	4-2	N	N
1969 New York (N)	8-4	4-2	Y	Y
1974 Pittsburgh	8-4	6-0	N	N
1973 Cincinnati	8-4	4-2	N	N
1980 Kansas City	8-4	4-2	N	Y
1979 Cincinnati	8-4	3-3	N	N
1972 Oakland	8-4	4-2	N	Y
1972 Cincinnati	8-4	4-2	Y	Y
1981 Los Angeles	5-2	3-0	N	Y

Based on performance in both halves of the strike-shortened 1981 season, only two of the four series had the team with the best record enjoying the HFA. This is open to debate because of the disparity in total number of games played during that year. This also occurred in 1972 when the Pittsburgh Pirates went 96-52 but ceded the HFA to the 95-52 Cincinnati Reds. In the American League the home team won only twice, but in the Senior Circuit host clubs lost just once.

In playoff series that went the full five games (up until 1984) or seven games (since 1985), the home team won nine of fourteen. However, only four of nine victors deserved to have the HFA on the basis of their record. Among teams that lost that last game, three of five deserved the HFA.

1981 American League

Team		Season Record	Had HFA	De-served HFA	Home Rec. in Div. Plyoff.
New York	(1st half winner 34-22)	59-48 .551	Y	N	1-2
Milwaukee	(2nd half winner 31-22)	62-47 .569	N	Y	0-2
Oakland	(1st half winner 37-23)	64-45) .587	Y	Y	1-0
Kansas City	(2nd half winner 30-23)	50-53 .485	N	N	0-2
					2-6

1981 National League

Team		Season Record	Had HFA	De-served HFA	Home Rec. in Div. Plyoff.
Philadelphia	(1st half winner 34-21)	59-48 .551	Y	N	2-1
Montreal	(2nd half winner 30-23)	60-48 .556	N	Y	2-0
Los Angeles	(1st half winner 36-21)	63-47 .573	Y	Y	3-0
Houston	(2nd half winner 33-20)	61-49 .555	N	N	2-0
					9-1

Won Deciding Game		Lost Deciding Game	
Team	Deserved HFA	Team	Deserved HFA
1972 Cincinnati	N	1972 Detroit	N
1973 New York (N)	N	1977 Kansas City	Y
1973 Oakland	N	1980 Houston	Y
1976 New York (A)	Y	1981 Montreal	N
1982 Milwaukee	Y	1985 Toronto	Y
1984 San Diego	N		
1986 Boston	Y		
1987 St. Louis	Y		
1988 Los Angeles	N		

Teams with the home-field advantage are not guaranteed to clinch their league's pennant, but the leagues should uphold the teams who have proven themselves over the course of the regular season.

In the forty league championship series that have been played, only twenty-three teams that earned the HFA with their record actually had it in the LCS. Furthermore, only fourteen league champions had the best regular season record, with those teams compiling a collective 23-5 record in home playoff games. On the other hand, the remaining nine who had the best regular season but lost their LCS were a poor 4-15 at home in the playoffs.

It is the responsibility of a team to take advantage of every opportunity that it can, but no one should be denied the HFA simply because it is not that team's "turn to have it." Fourteen of twenty-three clubs, or sixty-one percent of the teams, who deserved the home-field advantage by right of a superior record won their league championship series. That number should increase if more teams are given their due on merit, based on the high winning percentage (23-5, .821) of those teams listed above.

Two decades of playoffs have provided us with a multitude of great games, memorable plays, heroes, and villains, but compared to its other sporting brethren, baseball has some catching up to do when the home-field advantage is at stake.

LCS Winners That Had the Deserved HFA

Team	Home Playoff Record
1969 New York (N)	1-0
1970 Baltimore	1-0
1970 Cincinnati	1-0
1971 Pittsburgh	2-0
1974 Los Angeles	1-1
1976 Cincinnati	1-0
1976 New York (A)	2-1
1978 Los Angeles	1-1
1978 New York (A)	2-0
1979 Pittsburgh	1-0
1982 Milwaukee	3-0
1984 Detroit	1-0
1986 Boston	3-1
1087 St. Louis	3-1
	23-5

Deserving HFA Teams That Lost the LCS

Team	Home Playoff Record
1974 Baltimore	0-2
1975 Oakland	0-1
1977 Kansas City	1-2
1977 Philadelphia	0-2
1980 Houston	1-2
1980 New York (A)	0-1
1981 Oakland	0-1
1983 Chicago (A)	0-2
1985 Toronto	2-2
	4-15

Master Playoff Data

Team	Season	Home	Road	Season Series	Rec. Sea.	Had HFA	DSV HFA	Home Ply. Rec.	Won Ply.
88 BOS	89-73	53-28*	36-45	3-9	3-3	Y	N	0-2	N
88 OAK	104-53	54-27*	50-31*	9-3	6-0	N	Y	2-0	Y
88 NY	100-60	56-24*	44-36*	10-1	4-1	N	Y	1-2	N
88 LA	94-67	45-36	49-31*	1-10	0-6	Y	N	2-2	Y
87 DET	98-64	54-27*	44-37*	8-4	4-2	N	Y	1-2	N
87 MIN	85-77	56-25*	29-52	4-8	2-4	Y	N	2-0	Y
87 STL	95-67	49-32*	46-35*	5-7	3-3	Y	N	3-1	Y
87 SF	90-72	46-35	44-37*	7-5	4-2	N	N	2-1	Y
86 BOS	95-66	51-30*	44-36	5-7	3-3	Y	Y	3-1	Y
86 CAL	92-70	50-32	42-38*	7-5	4-2	N	N	2-1	N
86 NY	108-54	55-26*	53-28*	5-7	4-2	N	Y	1-2	Y
86 HOU	96-66	52-29*	44-37*	5-7	4-2	N	N	1-2	N
85 TOR	99-62	54-26	45-36*	5-7	2-4	Y	Y	2-2	N
85 KC	91-71	50-32	41-39*	7-5	3-3	N	N	2-1	Y
85 STL	101-61	54-27*	47-34*	5-7	3-3	Y	N	3-0	Y
85 LA	95-67	48-33*	47-34*	7-5	4-2	Y	N	2-1	N
84 DET	104-58	53-29*	51-29*	7-5	1-5	Y	Y	1-0	Y
84 KC	84-78	44-37	40-41	5-7	0-6	N	N	0-2	N
84 CHI	96-65	51-29*	45-36*	6-6	3-3	N	Y	2-0	N
84 SD	92-70	48-33*	44-37	6-6	3-3	Y	N	3-0	Y
83 BAL	98-64	50-31	48-33*	7-5	4-2	N	N	1-1	Y
83 CHI	99-63	55-26*	44-37*	5-7	3-3	Y	Y	0-2	N
83 PHI	90-72	50-32*	40-41	1-11	1-5	Y	N	2-0	Y
83 LA	91-71	48-32*	43-39	11-1	6-0	N	Y	1-1	N
82 MIL	95-67	48-34	47-33*	6-6	3-3	Y	Y	3-0	Y
82 CAL	93-69	52-29	41-40*	6-6	3-3	N	N	2-0	N
82 STL	92-70	46-35	46-35*	5-7	2-4	N	Y	2-0	N
82 ATL	89-73	42-39	47-34*	7-5	3-3	Y	N	0-1	N
81 NY	(1st 34-22)	32-19*	27-29	3-3	2-1	Y	N	1-2	Y
81 MIL	(2nd 31-22)	28-21	34-26*	3-3	2-1	N	Y	0-2	N
81 OAK	(1st 37-23)	35-21*	29-24	3-3	1-2	Y	Y	1-0	Y
81 KC	(2nd 30-23)	19-28	31-25*	3-3	1-2	N	N	0-2	N
81 NY	59-48	32-19*	27-29	4-3	2-1	N	N	2-0	Y
81 OAK	64-45	35-21*	29-24	3-4	2-2	Y	Y	0-1	N

Master Playoff Data (cont.)

Team	Season	Home	Road	Season Series	Rec. Sea.	Had HFA	DSV HFA	Home Ply. Rec.	Won Ply.
81 PHI	(1st 34-21)	36-19	23-29	4-7	4-2	Y	N	2-1	N
81 MIL	(2nd 30-23)	38-18*	22-30	7-4	5-0	N	Y	2-0	Y
81 LA	(1st 36-21)	33-23	30-24	8-4	5-1	Y	Y	3-0	Y
81 HOU	(2nd 33-20)	31-20	30-29	4-8	3-3	N	N	2-0	N
81 MTL	60-48	38-18*	22-30	2-5	2-2	Y	N	1-2	N
81 LA	63-47	33-23	30-24	5-2	3-0	N	Y	1-1	Y
80 NY	103-59	53-28*	50-31*	4-8	2-4	Y	Y	0-1	N
80 KC	97-65	49-32*	48-33*	8-4	4-2	N	N	2-0	Y
80 PHI	91-71	49-32	42-39*	9-3		N	N	1-1	Y
80 HOU +	93-70	55-26*	38-44	3-9	2-4	Y	Y	1-2	N

+ Defeated LA in one game playoff at LA (HOU was 3-6 at LA)

Team	Season	Home	Road	Season Series	Rec. Sea.	Had HFA	DSV HFA	Home Ply. Rec.	Won Ply.
79 BAL	102-57	55-24*	47-33*	9-3	5-1	N	Y	2-0	Y
79 CAL	88-74	49-32*	39-42	3-9	2-4	Y	N	1-1	N
79 PIT	98-64	48-33	50-31*	4-8	1-5	Y	Y	1-0	Y
79 CIN	90-71	48-32	42-39*	8-4	3-3	N	N	0-2	N
78 NY#	100-63	55-26	45-37*	5-6	3-3	Y	Y	2-0	Y
78 KC	92-70	56-25*	36-45	6-5	3-2	N	N	1-1	N
78 PHI	90-72	54-28	36-44*	5-7	3-3	N	N	0-2	N
78 LA	95-67	54-27*	41-40	7-5	4-2	Y	N	1-1	Y

Defeated BOS in one game playoff at BOS (NY was 5-3 at BOS)

Team	Season	Home	Road	Season Series	Rec. Sea.	Had HFA	DSV HFA	Home Ply. Rec.	Won Ply.
77 NY	100-62	55-26*	45-36	5-5	4-1	N	N	1-1	Y
77 KC	102-60	55-26*	47-34	5-5	4-1	Y	Y	1-2	N
77 PHI	101-61	60-21*	41-40*	6-6	4-2	Y	Y	0-2	N
77 LA	98-64	51-30*	47-34*	6-6	4-2	N	N	1-1	Y
76 NY	97-62	45-35	52-27*	5-7	2-4	Y	Y	2-1	Y
76 KC	90-72	49-32	41-40	7-5	3-3	N	N	1-1	N
76 PHI	101-61	53-28*	48-33*	7-5	4-2	N	N	0-2	N
76 CIN	102-60	49-32*	53-28*	5-7	3-3	Y	Y	1-0	Y
75 BOS	95-65	47-34	48-31*	6-6	4-2	N	N	2-0	Y
75 OAK	98-64	54-27*	44-37	6-6	4-2	Y	Y	0-1	N
75 PIT	92-69	52-28*	40-41*	6-6	4-2	Y	N	0-1	N
75 CIN	108-54	64-17*	44-37*	6-6	4-2	N	Y	2-0	Y
74 BAL	91-71	46-35	45-36*	6-6	2-4	Y	Y	0-2	N
74 OAK	90-72	49-32*	41-40	6-6	2-4	N	N	1-1	Y
74 PIT	88-74	52-29*	50-31*	4-8	4-2	Y	Y	1-1	Y
73 BAL	97-65	50-31*	47-34*	5-7	2-4	N	N	1-1	N
73 OAK	94-68	50-31*	44-37*	7-5	3-3	Y	N	2-1	Y
73 NY	82-79	43-38*	39-41*	4-8	2-4	Y	N	2-1	Y
73 CIN	99-63	50-31*	49-32*	8-4	4-2	N	Y	1-1	N
72 DET	86-70	44-34	42-36	4-8	2-4	Y	N	2-1	N
72 OAK	93-62	48-29	45-33*	8-4	4-2	N	N	2-0	Y
72 PIT	96-59	49-29*	47-30*	4-8	2-4	N	N	1-1	N
72 CIN	95-59	42-34*	53-25*	8-4	4-2	Y	N	2-1	Y
71 BAL	101-57	53-24*	48-33*	7-4	3-2	N	Y	2-0	Y
71 OAK	101-60	46-35*	55-25*	4-7	2-4	N	N	0-1	N
71 PIT	97-65	52-28*	45-37	3-9	2-4	Y	Y	2-0	Y
71 SF	90-72	51-30*	39-42	9-3	5-1	N	N	1-1	N
70 BAL	108-54	59-22*	49-32*	5-7	2-4	Y	Y	1-0	Y
70 MIN	98-64	51-30*	47-34	7-5	3-3	N	N	0-2	N
70 PIT	89-73	50-32*	39-41	4-8	3-3	N	N	0-2	N
70 CIN	102-60	57-24*	45-36	8-4	5-1	Y	Y	1-0	Y
69 BAL	109-53	60-21*	49-32*	8-4	5-1	N	Y	2-0	Y
69 MIN	97-65	57-24*	40-41*	4-8	3-3	Y	N	0-1	N
69 NY	100-62	52-30*	48-32*	8-4	4-2	Y	Y	1-0	Y
69 ATL	93-69	50-31	43-38*	4-8	2-4	N	N	0-2	N

* Indicates best or tied for best record among teams in the division.

Umpiring in the 1890's

RICH ELDRED

You think umpires take too much abuse from players? Late last century they often had to fight their way off the field. Here's a sampling of epithets and brawlgames.

UMPIRING IN THE LATE NINETEENTH CENTURY was often perilous. Virulent and sometimes violent abuse from players, fans, owners, and reporters was common. Although baseball fans were disgusted by the constant turmoil, the magnates did nothing.

"The pay is good and you can't beat the hours," umpire Tim Hurst said, but in fact few men long endured working a game alone. Half a season, a year, were routine tenures. Most umpires were hired sight unseen by National League president Nick Young, and many were ex-ballplayers with no experience. Young's failure to rotate umpires — one man commonly worked an entire homestand or more — allowed minor tiffs to escalate into running feuds.

In one stretch of 1897, Tom Lynch handled 63 games involving Boston. On Labor Day, manager Frank Selee wrote Young asking for somebody else.

"I can only give decisions as I see them," Lynch told Tim Murnane of the Boston Globe. Dropping by the Boston Herald office before leaving town, he thanked baseball writer Jake Morse. "If all papers were as fair as the Herald, it would not be such bad work umpiring," Lynch told the Herald. Lynch's work was a "treat," Morse wrote on September 8, but he added his opinion that the league should use two umpires.

In times of inertia it takes a crisis to stir some action. One crisis occurred in August 1897 and the league's response had far-reaching implications.

On August 8 the Baltimore Orioles were in Boston. Naturally, Lynch was the umpire. In the eighth inning he kicked Joe Kelley and Arlie Pond off the Orioles' bench. "You're a big stiff," yelled Jack Doyle, Baltimore's first baseman. Lynch looked away. Passing by after the inning, Doyle suggested Lynch would get "trimmed" in Baltimore. Lynch thumbed him.

"Doyle followed Lynch up, thrice applying to him an epithet so vile and offensive as not to excuse but to demand physical retaliation," Bert Smalley wrote in the Boston Record, adding, "The epithet Doyle then used was too much to be endured, even by an umpire." When Doyle repeated it the second time, Lynch whirled around. "What's that you say?" As Smalley described it, "A third time the foul-mouthed player flung the insult in Lynch's teeth and Lynch struck him fairly between the eyes. The fierce minute's work that followed before the police and the players could pry the men apart had best be forgotten."

Observed Murnane: "The time will soon come when no person above the rank of garrotter can be secured to umpire a game."

"I for one admire Lynch's pluck and sand," Smalley declared. "Players of Doyle's stripe are fast making the game one that only a prize fighter or a thug has any business in."

The plucky Lynch, unable to open his left eye because of Doyle's head butt, went home to New Britain, Connecticut. He told Murnane that except in Boston, the team owners failed to back the umpires. New York owner Andrew Freedman, who complained that the umpires were incompetent and dishonest, was the worst crank, Lynch said.

Baltimore's owner/manager, Ned Hanlon, illustrated Tom's point. "Is it any wonder after the deal that Lynch gave the Baltimores on Friday that some of the players would have resented it?" he said. "It has been a general roast and this man Lynch is at heart a Boston man and I know it," he told the Globe.

Doyle defended his attack on Lynch. "I want to tell you one thing, that all with Irish blood in their veins will never stand being openly assaulted without retaliating," he told the Boston Post. ". . . That is the first time in my life I ever

---

Rich Eldred is researching the origins of the Boston Red Sox.

raised my hand on the ballfield at any umpire."

Ashamed of the incident, Lynch sent Young his resignation. Nick refused it; he couldn't spare Lynch because umpire Tim Hurst was in jail. (More on this later.)

To fill in for Lynch while he was away, Young hired Bill Carpenter, a twenty-three-year-old umpire in the Maine State League. When Doyle batted, the crowd hissed. "Doyle has a crust like an alligator. . . . He simply faced the pavilion and clapped his hands," Murnane observed. One fan hollered, "Dirty ball, dirty ball." Baltimore catcher Bill Clarke told Carpenter, "Don't judge us by the action of one man." He's right, Murnane said. "Ed Hanlon must blush at the language used by his men." Carpenter twice called for policemen when he ordered Baltimore players off the field. When Boston's Hugh Duffy ran in from left to argue, the Oriole bench "to a man commenced to cry, 'Police! Police!'"

And why was Tim Hurst in jail? It was because of something that happened in Cincinnati.

You could buy a mug of beer at the park in Cincinnati. Occasionally, unhappy fans gave the umpire a "crystal shower."

Later, explaining what had happened that fateful day, Hurst said, "I am sorry . . . but it is done and cannot be helped now. . . . The crowd kept jeering me but I paid no attention until a heavy beer mug struck me on the foot. I turned in time to see another coming. I picked up the first one and threw it underhanded into the crowd. I did not throw it at any particular person. . . . I lost my temper and this is the result." The "result" was that a fan was hospitalized with severe head injuries.

HURST WAS ARRESTED and charged with assault to kill. He put up a $300 bond and left town, but the man's condition slipped and, at the request of the Cincinnati police chief, Hurst was picked up during the Pittsburgh-St. Louis game. After spending the night on a bed in the jury room, he was released on $500 bond.

Reappointment is out of the question, Murnane thought. "Hurst is a most companionable fellow, the wittiest of entertainers and a good friend. He never drinks or uses tobacco." But "public sentiment will condemn him."

Despite his occasional problems Hurst had long success, and it wasn't owing to gentle diplomacy. One time, Bert Smalley wrote in the Boston Record on July 28, 1897, Tim "put his mouth close to the player's ear and said coolly, 'Now you're getting a bit chesty, I see you've made a couple of good stops, knocked out a couple of hits and you think you're solid with the crowd. Well, I'll just tell you something. I'll give you the key to my room at the hotel, where everything is nice and quiet, and when we get in there alone I'll break that jaw of yours so you can't kick for the rest of the season. I'll see that you get out quietly so you can explain your injury by saying you fell down somewhere.' " The kicker didn't take the key.

Joe Kelley told Hurst, "If I was Hanlon you'd never umpire another game in Baltimore."

"What? Not be allowed to umpire in this city for a lot of swell gentlemen like your crowd? Now, Kel, don't say that, old boy, for you know all the umpires are stuck on you people."

Hurst called a Brooklyn player out at home. The player retorted, "You're a nice duck, ain't you. Why, he didn't come within a yard of me. Say, Tim, I know your girl in Philadelphia." Hurst whipped out his notebook and pencil. "When any of my friends so forgets themselves as to speak to such a yellow ballplayer as you, I scratch them," he said as he erased the name.

As Hurst explained to Tim Murnane, "You see, I don't let these people bother me in the least. . . . If a man takes these ballplayers seriously it is only a matter of a very short time until they drive him to drink or to a madhouse."

But unfortunately for league president Young, the players were winning. Jack Sheridan quit and Bob Emslie was hurt. Four of Young's seven-man staff were in trouble.

"Altogether I am very badly off for umpires and don't know where to look for recruits," Young said. "I sincerely hope there may be extenuating circumstances in Hurst's case."

Young, sitting in his Washington office (besides serving as league president he worked as a clerk for the Treasury Department), reflected on "the toughest week for umpires in all my experience," which dated from 1871. Heaving a sigh and looking forlorn, he remarked, "I don't know where to get acceptable men to umpire if this thing continues. . . . Here is Connolly of the New England League, said to be one of the best men in the business, [he] positively declines to accept an appointment." (Connolly had refused in '96 also.) "And Dan Campbell begged off until umpiring was semi-respectable. . . . John Sheridan sat in a chair right at my desk and vowed he could not stand the personal abuse heaped on him by certain players, managers and newspapers. He vowed to me that he had not taken a drink of liquor since the season began, notwithstanding the charge made against him by Ned Hanlon."

Young noted that he'd be in a "pretty fix" if not for Bob Emslie and Lynch. "Lynch is a sick man and he needs a few weeks' rest. He intended to go to the seashore to build up his constitution," but could not be spared. "Bob Emslie received a sharp blow over his left lung and coughed up a large clot of blood," but was still calling them. Al Reach recommended John Kelly of the Pennsylvania Interstate

League, and Nick signed him pronto.

Eventually, Young felt himself compelled to resign from his federal sinecure to give full attention to the umpire problem.

The Globe's Tim Murnane went to New Britain, Connecticut, to talk with Tom Lynch. (Lynch, who worked at the Opera House during the winter and was "considered a man of executive ability," was himself the National League president years later.) Murnane and Lynch discussed Jack Sheridan. "The players simply broke poor Jack's heart," Lynch said. "I saw him at the Ashland House yesterday and he told me the players abused him until he could stand it no longer. While he was in Pittsburgh I sent him a telegram telling him to stick it out. . . . He told me that the message cheered him up for several days. . . The poor fellow cried like a child as he went over his troubles for Sheridan was the soul of honor," Lynch said. Murnane concurred: Sheridan was "always impartial and fearless until slimy-tongued players abused him and he lost heart for the position."

On August 9, Murnane reviewed the season up to then, and one wonders why only Sheridan quit.

Early on, Cleveland's Jesse Burkett, "well educated by [manager Patsy] Tebeau," threatened to "whip" Michael McDermont after a game. A Louisville crowd mobbed Sheridan and when he called Lajoie out for deliberately getting hit by a pitch, several Philadelphia players tried to slug him.

In Pittsburgh, a mob "grossly insulted" Tim Hurst. Tim knocked down one fan, precipitating a general row, and fifteen police escorted him out. "A block away a man hit Hurst in the back of the head and the umpire promptly sent his assailant to the grass too. The mob was closing in now and Hurst, breaking through, jumped on a trolley car and took the first train out of town."

When McDermont forfeited a game to New York and fined Pittsburgh's Dick Padden, Frank Killian, and Pat Donovan $25 each, the Pirates kicked out the dressing-room windows. Later, McDermont fired a punch at Jim Rogers of Louisville.

In Chicago, Lynch called a Colt safe at home. Boston catcher Fred Lake protested and Cap Anson got into it. Lake tried to bop Cap. "Lynch, in trying to separate the belligerents, handled the 'old man' [Anson] a bit roughly, whereupon Anse squared off at him. Lynch then grabbed the broom with which he swept the plate and made a swipe at the Chicago captain, who ducked. Then Lynch put Anson out of the game." The police dragged Monte Cross off the field and fined him $25.

On July 10, Sheridan was pelted with rotten eggs. On the same day, in Louisville, Lynch tossed Clarke and Davis out of the first game of a doubleheader, then, after a "wild

row," refused to umpire the second game. Jim Wolf filled in. New York, Louisville's opponent, was ahead 7-2 in the ninth when Mike Sullivan and then Amos Rusie lost the plate. When Tom McCreary walked, forcing in the tying run, and the Giants surrounded Wolf, the crowd charged the field, "Joyce tried to punch Wolf and Parke Wilson struck Hach of Louisville in the face. In the midst of the row, when a policeman was hauling Wilson off the field, Pickering of Louisville scored the tying run."

On July 22, Pink Hawley of Cincinnati decked Sheridan with a shot to the jaw. Jack ejected him. In the second game, the crowd brought bags of rotten eggs and bombarded Sheridan again. In another game, Heine Peitz, the Reds' catcher, charged Hurst. Tim jolted him in the tummy with his mask and Peitz smashed Hurst in the mouth, drawing blood.

Murnane concluded: "There are more games lost by woodenheaded players failing to exercise their alleged 'thinkers' . . . than by erroneous decisions of the umpires." About the latter, Murnane said, Hurst, Lynch, and Emslie were the best men. Sheridan was before he went backsliding. "O'Day is honest but loses his head too easily," McDonald is good if he's left alone and McDermont is "just fair."

BUT NOT ALL MEN were as nifty with their fists as Mr. Hurst, and the $1,500 salary wasn't attracting anyone. Cincinnati pitcher Frank Dwyer donned the mask for a day. The Reds were down 3-2 in the ninth with two out and the bases loaded. Dwyer called Bid McPhee out on strikes. "The air became blue," Murnane wrote. "Dwyer's associates were hot enough to mob him. Few players would have acted as honestly as Dwyer." (Dwyer and Bill Carpenter later became full-time umpires.)

With all this happening, the time was never better for strong, united action by the magnates. Typically, they did nothing.

Lynch returned to his post. Hurst, found guilty of attempted murder in Cincinnati (the victim recovered), was fined $100 plus court costs. Jack Sheridan was gone for good.

In September, Andrew Freedman docked in New York City, fully rejuvenated from his annual European vacation, and immediately blasted his favorite targets.

The Giants would be second except for rotten umpires in Cincinnati, he told Murnane. "The players there are a lot of loafers and the umpires we had to submit to were thoroughly incompetent." Who was to blame? "Nick Young. He is dominated by a bad influence [John T. Brush]. When we were in the west we were furnished with the worst and now that we have returned home we have two umpires and always the best the league affords. I have

Jack Sheridan

no complaint to make to this, because we play only clean ball."

Sure you do, but what about the Reds? "They are a lot of loafers and will not receive any courtesies from me. They have won game after game by unfair means and their tactics are sanctified by the Cincinnati management. . . . As long as that team is in the hands that it is, it will not succeed."

The other owners were not pleased with Freedman's comments. "Mr. Freedman has made some serious charges in his recent interviews," said Brooklyn owner Charles Byrne. "He has charged umpires with being drunk," and picking on New York. ". . . He is reckless and doesn't care what he says."

In case he hadn't assured his termination, Tim Hurst chattered away with Murnane: "What do you think of that stiff Freedman? Here he goes and abuses Mr. Young as if he were a pickpocket. . . . Why that man works 20 out of every 24 hours of his life for the National League. . . . Making such cracks about Nick Young is enough to give a decent man the pip. The league ought to get after this Bowery boy and throw him into a tank."

The Herald's Jake Morse concurred: "The league could not replace Mr. Young."

But of course they could replace Mr. Hurst.

The American League, just over the horizon in the late 1890s, succeeded where others failed, for many reasons.

By 1900 people were sick of lawless National League ball. Ban Johnson's reputation was that he brooked no challenge to the umpire's authority, and the press expended barrels of ink extolling him in 1901, when Ban faced similar troubles. While Johnson's disciplinary actions were tempered by box-office considerations, he won nearly unanimous approval in print, even from National League partisans. And across the tracks, Andy Freedman banned umpire Billy Nash from the New York grounds and openly mocked and threatened Nick Young. The contrast wasn't lost on the fans.

Maybe the American League would have made it even if the National League had run a tighter ship, but no other rival had.

One of Johnson's original umpires was Tommy Connolly, who had twice turned Young down. He lasted until 1931 and was elected to the Hall of Fame in 1953.

"I am glad to have the opportunity to be with Johnson," Connolly told Sporting Life. "I'll get a chance to get backed up. In my last venture in the National League, I fined 14 men in two weeks and not a fine went. All the rules in the world will not help the game if the umpires are not supported."

Johnson also hired Jack Sheridan. On the way to his first assignment, Jack got off the train in Missouri and began directing an imaginary game in the middle of Main Street. He was hospitalized for "mental derangement." Drink was responsible, Johnson lamented. Fortunately, Sheridan recovered rapidly and went on to umpire 14 years in the American League.

After being fired by Nick Young, Hurst signed on as manager of St. Louis for 1898. His team had a dismal (39-111) record. Amazingly, Hurst was rehired by Young.

He didn't last long. This time, Murnane wrote, Hurst "has himself to blame for his luck, for besides poor umping, he has added a foul mouth to his work."

There's no backing, Tim told his pal Jake Morse. "I got tired of it. What's the use? There was only one way — grin and bear it."

Even on the fringes of baseball, Hurst was beloved by the scribes and remained one of sport's most quoted men. Annually, Morse and others wondered why Ban Johnson didn't grab such a fine ump. In 1905 Ban broke down and signed him up.

But Tim's pugnacious, both-guns-blazing approach was not what Johnson wanted. When Tim spat in Eddie Collins' face, "because I don't like college men," Ban let him go.

In a way it was the end of an era. There have been incidents since then, but never again would an umpire have to brawl his way to the top or face the relentless barrage of scorn that defined umpiring in the 1890s.

Unusual Extra-Base Feats
STEVE KREVISKY

It's one thing to lead a league in doubles, triples, or homers, quite another to lead in two or three of these categories the same year. It's truly remarkable—and rare—to hit 20 of each.

THREE HALL-OF-FAMERS, one active player who could make the Hall, and one old-timer who probably never will, share an unusual extra-base feat: Each one led his league in both home runs and triples in the same season.

The Hall-of-Famers are Jim Bottomley, Mickey Mantle, and Willie Mays. The possible entrant is Jim Rice. The old-timer is Harry Lumley, who played for Brooklyn in the first decade of this century.

TABLE 1: LEADERS IN HR AND 3B IN THE SAME SEASON

Player	Year	3B	HR	Other categories led
Lumley	1904	18	9	
Bottomley	1928	20	31	136 RBI
Mantle	1955	11	37	113 BB, .611 SA
Mays	1955	13	51	8.8 HR%, .659 SA
Rice	1978	15	46	139 RBI, .600 SA, 213 H

Note that Mantle and Mays performed this feat in 1955. Mantle was not a big doubles hitter; only once did he exceed 30 (1952). In 1961, while Mantle and Roger Maris both chased Babe Ruth's one-season home run record of 60, each hit only 16 doubles.

Mays hit only 18 doubles in 1955, although he substantially increased his doubles totals in San Francisco. He led the National League three times in triples but never in doubles or RBIs.

Bottomley had double figures in doubles, triples, and homers (the "triple double") in six consecutive years (1924-29). He led the National League in hits and doubles in 1925, doubles and RBIs in 1926, and had 100 or more RBIs in each of the six years. Sunny Jim also holds the major-league record for most RBIs in one game, 12, set on Sept. 16, 1924.

In Rice's big 1978 year, he also led the American League in three other categories (see table). Rice had three consecutive years of 100 runs, 100 RBIs, and 200 hits (1977-79) and two straight seasons of leading in home runs and slugging average (1977-78).

How about leaders in both doubles and triples in the same season? There are more of those.

TABLE 2: LEADERS IN 2B AND 3B IN THE SAME SEASON

Player	Year(s) leading in 2B and 3B	
Musial	1943, 1946, 1948, 1949	(MVP in '43, '46, '48)
Hornsby	1921	.397 BA
Gehringer	1929	had 60 doubles in 1936
Cobb	1908, 1911, 1917	(1911: 147 R, 144 RBI, 248 H, .420 BA)
H. Wagner	1900, 1908	(1908: led league in several areas)
B. Veach	1919	
Vosmik	1935	
Versalles	1965	
Brock	1968	
Tovar	1970	

Note Musial's frequency. He's also a member of the 50-20 club (50 2B, 20 3B). He did the triple double in seven consecutive years as well (1942-49, excluding 1945, when he was the service).

In 1948 Musial just missed leading the league in 2B, 3B, and HR (Mize beat him out by 1 HR); however, Musial also led the National League that season in runs, hits, RBIs, batting average, and slugging average. Not a bad year's work.

TABLE 3: LEADERS IN 2B AND HR IN THE SAME SEASON

Player	Year	Other feats
Lajoie	1901	Triple Crown
Speaker	1912	.383 BA, 136 R
Zimmerman	1912	Triple Crown
Hornsby	1922	Triple Crown
Klein	1933	Triple Crown
Medwick	1937	Triple Crown
Greenberg	1940	129 R, 150 RBI (led), .670 SA (led)
Williams	1949	Led in R (150), RBI (159), BB (162), SA (.650)
Stargell	1973	Led in RBI (119), SA (.646)

Near misses: George Sisler (1920), with 49 2B, 18 3B, 19 HR, .407 BA, 257 H (the record); Lou Gehrig (1927), 52 2B, 18 3B, 47 HR, 175 RBI and .373 BA; Stan Musial (1948), with 46 2B, 18 3B, 39 HR, .376 BA.

Steve Krevisky teaches math at Middlesex (Ct.) Community College.

Jim Bottomley

TABLE 4: MEMBERS OF THE 20-20-20 CLUB

Player	Year	2B	3B	HR	Other feats
W. Schulte	1911	30	21	21	121 RBI (led): .534 SA (led)
Bottomley	1928	42	20	31	136 RBI (led)
Heath	1941	32	20	24	Rebounds from off-1940
Mays	1957	26	20	35	38 SB (led); .626 SA (led)
Brett	1979	42	20	23	212 H (led)

Some unusual or fluky batting feats:

1. Larry Bowa (1972), 11 2B, 1 HR, 13 3B (led league).

2. Owen Wilson (1912), a record 36 3B; never led league or approached this total again.

3. Earl Webb (1931), 67 2B; never more than 30 in any other season, 155 lifetime.

4. Speaker (1920-23) and Wagner (1906-09) each led the league in 2B for four consecutive years. Crawford (1913-15) led in 3B for three consecutive seasons.

5. Medwick had seven consecutive seasons of 40 or more doubles, leading the National League from 1936 through 1938 with totals of 64, 56, and 47.

6. Paul Waner (1926, 1927) and Ival Goodman (1935, 1936) each led the league in 3B in each of their first two years. Waner then led in 2B in 1928 with 50, and also led in 1932 with 62.

7. Billy Jurges (1935) 33 2B, 1 3B, 1 HR; (1937) 18 2B, 10 3B, 1 HR.

8. Adam Comorosky (1930) 47 2B, 23 3B, never again approached those numbers (it was a hitter's year).

9. Lou Boudreau (1941, 1944, 1947), led in 2B with 45 in each of those years. In 1940, when he hit 46 2B, Greenberg led with 50.

Some analogous feats in the 19th century: Tip O'Neill (1887) led in 2B, 3B, and HR, as well as H, R, BA, and SA. Harry Stovey (1884) led in 3B, HR, H, R, BA, and SA. Others who led in 2B and HR (not a complete list): Jimmy Ryan (1888), Dan Brouthers (1886), and Hugh Duffy (1884), who also batted .438 and won the Triple Crown.

1930 Negro National League

DICK CLARK AND JOHN B. HOLWAY

In the latest edition of an ongoing SABR project, researchers tabulated a banner year for Willie Wells, Rube Foster, and other Negro-league immortals.

LATIN AMERICANS called Willie Wells "Diablo" — the Devil. In 1930 he showed why.

The little shortstop hit .404 to lead the western clubs in hitting. (Bill Terry led the white majors with .401; it would have been exciting to see the two compete in the same league.)

Willie also slugged 14 homers, the best in the West, though second to big George (Mule) Suttles, his St. Louis Stars' teammate who hit 20 splitting his season between St. Louis and New York. A short left-field fence in St. Louis aided both men.[1]

Wells was also tops in doubles, hits, and total bases, and second in stolen bases. His 17 steals were two more than his close friend and teammate, Cool Papa Bell, and one behind the league leader, Terris McDuffie of Birmingham.[2]

These figures were compiled by a team of researchers, in and out of SABR, who scoured hundreds of box scores in both black and white newspapers of that year. Although some games will be forever missing from the record, we believe these to be the definitive totals, as complete as they will ever be.

This is part of an on-going project, under editor Dick Clark, to compile the most compete statistics possible for the Negro leagues, whose stats were rarely published, and, when they were, were often inaccurate. The 1921 Negro National League stats were published in the 1985 "Baseball Research Journal."

We have counted all league games in 1930, about 60 games per team. We have also counted additional games, about 10 or so per team against other top black clubs, such as the independent Homestead Grays. This gives us two sets of figures — league games and total black games. (We did not, however, count contests against white semipro clubs.)

In league games only, rookie Herman (Jabbo) Andrews

of Memphis and Birmingham was the batting champ with .399 to Wells' .397. (If Jabbo or Willie had known how close they were to .400, they might have sat out some games or dropped a few bunts, as Ty Cobb, Roger Hornsby, and others had been known to do, to top the goal.) And Andrews and Dale Alexander are the only batting champions ever traded midway through the season. Andrews remained in the black leagues for 13 years but never approached his 1930 performance again.

Among the pitchers, Eggie Hensley of first-place St. Louis edged Big Bill Foster of the Chicago American Giants as the biggest winner in the West. Hensley was 17-6, compared to Foster's 16-10 with a sixth-place team overall.

Foster was the younger brother of Hall-of-Famer Rube and is considered by many the best lefty in Blackball annals[3]. In addition to managing the American Giants, he was also the strikeout king that year, with 134 in 199 innings.

---

[1] Wells set the Negro league single-season home-run record with 27 in 1929. That October he bedeviled a white big-league all-star team of Charlie Gehringer, Heinie Manush, Harry Heilmann, and others, hitting .500 with two triples and two steals of home, as the blacks won three games of four. Wells' lifetime average against white big leaguers was .396.

[2] McDuffie would later take up pitching and receive a reluctant tryout from Branch Rickey of the Dodgers in 1944.

[3] Foster leads all Negro leaguers in lifetime victories, with a 129-62 record for games researched so far. Paige is fifth with 80-37.

Dick Clark and John B. Holway are leading Negro-league historians.

Satchel Paige, who jumped to the East for the first half of the season, finished with a 9-4 record for fifth-place Birmingham. (He was 3-1 at Baltimore for 12-5 overall.)

Paige had 69 Ks in 102 innings. (His Baltimore totals are not yet available.) At Birmingham Satch scored well in TRA (Total Run Average — earned runs were not given in box scores). He had a 3.17, second best in the hard-hitting black league.

The league leader was Ted (Double Duty) Radcliffe, the popular speaker at the 1986 SABR Chicago convention, with 2.80. Duty had a 9-3 record for the champion Stars and tied Foster for the lead in saves, with three. He also batted .289, splitting his time between pitching and catching, hence the monicker "Double Duty," given him by Grantland Rice.

Two other Birmingham hurlers, who taught Paige his fabled control, also did well in 1930. Harry Salmon was second in strikeouts, and Sam Streeter (see "Smartest Pitcher in Negro Leagues," BRJ, 1984) led in complete games.

As the season opened, the two top sluggers in the West — indeed, the two top homer hitters in Blackball history — Suttles and Detroit's Turkey Stearnes[4] — joined Paige in jumping to the East. The Depression had settled over the league, and they hoped to make more money from the move.

St. Louis replaced the big Mule with speedy, fancy-fielding George Giles (pronounced Guiles), sometimes called "the Black Terry" and grandfather of Brian Giles, who played infield for the Mets in 1981-83. But the Detroit Stars had no way to replace Stearnes, a seven-time home-run champ. The powerhouse St. Louis club, with a **team** batting average of .327, won the first half of the split season, beating Kansas City, whose 17-game winning streak was not enough.

Both Suttles and Stearnes returned for the second half. Mule moved to left field, leaving Giles on first.

Stearnes hit only three homers, playing in huge Hamtramck Stadium, but he pumped new life into the Detroiters, who captured the second-half title.

The Monarchs, meanwhile, went on an extended barnstorming tour against the Grays. A bus accident put several key Monarchs out of action, including the great Bullet Joe Rogan, and the Grays won 13 of the 15 contests. The most famous one pitted Homestead's forty-four-year-old Joe Williams against the Monarchs' Chet Brewer[5]. They dueled for 12 innings under the lights, Brewer striking out 19 men and Williams 27 before Joe won it on a one-hitter. Homestead's eighteen-year-old rookie Josh Gibson got his baptism in the series, hitting .243, with one home run.

In the NNL playoff, St. Louis and Detroit split the first two games in the cozy St. Louis park. Stearnes ripped two homers in the first game and went five-for-five in the second, including a homer. Moving to Hamtramck, Wells and Suttles homered, but Stearnes' two doubles gave Detroit a 7-5 win. The next day Turkey tripled and became the first man to hit a ball over the park's distant right-field wall; Wells trumped him with two singles and an inside-the-park homer, as St. Louis won 4-3 to even the Series. Willie got three more hits in Game Seven, while the St. Louis pitchers finally stopped Stearnes, and St. Louis won 13-7. St. Louis went on to win the Series in nine games. Turk hit .481, the Devil .438.

There was no Black World Series that year against the champions of the East, the Grays (Williams, Gibson, Oscar Charleston), who defeated the New York Lincoln Giants (Pop Lloyd, Chino Smith) in a challenge series. That's the series when Gibson reportedly hit one ball over the roof of Yankee Stadium and another over the center-field fence of Forbes Field.

The year came to an end with the death of Rube Foster in the Kankakee insane asylum in December. With him, coincidentially, died his creation, the Negro National League, a victim of the Depression.

But perhaps the most historic event of the year was the birth of night ball. The Monarchs unveiled their lights at Enid, Oklahoma, on April 28 in a game against Phillips University, the same night that Organized Ball saw its first night game about 100 miles away at Independence, Kansas. (The putative pioneer, Des Moines, played its first night game May 2.)

"What talkies are to movies, lights will be to baseball," Monarch owner J.L. Wilkinson predicted. He took his lights all over the country, including Sportsmen's Park in St. Louis and Forbes Field in Pittsburgh. Cardinal president Sam Breadon ordered a set for his Houston farm team.

The leagues began to crumble under the hard times, and many veteran teams succumbed. But the new invention of lights probably saved both the Negro-league teams and the white leagues in the long decade to come.

The following persons have contributed to the Negro leagues statistics project: Terry Baxter, John Bourg, Harry

---

[4] Stearnes hit 160 homers in games found so far; Suttles hit 150, and Gibson 137 (most of them in Latin America). Wells is sixth on the list with 111. All totals are incomplete.

[5] Brewer now lives in Los Angeles, where his boys' baseball program has rescued many youths in trouble and has sent Dock Ellis, Enos Cabell, Bob Watson, and many others to the major leagues.

Brunt, C. Baylor Butler, Elizabeth Cale, Dick Clark, Harry Conwell, Dick Cramer, Deborah Crawford, Paul Doherty, Garrett Finney, Bob Gill, Troy Greene, Richard Hall, John B. Holway, John Holway Jr., Merl Kleinknecht, Larry Lester, Jerry Malloy, Joe McGillen, Bill Plott, Jim Riley, Susan Scheller, Mike Stahl, A. D. Suehsdorf, Lance Wallace, Edie Williams, and Charles Zarelli.

1930 NEGRO NATIONAL LEAGUE

							(League Only)	
Club	W	L	Pct.	GB	R/G	OR/G*	R	OR
St. Louis Stars	62	21	.747	—	7.99	5.02	663	417
Detroit Stars	48	33	.593	13	5.58	4.52	452	366
Kansas City Monarchs	36	22	.621	13½	6.09	4.76	353	276
Chicago American Giants	47	47	.500	20½	4.57	5.18	430	487
Birmingham Black Barons	42	47	.472	23	4.63	5.20	412	463
Memphis Red Sox	29	45	.392	28½	4.64	6.06	343	448
Cuban Stars	21	37	.362	28½	4.41	5.29	256	307
Nashville Elite Giants	18	52	.257	37½	4.39	7.73	307	541
Louisville Red Caps	14	27	.341		4.23	5.45	173	223

Non-League Affiliate Member Record Against League Teams

Homestead Grays	28	8	.778		7.22	4.33	260	156

* Opposition runs per game

RECORDS FOR ALL GAMES

Club	W	L	Pct.
St. Louis Stars	78	29	.729
Detroit Stars	59	40	.596
Chicago American Giants	59	55	.518
Kansas City Monarchs	39	40	.494
Birmingham Black Barons	44	48	.478
Cuban Stars	23	38	.377
Memphis Red Sox	32	53	.376
Nashville Elite Giants	22	54	.289

CLUB BATTING — LEAGUE GAMES ONLY

Club	% of Boxes	2B	3B	HR	SB	Pct.
St. Louis Stars	.74	118	37	62	58	.327
Detroit Stars	67	94	59	28	51	.283
Kansas City Monarchs	90	97	32	20	68	.297
Chicago American Giants	65	84	33	14	30	.267
Birmingham Black Barons	77	80	58	35	65	.286
Memphis Red Sox	82	96	31	14	24	.282
Cuban Stars	67	41	20	18	34	.243
Nashville Elite Giants	57	53	33	14	15	.257
Louisville Red Caps	34	23	11	8	6	.238

CLUB PITCHING — LEAGUE GAMES ONLY

Club	CG	SH	SV	BB	SO	OR/G
St. Louis Stars	51	4	9	162	248	5.02
Detroit Stars	56	8	1	100	249	4.52
Kansas City Monarchs	47	7	1	134	310	4.76
Chicago American Giants	56	6	7	202	268	5.18
Birmingham Black Barons	66	3	2	159	275	5.20
Memphis Red Sox	34	3	2	207	254	6.06
Cuban Stars	38	2	0	118	167	5.29
Nashville Elite Giants	34	4	0	131	169	7.73
Louisville Red Caps	21	2	3	35	58	5.45
Homestead Grays	18	1	0	29	74	4.33

BATTING LEADERS

LEAGUE GAMES

Batting Average

Andrews, Birm. Mem.	.399
Wells, St. Louis	.397
Duncan, K.C.	.388
Bell, St. Louis	.367
Suttles, St. Louis	.367

Hits

Wells, St. Louis	92
Andrews, Birm. Mem.	85
B. Russell, St. Louis	84
Rogers, Birm. Mem.	79

Doubles

Wells, St. Louis	26
Rogers, Birm. Mem.	21
Young, K.C.	15

Triples

Johnston, Detroit	12
Stearnes, Detroit	9
Rile, Detroit	9
Crutchfield, Birm.	9

Home Runs

Wells, St. Louis	12
Suttles, St. Louis	9
Livingston, K.C.	9

Total Bases

Wells, St. Louis	158
Andrews, Birm. Mem.	129
Rogers, Birm. Mem.	127
Bell, St. Louis	123

Slugging Average

Suttles, St. Louis	.733
Stearnes, Detroit	.681
Wells, St. Louis	.681
Andrews, Birm. Mem.	.606

Stolen Bases

McDuffie, Birm.	16
C. Smith, Birm.	16
Wells, St. Louis	15

ALL GAMES

Batting

Wells, St. Louis	.404
Suttles, St. Louis	.400
Andrews, Birm. Mem.	.388
Fernandez, Chicago	.373
Duncan, K.C.	.372

Hits

Wells, St. Louis	111
Bell, St. Louis	93
B. Russell, St. Louis	92
Andrews, Birm. Mem.	90

Doubles

Wells, St. Louis	30
Rogers, Birm. Mem.	21
Rile, Detroit	17
Bell, St. Louis	17

Triples

Johnston, Detroit	13
Stearnes, Detroit	10
Rile, Detroit	9
Crutchfield, Birm.	9

Home Runs

Wells, St. Louis	14
Suttles, St. Louis	12
Livingston, K.C.	9

Total Bases

Wells, St. Louis	189
Bell, St. Louis	143
Andrews, Birm. Mem.	136
Rogers, Birm. Mem.	134

Slugging Average

Suttles, St. Louis	.820
Wells, St. Louis	.687
Stearnes, Detroit	.661
Andrews, Birm. Mem.	.586

Stolen Bases

McDuffie, Birm.	18
Wells, St. Louis	17
C. Smith, Birm.	16
Bell, St. Louis	15

PITCHING LEADERS

LEAGUE GAMES

Winning Percentage

Army Cooper, K.C.	.909
Trent, St. Louis	.800
Andy Cooper, Detroit	.778

Victories

Hensley, St. Louis	16
Andy Cooper, Detroit	14
Foster, Chicago	12

Games

Streeter, Birm.	29
Foster, Chicago	28
C. Bell, Memphis	26
Salmon, Mem. Birm.	26

Complete Games

Streeter, Birm.	19
Foster, Chicago	15
Andy Cooper, Detroit	14
Hensley, St. Louis	14

ALL GAMES

Winning Percentage

Army Cooper, K.C.	.909
Trent, St. Louis	.846
Matlock, St. Louis	.786

Victories

Hensley, St. Louis	17
Foster, Chicago	16
Andy Cooper, Detroit	15

Games

Foster, Chicago	34
Streeter, Birm.	30
McDonald, Chicago	30
C. Bell, Memphis	29

Complete Games

Streeter, Birm.	20
Foster, Chicago	18
Andy Cooper, Detroit	16
Hensley, St. Louis	15

Innings

Streeter, Birm.	177.2	Foster, Chicago	199
Hensley, St. Louis	167	Streeter, Birm.	186.2
Salmon, Mem. Birm.	166.1	Hensley, St. Louis	179

Runs Per Game

Radcliffe, St. Louis	3.03	Radcliffe, St. Louis	2.80
C. Bell, K.C.	3.03	W. Bell, K.C.	3.12
Paige, Birm.	3.38	Paige, Birm.	3.17
Shaw, Detroit	3.44	Dean, Detroit	3.29

Strikeouts

Foster, Chicago	113	Foster, Chicago	134
Salmon, Mem. Birm.	94	Salmon, Mem. Birm.	101
Army Cooper, K.C.	85	Holsey, Chicago	90

Shutouts

10 Players Had 2 Each		Foster, Chicago	3
		Shaw, Detroit	3

1930 NASHVILLE ELITE GIANTS

League (18-52)   **All Games (22-54)**

We have no box scores of non-league games; therefore below are league averages only.

G	AB	H	2B	3B	HR	SB	Pct.	Pos.	Player
43	128	37	4	6	3	3	.298	1B	Willie Bobo
42	159	45	8	2	2	5	.276	2B	Black Bottom Buford
44	166	41	3	6	4	0	.258	SS	Leroy Stratton
19	46	7	1	1	0	0	.152	3B	Jesse Edwards
31	123	39	4	2	0	2	.322	LF	Hannibal Cox
47	166	46	7	8	2	4	.283	CF	Jack Ridley
34	123	36	6	2	0	0	.302	RF	Nish Williams
15	52	15	2	2	0	0	.286	C	Poindexter Williams
21	45	12	3	0	0	0	.267	P-OF	Henry Wright
15	46	10	0	1	3	0	.217	C-OF	Louis English
14	41	9	2	1	0	0	.229	Inf	Joe Wiggins

Pitching

G	IP	GS	CG	ShO	Sv	W-L	RPG	Player
25	113	15	9	2	0	6-11	8.20	Henry Wright
18	104.2	13	8	1	0	5-8	4.64	Jim Willis
15	58.2	11	6	0	0	2-7	5.83	Clarence Red White
13	51.2	8	4	1	0	1-8	9.05	? McCauley

1930 LOUISVILLE RED CAPS

Games against NNL teams (14-27)

G	AB	H	2B	3B	HR	SB	Pct.	Pos.	Player
21	78	22	3	0	1	3	.282	1B	Willie Lee Scott
16	54	14	0	2	1	0	.259	2B	Sammy Hughes
20	70	16	3	1	0	1	.229	SS	Henry Harris
11	34	10	4	1	0	0	.294	3B	? Norris
20	74	17	2	2	1	1	.230	LF	Red McNeil
13	32	3	1	1	0	1	.094	CF	? Palmer
16	54	16	3	1	2	0	.296	RF	? Massey
18	59	12	2	0	2	0	.203	C	Poindexter Williams
19	66	17	4	2	1	0	.258	P-OF	Willie Gisentaner
17	48	13	1	1	0	0	.271	2B-OF	Connie Wesley

Pitching

G	IP	GS	CG	ShO	Sv	W-L	RPG	Player
10	62.1	9	6	1	0	3-6	6.36	Richard Cannon
9	49.2	5	5	1	2	3-3	3.62	? Hudson
7	40	5	3	0	0	3-3	6.53	Willie Gisentaner
7	40	6	4	0	0	0-6	7.20	Lefty Capers

1930 CUBAN STARS

League (21-37)   **All Games (23-38)**

We have no box scores of non-league games; therefore below are league averages only.

G	AB	H	2B	3B	HR	SB	Pct.	Pos.	Player
41	140	39	3	2	2	2	.279	1B-OF	Felipe Sierra
45	157	44	7	2	4	10	.280	2B	Angel Alfonso
42	144	23	3	1	1	0	.160	SS	Marcelline Bauza
43	145	32	5	1	4	0	.221	3B	Ramon Hernandez
39	138	31	3	1	1	1	.225	LF-P	Lazaro Salazar
43	176	36	4	2	2	10	.205	CF	Cando Lopez
41	160	49	5	3	1	4	.306	RF	Rogelio Alonzo
39	123	36	3	3	1	3	.293	C	? Cortez
31	80	24	4	4	2	2	.300	1B-C	Pablo Diaz

Pitching

G	IP	GS	CG	ShO	Sv	W-L	RPG	Player
24	133.1	17	13	1	0	10-7	4.01	Yo-Yo Diaz
21	115	17	10	1	0	4-12	4.92	Luis Tiant Sr.
15	69.1	7	6	0	0	3-8	6.49	Jesus Lorenzo
10	46.2	6	3	0	0	2-3	5.30	? Molina

1930 ST. LOUIS STARS

			League (62-21)									All Games (78-29)					
G	AB	H	2B	3B	HR	SB	Pct.	Pos.	Player	G	AB	H	2B	3B	HR	SB	Pct.
54	223	76	14	4	3	6	.341	1B	George Giles	66	271	87	15	4	3	7	.321
63	233	69	11	6	4	2	.296	2B	John Henry Russell	72	260	79	11	6	5	2	.304
61	232	92	26	2	12	15	.397	SS	Willie Wells	73	275	111	30	3	14	17	.404
60	244	69	4	4	5	7	.308	3B	Dewey Creacy	73	270	77	4	5	7	7	.285
33	120	44	5	6	9	5	.367	LF	Mule Suttles	43	150	60	11	8	12	8	.400
49	210	77	13	6	7	11	.367	CF	Cool Papa Bell	62	263	93	17	6	7	15	.354
62	244	84	10	3	7	6	.344	RF	Branch Russell	72	278	92	11	3	8	7	.331
41	157	47	4	1	2	1	.299	C	Henry Williams	48	181	56	4	2	2	1	.309
46	152	44	9	2	6	3	.289	P-C	Ted Radcliffe	55	180	51	11	2	6	4	.283
37	119	41	8	1	1	1	.345	OF-P	John Williams	44	141	45	8	1	1	1	.319
23	76	24	8	0	5	1	.316	OF	Wilson Redus	33	106	32	9	3	5	3	.302

1930 ST. LOUIS STARS (cont.)

Pitching

G	IP	GS	CG	ShO	SV	W-L	RPG	Player	G	IP	GS	CG	ShO	SV	W-L	RPG
25	167	20	14	0	1	16-5	4.74	Slap Hensley	27	179	22	15	0	1	17-6	4.93
17	78.2	8	5	1	1	8-2	4.57	Ted Trent	20	103.2	11	7	1	1	11-2	4.69
16	83.3	9	8	1	3	7-3	3.03	Ted Radcliffe	19	93.3	11	9	1	3	9-3	2.80
16	91	14	8	0	1	7-3	4.85	Joe Strong	20	103.3	16	9	0	2	9-3	4.88
15	72.2	12	6	1	0	9-3	5.82	Leroy Matlock	17	88.2	14	8	1	0	11-3	5.28
14	67	9	4	0	1	6-2	5.24	Rosey Davis	18	95	12	7	1	1	8-3	4.64
14	72	10	6	1	2	7-2	4.88	John Williams	16	83.2	11	7	1	2	7-3	5.27

1930 DETROIT STARS

League (48-33)									All Games (59-40)							
G	AB	H	2B	3B	HR	SB	Pct.	Pos.	Player	G	AB	H	2B	3B	HR	SB	Pct.
56	210	65	13	9	7	6	.310	1B	Ed Rile	61	226	73	17	9	8	6	.323
47	165	37	6	0	3	2	.224	2B	Grady Orange	55	190	44	6	0	3	2	.232
57	215	64	10	7	3	7	.298	SS	Jake Dunn	65	240	67	11	7	4	7	.279
54	206	55	9	4	0	3	.267	3B	William Robinson	62	231	60	9	4	0	4	.260
55	216	73	8	12	3	5	.338	LF	Wade Johnston	63	242	78	10	13	3	7	.322
34	119	42	12	9	3	6	.353	CF	Turkey Stearnes	36	127	43	12	10	3	6	.339
55	223	58	7	8	0	10	.260	RF	Crush Holloway	63	256	64	9	8	0	10	.250
37	113	34	8	3	4	3	.301	C	Clarence Palm	41	127	40	8	3	5	4	.315
34	100	26	5	1	0	4	.260	C-1B	Leon Daniels	40	113	30	7	1	0	4	.265
21	59	16	6	2	2	2	.271	OF-1B	Lou Dials	29	80	22	6	4	3	3	.275
21	70	20	6	0	2	2	.286	1B-OF	William Love	26	86	24	7	0	2	2	.279
11	39	10	2	0	0	1	.256	2B	Bingo DeMoss	11	39	10	2	0	0	1	.256

Pitching

G	IP	GS	CG	ShO	SV	W-L	RPG	Player	G	IP	GS	CG	ShO	SV	W-L	RPG
23	136.2	17	14	2	1	14-4	5.20	Andy Cooper	27	161	20	16	2	2	15-6	4.97
21	116.2	16	10	1	0	6-10	5.78	Willie Powell	25	143.1	19	12	1	1	9-10	5.15
21	120.1	16	12	2	0	10-5	3.44	Ted Shaw	24	130.1	18	13	3	0	11-5	3.38
19	126	14	10	2	0	9-5	4.29	Albert Davis	22	137	17	12	2	0	9-7	4.73
17	111.2	11	8	1	0	8-7	3.46	Nelson Dean	20	136.2	14	10	2	0	10-8	3.29

1930 KANSAS CITY MONARCHS

League (36-22)									All Games (39-40)							
G	AB	H	2B	3B	HR	SB	Pct.	Pos.	Player	G	AB	H	2B	3B	HR	SB	Pct.
44	144	48	15	4	1	7	.333	1B	Tom Young	47	155	50	16	4	1	8	.323
53	216	77	12	4	2	9	.356	2B	Newt Allen	57	235	81	12	4	2	9	.345
49	195	53	7	3	0	9	.272	SS	Hallie Harding	51	201	54	7	3	0	9	.269
48	158	43	9	2	3	11	.272	3B	Newt Joseph	52	175	47	10	3	3	12	.269
45	159	48	10	1	0	10	.302	LF	Leroy Taylor	49	177	49	10	1	0	10	.277
28	103	32	5	0	1	5	.311	CF	Bullet Joe Rogan	28	103	32	5	0	1	5	.311
53	201	61	11	5	9	2	.303	RF	L.D. Livingston	55	210	63	11	5	9	2	.300
47	139	54	9	5	1	4	.388	C	Frank Duncan	50	148	55	9	5	1	4	.372
54	199	52	7	8	2	8	.261	Utl.	Dink Mothel	58	218	58	9	8	3	8	.266
21	61	17	3	0	1	0	.279	P-OF	William Bell	23	69	19	3	0	1	0	.275
20	52	10	2	0	0	2	.192	P-OF	Chet Brewer	23	65	11	2	0	0	2	.169

Pitching

G	IP	GS	CG	ShO	SV	W-L	RPG	Player	G	IP	GS	CG	ShO	SV	W-L	RPG
16	100.2	12	11	2	1	8-6	5.09	Henry McHenry	18	100.2	13	11	2	1	8-7	5.09
14	113.2	12	12	2	0	8-5	4.04	Chet Brewer	17	145.1	15	15	2	0	8-8	3.90
14	102.1	14	9	0	0	10-1	4.66	Army Cooper	14	102.1	14	9	0	0	10-1	4.66
12	73.2	9	5	1	0	2-6	6.23	John Markham	14	77.2	10	6	1	0	2-7	6.26
12	92	10	10	2	0	8-3	3.03	William Bell	13	101	11	11	2	1	9-3	3.12

1930 CHICAGO AMERICAN GIANTS

League (47-47)									All Games (59-55)							
G	AB	H	2B	3B	HR	SB	Pct.	Pos.	Player	G	AB	H	2B	3B	HR	SB	Pct.
60	189	68	13	7	5	5	.360	1B	Walter Davis	71	214	72	15	7	5	5	.336
62	202	53	4	2	1	1	.262	2B	Charlie Williams	74	231	59	5	4	2	1	.255
55	176	39	4	4	0	0	.222	SS	Eddie Buck Miller	57	184	41	5	4	0	0	.223
47	144	29	2	1	0	3	.201	3B	Harry Jeffries	51	156	31	3	1	0	3	.199
61	191	45	6	2	0	1	.236	LF	James Sandy Thompson	69	214	52	7	2	0	1	.243
65	235	62	9	5	0	5	.264	CF	Stanford Jackson	75	273	67	10	5	0	5	.245
38	98	24	5	0	1	4	.245	RF	Melvin Powell	46	119	31	7	1	1	4	.261
31	94	33	8	0	0	0	.351	C	Mitch Murray	31	94	33	8	0	0	0	.351
43	137	42	11	5	2	3	.307	Utl.	Jim Brown	52	158	51	11	7	2	4	.323
30	86	20	3	0	0	1	.233	OF	Jelly Gardner	30	86	20	3	0	0	1	.233

1930 CHICAGO AMERICAN GIANTS (cont.)

G	AB	H	2B	3B	HR	SB	Pct.	Pos.	Player	G	AB	H	2B	3B	HR	SB	Pct.
				League (47-47)									All Games (59-55)				
27	81	30	1	1	0	2	.370	C	Jose Fernandez	37	110	41	4	1	0	2	.373
32	54	15	4	1	0	0	.278	P-1B	George Mitchell	32	54	15	4	1	0	0	.278
23	70	24	4	4	3	3	.343	OF	Rap Dixon	35	99	30	8	4	3	7	.303

Pitching

G	IP	GS	CG	ShO	SV	W-L	RPG	Player	G	IP	GS	CG	ShO	SV	W-L	RPG
28	165.2	17	15	2	3	12-9	4.13	Willie Foster	34	199	20	18	3	3	16-10	3.71
25	129.2	19	10	1	1	10-9	5.10	Webster McDonald	30	131.2	20	10	1	1	11-10	4.92
24	134.1	19	11	0	0	10-8	4.96	George Mitchell	25	139	19	11	0	0	11-8	4.99
21	136.2	16	12	2	1	7-10	5.33	Frog Holsey	23	150.1	18	13	2	1	8-10	5.39
16	61	8	3	1	2	4-5	6.34	Harold Morris	19	76.2	11	4	1	2	5-5	6.10

1930 BIRMINGHAM BLACK BARONS

G	AB	H	2B	3B	HR	SB	Pct.	Pos.	Player	G	AB	H	2B	3B	HR	SB	Pct.
				League (42-47)									All Games (44-48)				
45	149	50	5	4	6	3	.336	1B	L. Thomas	45	149	50	5	4	6	3	.336
45	154	44	2	1	1	2	.286	2B	John Shackleford	48	162	48	2	1	1	2	.296
64	220	48	3	7	3	2	.218	SS	Anthony Cooper	67	229	51	3	7	3	2	.223
35	109	27	5	2	0	0	.248	3B	E.C. Pop Turner	38	118	31	6	2	0	0	.263
61	186	54	10	2	3	16	.290	LF	Terris McDuffie	64	195	58	11	2	3	18	.297
64	236	67	5	9	2	5	.284	CF	Jimmy Crutchfield	67	248	71	5	9	3	5	.286
33	114	35	9	2	3	1	.307	RF	William Nat Rogers	36	123	39	9	2	3	2	.317
59	198	62	7	3	5	6	.313	C	Bill Perkins	62	205	63	7	3	5	6	.307
37	112	40	4	7	1	16	.357	Utl.	Clarence Smith	37	112	40	4	7	1	16	.357
32	103	25	3	2	0	4	.243	SS	Willie Owens	34	107	26	4	2	0	4	.243
29	104	40	7	1	3	2	.385	OF	Herman Jabbo Andrews	29	104	40	7	1	3	2	.385
27	67	18	2	0	0	0	.269	C	Robert Smith	29	69	19	2	0	0	0	.275
19	68	21	1	2	0	0	.309	1B	Nat Trammel	22	78	23	2	2	0	0	.295
19	74	19	6	1	2	3	.257	3B	G. Johnson	19	74	19	6	1	2	3	.257
16	66	20	2	2	1	1	.303	2B	Otto Mitchell	16	66	20	2	2	1	1	.303
12	37	9	2	1	1	1	.243	1B	Jim West	12	37	9	2	1	1	1	.243

Pitching

G	IP	GS	CG	ShO	SV	W-L	RPG	Player	G	IP	GS	CG	ShO	SV	W-L	RPG
29	177.2	23	19	0	0	11-11	4.31	Sam Streeter	30	186.2	24	20	0	0	12-11	4.15
20	119	19	11	0	0	8-10	6.20	Columbus Vance	21	124.1	20	11	0	0	8-11	6.37
18	104.3	14	10	0	0	4-10	6.13	Julian Bell	18	104.3	14	10	0	0	4-10	6.13
15	97	8	7	0	1	7-4	5.38	Harry Salmon	15	97	8	7	0	1	7-4	5.38
14	93.1	10	9	2	1	8-4	3.38	Satchel Paige	15	102.1	11	10	2	1	9-4	3.17
13	80.2	10	7	1	0	3-7	5.69	Willie Cornelius	14	82.1	10	7	1	0	3-7	5.58

1930 MEMPHIS RED SOX

G	AB	H	2B	3B	HR	SB	Pct.	Pos.	Player	G	AB	H	2B	3B	HR	SB	Pct.
				League (29-45)									All Games (32-53)				
47	176	54	11	1	0	1	.307	1B	George McAllister	53	201	59	11	1	0	1	.294
54	187	42	9	3	0	1	.225	2B	Milton Laurent	60	212	53	12	4	0	2	.250
48	165	50	6	7	2	2	.303	SS	Chester Williams	52	178	53	6	7	2	2	.298
40	153	39	4	2	0	0	.255	3B	Jimmy Binder	45	172	47	4	2	0	0	.273
42	141	42	8	1	4	2	.298	LF	Johnny Robinson	48	162	50	10	1	4	3	.309
46	170	55	11	4	1	7	.324	CF	? Ronsell	47	174	56	11	4	1	7	.322
30	109	45	7	4	3	0	.413	RF	Herman Jabbo Andrews	35	128	50	9	4	3	0	.391
41	131	35	5	1	0	0	.267	C	John Fat Barnes	47	151	39	6	1	0	0	.258
30	119	44	12	4	2	2	.370	OF	William Nat Rogers	31	123	45	12	5	2	2	.366
28	86	25	3	0	2	3	.291	INF	Charles Zomphiers	29	90	26	3	0	2	3	.289
27	93	27	4	1	0	0	.290	1B	Jim West	32	112	30	6	1	0	0	.268
26	45	15	1	1	0	2	.333	P-OF	Homer Goose Curry	28	48	16	1	1	0	2	.333
20	27	7	1	0	0	1	.259	3B-PH	Candy Jim Taylor	21	28	7	1	0	0	1	.250

Pitching

G	IP	GS	CG	ShO	SV	W-L	RPG	Player	G	IP	GS	CG	ShO	SV	W-L	RPG
26	135	19	10	0	0	6-12	5.13	Cliff Bell	29	147	21	11	0	0	6-14	5.27
18	98.2	12	6	1	0	3-8	6.20	Harry Cunningham	23	126.2	16	9	1	0	5-10	6.11
18	55	4	1	0	1	4-3	7.53	Homer Goose Curry	20	64	5	2	0	1	5-3	6.75
14	83.1	12	6	1	0	5-5	4.86	Murray Gillespie	15	87.3	12	6	1	1	5-5	4.85
11	67.1	8	7	0	1	4-5	5.35	Harry Salmon	13	79.1	10	8	0	1	4-7	5.45
11	51	7	2	1	0	4-2	6.18	Willie Cornelius	13	51	8	2	1	0	4-3	6.18

From A Researcher's Notebook
AL KERMISCH

Ernie Banks was the first black manager, if only for a day.
Al Orth threw two complete games in one afternoon.
These findings and more from our staff archeologist.

SOME HEAVY HITTING IN FIRST PRO LEAGUE

During the five years that baseball's first professional league — the National Association of Professional Baseball Players — operated, there were some heavy hitting performances that deserve special recognition. Following are some of the most noteworthy:

June 28, 1871 — In an extraordinary game played at Troy, New York, the Philadelphia Athletics defeated the Troy Haymakers 49-33, with both teams scoring in all nine innings. For the Athletics, pitcher Dick McBride and John Radcliffe each scored seven runs while Ned Cuthbert, Wes Fisler, Al Reach, and Levi Meyerle tallied six times each.

October 5, 1872 — The Lord Baltimores of Baltimore defeated the Atlantics on the Capitoline Grounds in Brooklyn 39-14. Baltimore scored in all nine innings and catcher Scott Hastings registered seven hits and scored six runs.

July 4, 1873 — The Resolutes of Elizabeth, New Jersey, surprised the Red Stockings at Boston by winning the morning game 11-2. In the afternoon contest the Resolutes gave the home club a tussle for six innings but the Red Stockings broke the game wide open by scoring five runs in the seventh, two in the eighth and an unbelievable 21 runs in the ninth for a 32-3 victory.

July 28, 1873 — The Lord Baltimores overcame a 14-4 deficit by rallying for 13 runs in the last three innings to defeat the Red Stockings 17-14 on the Union Grounds in Boston. The victim of the uprising was Al Spalding, who was knocked out of the box in the eighth inning. The Baltimore victory spoiled an outstanding performance by Boston shortstop George Wright, who hit two home runs in the third inning, when the Red Stockings scored eight times. He led off the inning with a drive over the fence and later in the frame hit one into the left-field corner. The home runs were hit off Candy Cummings.

June 18, 1874 — The Mutuals of New York scored in every inning and completely overwhelmed the Chicago White Stockings 38-1 on the Union Grounds in Brooklyn. Bobby Mathews set the White Stockings down with two hits.

October 1, 1874 — The Red Stockings defeated the Atlantics 29-0 on the South End Grounds in Boston. Al Spalding held the Atlantics to three hits.

HARRINGTON HOMERED IN FIRST AT BAT IN N.L.

For years Bill Duggleby, a pitcher who hit a grand slam home run in his first time at bat for the Philadelphia Phillies on April 21, 1898, was considered the first player to homer in his first at bat. Several years ago I discovered that Mike Griffin had homered in his first at bat for Baltimore of the American Association on April 16, 1887. Later I found that Griffin had to share the honor with George Tebeau who had done the same thing on the same day in the same league for Cincinnati. That still left Duggleby as the first in the National League. Recently I ran across a National League player who performed the feat for Boston on September 10, 1895.

Joe Harrington joined Boston from Fall River after the close of the New England League season. He was immediately placed at second base and when he came to bat for the first time in the second inning he was given a great ovation by the Boston fans. He responded with a home run over the left-field fence off pitcher Bill Kissinger. Harrington had three hits in four times up in his debut, but St. Louis won 8-4.

ERNIE BANKS — MAJOR LEAGUE MANAGER FOR A DAY

Frank Robinson was the first black manager in the majors with Cleveland in 1975. Nonetheless, Ernie Banks, the popular Mr. Cub, likes to remind everyone that he managed in the majors before Robinson — even if only for a day.

Ernie was a coach with the Cubs under Manager Whitey Lockman in 1973. In a game at San Diego on May 8, Lockman was ejected in the eleventh inning for arguing a called strike on Billy Williams. The Cubs were short of

---

Al Kermisch is an original SABR member who contributed to the first 15 issues of "BRJ."

coaches that day. Larry Jansen was with his wife, who had undergone surgery, while Pete Reiser was at home recuperating from a scuffle in San Francisco a few days earlier. That left coaches Banks and Hank Aguirre, and Ernie got the job. The Cubs won the game in the twelfth inning on Ken Rudolph's double, Don Kessinger's sacrifice bunt, and a pinch-hit double by Joe Pepitone, making Banks a winner in his first stint as a major-league manager.

BILL WHITE SPARKLED IN DEBUTS

Bill White, former major league player and broadcaster and now president of the National League, had exceptional debuts in both the minor and major leagues. He broke into Organized Baseball as a New York Giant farmhand for Danville in the Carolina League in 1953. White made his debut on April 22 in the opening game of the season at Reidsville. He led the Danville attack with a home run, double, single and four RBI in five times at bat as his club won 13-11.

White was called up to the Giants on May 6, 1956, from Minneapolis of the American Association. The Giants were in St. Louis, and White was placed in the starting lineup as the No. 6 hitter. In his first major-league at bat, in the second inning, he hit a home run off Ben Flowers into the pavilion seats in right-center. On his second at bat his drive missed the right field pavilion roof by a few feet for a double. White took a called third strike from Lindy McDaniel in the sixth and singled off Gordon Jones in the ninth. Despite his successful debut, the Giants lost to the Cards 6-3.

JENNINGS TOPS IN MULTIPLE HIT BY PITCHER GAMES

Don Baylor and Ron Hunt are the all-time leaders in getting hit by pitches, but before 1900 it was Hugh Jennings, of the old Orioles, who specialized in HP's. He was hit three times in a game on a record three occasions — in 1894, 1896 and 1898 — all while with the Orioles, or so says the record book. But Jennings was hit thrice a fourth time while with Brooklyn, where Ned Hanlon had moved most of his Oriole stars. On July 8, 1899, Jennings was plunked three times by Chick Fraser of the Phillies as Brooklyn beat the visiting Phillies 6-2.

ORTH WON TWO COMPLETE GAMES IN ONE DAY

On October 13, 1898, Phillie pitcher Al Orth threw two complete game victories over Brooklyn, but his feat is not listed in the record books. Delighting the Philadelphia crowd, he won the first game 5-1 on four hits and the second, halted by darkness after five innings, 9-6 on six hits. The White Sox' Ed Walsh is credited with two

Bill White

complete game victories at Boston on September 26, 1905. Actually, he did not start the first game even though he was in the contest for all 27 putouts. Doc White, the starter, gave up a single to Fred Parent, who took second on a fumble by outfielder James Callahan. With the count two balls on Chick Stahl, White asked to be relieved; he said the wind was blowing against his curveball and it wouldn't break over the plate. Manager Fielder Jones sent in Walsh, who had no chance to warm up. Boston scored five runs in the inning, but Walsh pitched shutout ball the rest of the way and won 10-5. He won the second game 3-1 in eight innings, the game being curtailed by darkness.